British History in
General Editor: Je

Please note that a sister series, *Social History in Perspective*, is available covering the key topics in social and cultural history.

British History in Perspective
Series Standing Order:
ISBN 0–333–71356–7 hardback
ISBN 0–333–69331–0 paperback

You can receive future titles in this series as they are published by placing a standing order. Please contact your bookseller or, in case of difficulty, write to the address below with your name and address, the title of the series and one of the ISBNs quoted above.

Customer Services Department, Macmillan Distribution Ltd
Houndmills, Basingstoke, Hampshire RG21 6XS, England

Political Movements in Urban England, 1832–1914

MATTHEW ROBERTS

First published 2009 by
PALGRAVE MACMILLAN

Palgrave Macmillan in the UK is an imprint of Macmillan Publishers Limited,
registered in England, company number 785998, of Houndmills, Basingstoke,
Hampshire RG21 6XS.

Palgrave Macmillan in the US is a division of St Martin's Press LLC,
175 Fifth Avenue, New York, NY 10010.

Palgrave Macmillan is the global academic imprint of the above companies
and has companies and representatives throughout the world.

Palgrave® and Macmillan® are registered trademarks in the United States,
the United Kingdom, Europe and other countries.

ISBN-13: 978-1-4039-4911-0 hardback
ISBN-10: 1-4039-4911-5 hardback
ISBN-13: 978-1-4039-4912-7 paperback
ISBN-10: 1-4039-4912-3 paperback

This book is printed on paper suitable for recycling and made from fully
managed and sustained forest sources. Logging, pulping and manufacturing
processes are expected to conform to the environmental regulations of the
country of origin.

A catalogue record for this book is available from the British Library.

A catalog record for this book is available from the Library of Congress.

10 9 8 7 6 5 4 3 2 1
18 17 16 15 14 13 12 11 10 09

Printed and bound in China

Contents

Acknowledgements

I would like to thank my colleagues at Sheffield Hallam, especially Peter Cain, Marie Hockenhull Smith, Merv Lewis, Roger Lloyd-Jones, Clare Midgley and Antony Taylor, who shared their knowledge and enthusiasm. Beyond Sheffield, I have received help and encouragement from James Gregory, Jon Lawrence, Matthew McCormack, Jon Parry, Jane Rendall, Edward Royle and Philip Salmon. I also thank the editors of *Parliamentary History* for allowing me to use a review article that I wrote for them as the basis for Chapters 6 and 7. Finally, special thanks must go to Rosalind Wolstenholme for her tolerance, support and love.

MATTHEW ROBERTS

Introduction

This book is a study of the mass political movements that came of age in England between the Great Reform Act of 1832 and the outbreak of the Great War in 1914, and explores the evolving relationship between these political movements and their popular supporters in urban England. Although there was nothing exclusively 'urban' about many of these political movements, their epicentres were usually to be found in the burgeoning towns and cities of Victorian and Edwardian England, hence the focus in this book on the urban dimensions of political mobilization.

Over the last twenty-five years, many of the traditional historical interpretations of these political movements have been challenged and, in many cases, overturned. The purpose of this book is to take stock of this historical revisionism, and subject it to critical scrutiny. Chapter 1 explores the relationship between the franchise and citizenship, and introduces some of the key aspects of British political culture. Chapters 2 to 9 have been written in pairs, each pair examining one of the four major popular political movements of the period: Chapters 2 and 3 discuss radicalism in the era of the Chartists, its culture and subsequent 'failure'; Chapters 4 and 5 focus on the growth of popular Liberalism and its problematic relationship with post-Chartist radicalism; Chapters 6 and 7 shed new light on the relatively neglected phenomenon of popular Conservatism; and Chapters 8 and 9 revisit the long-standing historical controversy surrounding the decline of the Liberal party and the rise of Labour. The first chapter in each pair provides a narrative history; the second engages with the revisionist historiography. The final chapter highlights the main changes and continuities in popular political culture between 1832 and 1914.

Although seldom explicitly identified or personified, the view presented in this book is largely that of the informed political activist, the crucial linking figure between the national leadership and the people.

But this is not merely a history of an activist minority; rather, the purpose is to explore how political movements and their activists used ideas to define and mobilize popular support. Historians have traditionally paid little attention to the role of ideas in popular politics, a neglect that stems in part from an assumption that the masses were, for the most part, apolitical. Even those who were involved in some of the great protest movements, such as Chartism, were thought to have been largely ignorant of the political aims and objectives. However, whilst some of those attending meetings and demonstrations might have lacked a sophisticated knowledge of aims and objectives, many had a broad understanding of the issues involved. This, in turn, enabled the masses to respond in ways that made political movements more responsive to their interests. For example, Marc Brodie has shown how the London poor perceived Chartism primarily as an anti-tax crusade, so much so that the London Chartists were forced to devote more attention to this aspect in their speeches.[1]

Politics became unprecedentedly 'popular' in the nineteenth century: more people than ever before participated in the political system as voters, activists and members; and political movements, if they were to be effective, had to become 'popular'. In the current climate of political apathy and cynicism, the notion of politics being 'popular' seems bizarre. This is largely the result of a perception that politics is about the doings of a self-enclosed and self-seeking world of politicians at the national centre of power who are cut off from wider society. Ironically, this perception chimes with an older historical approach that viewed politics as the preserve of an elite few who were largely ignorant of wider society, and who were motivated by personal ambition rather than ideological principles.[2] It would be unduly naïve to suggest that politicians were not motivated, in part, by such considerations; and yet correspondingly disingenuous to write them off as totally lacking in principle and civic virtue. Either way, political life exists beyond Westminster. Politics is about more than prime ministers, governments, elections and political parties; an 'informal politics' of everyday life also exists. As Jon Lawrence has argued, uncovering this politics involves tracing the political languages and practices that collect around aspects of popular culture and how these connect with the 'formal politics' of parties and political movements.[3] In so doing, we can see how issues that are seemingly far removed from politics and the concerns of the political historian were, and are, intensely politicized.

What so often shines through from the popular politics of nineteenth-century Britain is a tremendous faith in politics to bring about change: many of us have lost sight of this rich tradition. Kevin Jefferys has made the dubious claim in his recent book that Britain never really possessed a vibrant political culture. Even more controversial is his claim that one of the major causes of the prevailing political apathy in contemporary Britain is the way in which a more participatory political system came about in the nineteenth century, an assertion that he does not really substantiate.[4] His suggestion that few people ever make the connection between their everyday lives and the state of the political system is simply untrue, and is based on a narrow conception of what constitutes the political sphere (in this case, formal party politics and voting at elections). To take an example from the supposedly apathetic desert that was nineteenth-century Britain, at its height in the early 1840s, Chartism drew support from three million people (the majority of whom were working class) out of a total population of some 18.5 million. As Kelly Boyd and Rohan McWilliam rightly comment in their recent anthology on Victorian Britain:

> if we are to proclaim the values of democracy and citizenship, we will need to continue pondering how Victorian Britain became, in fits and starts, a kind of democracy. Even now, the Chartists and other champions of democratic rights do not have the prominence in British or international collective memory that they ought to have.[5]

The condescension evident in Jeffery's work is reminiscent of the disillusioned Marxism of the 1970s. This attributed the absence of revolutionary socialism in Britain to the limited horizons, fatalism and apathy of the British working class. Socialism was the only legitimate and rational popular politics for the working class, and it was argued that all else was 'false consciousness'.[6] The problem with this argument is that it rests on an idealized, deterministic and narrow conception of popular politics against which the working class is inevitably found wanting. Shorn of the Marxist sympathies of those historians who advanced this interpretation, no objective reason can be cited for why the working class should have developed a revolutionary class-consciousness. That consciousness might well have been absent; what was not absent was a vibrant popular political culture.

When and why this vibrant age of popular politics began to disintegrate, and result in the current political disengagement is not entirely clear. What is clear, as I hope to show in this book, is that the seeds of that disintegration were not to be found in the nineteenth century. As such, I reject the revisionist arguments of the postmodernists that suggest popular politics became *less* participatory and popular in the nineteenth century.[7]

The New Political History

It is something of an in-house joke amongst historians that political history is forever making new comebacks and reinventing itself. One of the most dramatic comebacks and significant reinventions occurred in the 1980s and 1990s. These decades witnessed the advent of the appropriately titled 'new political history' (hereafter NPH). This book explores how the NPH has reshaped the landscape of Victorian and Edwardian popular politics. The NPH was precipitated by contemporary political developments in the late 1980s and early 1990s: the continuing electoral success of the Conservative party, which belied assumptions about the historical inevitability of the triumph of the 'working-class' Labour party; the fall of the Berlin Wall and the collapse of Soviet Communism. These events played a significant part in fuelling the rise of new intellectual currents that called into question the intellectual credibility of Marxism, the assumptions of which had underpinned so much postwar writing on modern British history. The essence of Marxism was the division of society into the bourgeoisie (capitalists) and the proletariat (the workers), consequent on a process of dramatic industrialization. The resulting conflict between the two classes and the expectation that the proletariat would eventually triumph and establish a classless society provided the key to understanding past and present politics. The empirical moorings of this theory, and of social history more generally, were also in the process of being shaken by historical reassessments of the Industrial Revolution. What had once appeared as a 'big bang', based on sudden and pervasive industrialization, turns out on closer inspection to have been little more than 'a long and uneven whimper'.[8] The absence of a pervasive and relatively uniform industrializing process has called into question the Marxist assumption that people similarly placed in the socio-economic structure from all over the country came to recognize a shared class identity. The collective impact of these contemporary developments and linked historical reassessments was a dramatic challenge to the conventional class interpretation of popular politics.

This class interpretation came into its own in the 1960s and 1970s under the influence of Marxism, labour history and sociology. The unifying thread to this work was an 'expressive' view of the relationship between politics and society in which the political sphere was seen as a reflection of underlying socio-economic structural divisions, notably class. For Marxist and labour historians, the making of a unified, class-conscious working class between 1780 and 1850, the falling away of that class-consciousness in the relatively harmonious mid-Victorian decades, and its re-emergence from the 1880s down to the First World War, provided the dynamic for the popular politics of the period. In turn, these social developments were shaped by the state of the economy. Surely, it was no coincidence that Chartism peaked in the 1830s and 1840s at times of severe depression and began to lose its purchase in the 1850s when the economy improved. As the chronological trajectory of this interpretation suggests, this gave rise to the 'three-stage' model of popular politics: the making of the working class, 1780–1850; the 'unmaking' of the working class, 1850–1880; and the 'remaking' of the working class, 1880–1920.

It was not just Marxist historians who held to this expressive theory of popular politics. In fact, it has mainly been associated with a model of voting behaviour called 'electoral sociology'. This was constructed by political scientists in the 1950s and 1960s and used by historians to develop a model of electoral change in nineteenth- and twentieth-century Britain.[9] According to this model, the social composition and ideological makeup of political parties, the character of the state and, most importantly, voting behaviour were all a reflection of underlying social cleavages – status, religion and class. At its most reductionist, this model presented political movements as largely passive beneficiaries or victims of wider societal forces beyond their control; at best, political movements were endowed with a limited agency that enabled them to adapt to, but not shape, these forces. As with Marxist and labour historians, the electoral sociologists also gave a chronological shape to the nineteenth century. Prior to the 1880s, voting behaviour and the character of politics was essentially locally based and shaped by religious identity, occupation and broader deferential loyalty to urban elites such as factory owners. From the 1880s, this status-based politics, as it was termed, was replaced by a modernized, nationalized political culture organized along class lines: hence, the rise of an organized working-class Labour party; the coalescing of the middle class behind the defensive Conservative party; and the decline of the once formidable Liberal party on account of its unwillingness or inability to respond to class politics. While Marxists, labour historians and electoral sociologists disagreed over the timing of these developments, the eventual triumph of class-based politics was undisputed. Further, whether it was status or class that underpinned popular politics, there was a common, though by no means universal, assumption that the political ideas, beliefs and values in the form of ideology were largely irrelevant – mere epiphenomena. The social basis of political mobilization, refracted through the ephemera of party organization, bribery and treating, corrupt practices and deference, constituted the stuff of popular politics.[10]

Few of these assumptions have escaped the searching critique of the NPH. This new approach emphasizes the autonomy (to varying degrees) of politics from society; the role of language in shaping political behaviour; and the danger of reducing that behaviour to expressions of underlying socio-economic divisions. The NPH is associated with the 'linguistic turn' – a term denoting the recent focus by scholars on language and the growing awareness of the complex relationship between language and social structures. This 'turn to language' is a key feature of poststructuralism, itself a literary offshoot of postmodernism. As its name suggests, postmodernism is presented as a self-conscious rejection of modernism. In contrast to modernist assumptions of grand, totalizing narratives (such as Marxism) with their emphasis on fixity, unity and homogeneity, postmodernism stresses indeterminacy, openness, complexity, diversity and heterogeneity.

Poststructuralists have applied these assumptions to the study of the relationship between language and social structure. They have rejected (again, to varying degrees) the modernist fallacy that social structures exist prior to, or outside of, language. Language, they maintain, is an active constituent element in the construction of reality; not merely a reflection of that reality.[11] As Geoffrey Crossick puts it in relation to the Victorians, 'if the terms they used were an attempt to describe the world, they were at the same time an attempt to shape it'.[12]

When viewed through the lens of the 'linguistic turn' it has become clear that the language of class was nowhere near as dominant in Victorian popular politics as was once thought. Political movements appealed less to classes and more to 'the people' – or 'the nation'.[13] Although these identifications transcended socio-economic divisions, they were far from being universally inclusive. Even the most seemingly inclusive identities are based on exclusions – invariably along the mutually constitutive fault-lines of class, religion, gender and nation.[14] As a result of the 'linguistic turn', historians now devote closer attention to language by focusing on how it actually works. There is now a greater awareness of the multi-vocality of political language, and of the scope for popular political actors to subvert the meaning of 'official' political messages or appropriate them for their own ends. Historians have also adopted a much wider definition of what language actually entails, encompassing not just words but also symbols and other visual material. The attempt to read symbols as cultural artefacts is heavily indebted to anthropology. These new methodologies have made historians of popular politics more attentive to the techniques and technologies of political communication and to its diversity. As the NPH has shown, the medium could be just as important as the message in producing meaning.[15] The NPH has also restored previously neglected or caricatured political movements to the centre of serious historical enquiry. Labour historians used to dismiss or explain away popular Liberalism and Conservatism; they did not fit into theories of class development, hence the charges of 'false consciousness'. Popular Liberalism and Conservatism could be deeply rational forms of popular political loyalty, stemming from support for the political principles underpinning these ideologies. Finally, in contrast to the conventional stress on change, the NPH has highlighted continuities, thus calling into question the stark juxtaposition of early, mid and late Victorian popular politics as posited by the 'three-stage' model. As such, the NPH has 'flattened out' the chronological terrain of nineteenth-century popular politics.

The 'linguistic turn' has not just been about drawing attention to previously obscured forms of social identity or shifting the accent from change to continuity. It has also re-conceptualized the relationship between political movements and their popular supporters. More specifically, the NPH has shown how political movements used language to define and mobilize constituencies of popular support. Seminal here was the pioneering work of Gareth Stedman Jones on the language of Chartism.[16] In simple terms, the essence of the NPH as conceived by Stedman Jones and by those who have developed his ideas is that:

> The role of politics is to provide a set of languages and set of ideas that help individuals make sense of society. For example, working people often do not become militant even when they are suffering hardship. They only agitate when a political language provides a diagnosis of the sources of their problem and establishes a viable strategy to deal with it. In other words, hunger by itself does not spur action; politics is necessary to provide the idea that hunger is not something to be endured.[17]

This represents a reversal of the conventional view that politics reflects society. The 'linguistic turn' has revealed just how dynamic political movements are: they are not simply the mouthpieces of pre-existing socio-economic identities. Political actors are not ready made; they have to be constructed. The creative challenge facing political movements is to articulate a coherent and populist appeal that links political ideas and policies with the everyday concerns of the people. The creative power of politicians, however, is not unlimited; that power is subject to popular dissent and subversion. Some revisionist historians have become aware of these limitations and have responded by developing the idea of the 'relative autonomy of politics' (from society).[18] Central to the notion of the *relative* autonomy of politics from society is the assumption that language plays a crucial role in the translation of material forces; however, it is not a substitute for them.[19]

Material forces exist independent of words, but our understanding of those material forces is shaped by particular linguistic orderings of experience, orderings that are unstable and shift over time and place. In short, socio-economic forces constrain but do not determine the form and content of politics. The fact of the matter is that structural factors *are* important. As Jon Lawrence has rightly argued:

> the potential for individual and group mobilization is likely to be directly related to the distribution of social, economic and cultural capital – that is to say to issues such as hours of work (and thus of free time), levels of residential stability, the relationship between wages and subsistence, ethnic homogeneity, levels of literacy, etc.[20]

Although important to pay close attention to the words that historical actors used, there was more to the politics of the period than mere verbal tussle. To the uninitiated in the historiography of popular politics, these statements might appear facile. Yet, the more strident practitioners of the NPH have come close to developing a view of politics that is virtually autonomous from society, a view that critics have rightly lambasted as 'linguistic determinism'. What had been ambiguous and, to some extent, implicit in Stedman Jones' work was taken further in the work of Patrick Joyce and James Vernon.[21] In their work, the creative powers of politicians and parties appear virtually unlimited, at least in terms of their theoretical models, if not necessarily in their practice.[22] Speaking for the people in these narratives was about imposing visions of the people onto the people. As Mayfield and Thorne argue, the problem with such narratives is that they effectively reduce 'popular political identifications to the textual vocabularies through which they were articulated', thus denying individual agency to ordinary people. If voters were merely blank slates and political movements were simply in the business of manufacturing identities for them, then one wonders how individuals determine the relative merits of competing political programmes or how voters change their allegiance.[23] The issue of reception and response is conveniently sidestepped. The idea of the *relative* autonomy of politics addresses these issues head on: what emerges from this approach is a more subtle and nuanced interpretation that explores 'the complex and ambiguous interaction of language and social structure'.[24]

The distinction between those historians who have emphasized the *relative* as opposed to the virtually complete autonomy of politics from society serves to illustrate that the practitioners of the NPH do not speak with one voice. Contrary to the claims of Neville Kirk – one of the most outspoken critics of the NPH – not all revisionists who have emphasized the relative autonomy of politics have argued for the 'primacy of political non-class based' identities in their interpretations of nineteenth-century popular politics.[25] First, even Stedman Jones and Joyce – Kirk's historiographical *bête noires* – never denied the existence of class, or class politics; rather, they were sceptical that class could issue from an objective socio-economic reality existing independently of, and prior to, its articulation in political language. Second, as Joyce acknowledges, the putative trans-class categories such as 'the people' could take on class meanings, but those meanings did not automatically translate into class conflict; that is, class without class conflict.[26] Third, Kirk's charge that the NPH has not devoted sufficient attention to the social determinants of politics is unfair, as the older historiography with which it has taken issue did not pay sufficient attention to the political sphere. As such, it was to be fully expected that the pioneering revisionist work of Stedman Jones and Joyce countered under-emphasis with over-emphasis. Nevertheless, as the NPH has matured over the last ten years, a methodological balance has been struck between social/material and political/linguistic forces, the outcome of continued historiographical debate. The present maturity of that debate is evidence that it is no longer possible to bemoan the intellectual insularity, empirical naïvety and anti-theory of British political and social historians, as was common twenty years ago. How, then, does the popular political landscape of Victorian and Edwardian England appear from the vantage point carved out by the NPH?

Chapter 1: Citizenship, the Franchise and Electoral Culture

In a letter to *The Times*, published on 30 July 1884, the trades unionist George Potter asked: 'If fitness is a matter of citizenship, are we not all Britons?' Potter went on to demonstrate that, in his opinion, many allegedly 'fit' Britons were, in fact, being denied citizenship (by which he meant the vote). Debates about citizenship, and who was deemed 'fit' to have that status conferred upon them, were central to the politics of Victorian Britain. The concept of citizenship might appear somewhat anachronistic in relation to nineteenth-century Britain – or even altogether alien. This is because citizenship has all too often been defined narrowly as a legal category that denotes membership of a national community, the acme of which is seen to be the possession of a passport. Yet, as new studies have made clear, citizenship needs to be defined more expansively as a status that mediates the relationship between individuals and the political community.[1] Citizenship can be understood in a British context as the mechanism whereby formal limits are placed on subjecthood (that is, the sovereign power of the state over its subjects) by allowing people to play a part in government. Hence the importance attached to the vote, especially by those who did not enjoy the privilege.[2] As the radical Joseph Chamberlain tellingly observed in the debates on the Third Reform Act of 1884–85, voting was 'the first political right of citizenship'.[3]

The three major reform acts (1832, 1867 and 1884), and the public debates to which they gave rise, were concerned with the question of what sorts of people should be included in – and who should be excluded from – the political life of the nation.[4] Put simply: who should be allowed to vote, and on what basis? These seemingly straightforward questions ranked amongst the most controversial of issues in modern British politics. This chapter explores how the 'political citizen' was

defined by the state. It also examines 'official' and 'popular' under-
standings of what it meant to have the vote between the First and Third
reform acts. In so doing, this chapter introduces some of the main
principles and assumptions that underpinned the evolving relationship between politics and the people in the nineteenth century. These
principles transcended political divisions, though individual political
movements tended to interpret these in different ways, as will become
clearer in later chapters.

Electoral Citizenship

By the early nineteenth century, a model of political citizenship had
emerged that was based on a fusion of English legal precedent and
continental theories of classical republicanism. That model would survive largely intact until 1914, although the structural integrity of that
model was weakened in the late nineteenth and early twentieth century.
This model of citizenship, as with the so-called 'English constitution'
from which it issued, had evolved somewhat haphazardly over time. Its
unwieldy nature was due to the absence of a formal written constitution,
such as existed in France and the United States of America. However,
the Constitution was no less real for that. Discussions about the Constitution – and, more importantly, what was thought to be constitutional –
saturated the language and practice of popular politics.[5]

Underpinning this model of citizenship was the notion of 'independence', a notion reinforced by ideas drawn from classical republicanism.
These ideas had been rediscovered by the Renaissance civic humanists
of fifteenth and sixteenth century Florence who wished to see a return
to the classical civic ideal of selfless participation in public life for the
wider public good.

This civic humanist creed was transported into Britain as a response
to the breakdown of constituted authority in the Civil War period.
Ideas of republican liberty did not displace the indigenous ideology
of Britain's unwritten constitution; rather, it was grafted onto that
ideology. The Civil War period had underlined how much English
liberty was located in a shifting ground of 'immemorial custom' that
had to be continuously interpreted and reinterpreted. In turn, this
necessitated a kind of active, republican citizenship as these customs
had to be preserved, refined and transmitted, especially in the face of
contestation.[6]

According to standard historical interpretations, this neo-classical
republican model of citizenship was displaced in the late eighteenth
century and, by the nineteenth century, had been replaced by a liberal

model. In contrast to neo-classical models of citizenship, which stressed duty, this liberal model emphasized abstract individual rights. However, a growing body of research suggests that republicanism was not entirely displaced by liberalism, and that it continued to shape notions of corruption, constitutionalism, civic duty and citizenship well into the nineteenth century.[7] As with their Florentine predecessors, English politicians, especially radicals and reformers, were concerned with creating the conditions for a durable republic of virtuous citizens. The problem was that reformers could not agree on what constituted a 'virtuous citizen'.

Republican ideas of citizenship also merged with English legal customs relating to property. Independence was the prerequisite for citizenship, and this was the exclusive preserve of male propertied householders. If the possession of property, as opposed to one's gender, was the cardinal criterion for political participation, the English legal system forged a very close association between the two. Under English common law, single and widowed women could own property on the same basis as men. As soon as women married, however, their legal existence was subsumed by their husbands, and this included their property. This legal disability was only partially overturned by the Married Women's Property Acts of 1870 and 1882.[8] Thus, it was widely accepted that only men in the condition of independence could and should participate in public life. Those who were in a state of 'dependency' would lack the necessary virtues – reason, temperament, education and a material stake in society – to resist the corruption and bribery that perennially threatened to reduce the political system to a state of servile effeminacy. Dependency could assume a number of forms: a client upon a patron, a tenant upon a landlord, a servant upon a master, a woman upon a man. Obligation and dependency were associated with femininity and effeminacy, and to be labelled as such was politically disempowering.[9] Independence was also contingent on the ability to support and defend one's dependents. This explains why the ideal citizen was usually conceived of as the head of a household. In a somewhat circular argument, the independence of men was underscored by having dependents in the form of wives, sisters, sons and daughters.[10] As the Liberal J. A. Roebuck argued in the parliamentary debates on the Second Reform Act of 1867, 'if a man has a settled house, in which he has lived with his family for a number of years, you have a man who has given hostages to the state, and you have in these circumstances a guarantee for that man's virtue'.[11]

The independent man was expected to exhibit certain characteristics in his behaviour: notably sincerity, assertiveness and straightforwardness. Embodying these characteristics 'fitted' one for political citizenship. Here is Gladstone, soon to be leader of the Liberal party, on the occasion of his much quoted House of Commons speech of May 1864 on the moral entitlement of respectable working men to the franchise: 'What are the qualities which fit a man for the exercise of a privilege such as the franchise? Self-command, self-control, respect for order, patience under suffering, confidence in the law, regard for superiors'. Earlier in the speech, Gladstone had declared that men who possessed such qualities 'are fit to discharge the duties of citizenship'.[12] Demonstrating a virtuous masculine self was the desideratum for enfranchisement.

For much of the eighteenth century, political commentators had mainly been concerned with ensuring the independence of public servants as a means to resist webs of corruption surrounding the King and his ministers. Governments at this time relied heavily on dispensing patronage to create and maintain parliamentary majorities. This gave rise to the 'country-party' ideology and the associated phenomenon of 'electoral independence'. 'Country-party' ideology was originally developed by opposition Whigs and later adopted by the Anglican tory squirearchy. It was the response by these 'outs' to their exclusion from power by the party of the 'court' (the 'ins' – the exclusive and corrupt recipients of royal patronage). This 'country' ideology maintained that only independent men who were free of this patronage network were able to restore balance and virtue to the polity. Hence the redemptive faith that Georgian reformers placed in the 'independent MP', so-called because of his public repudiation of patronage. Under the democratizing impact of the American and French revolutions and the rise of popular radicalism, the focus shifted from this exclusive preoccupation with the character of public men to the qualities of the electorate as well. Independence came to be thought of in more inclusive ways. The ability to support one's household and the possession of basic manly qualities such as sincerity and self-assertion became the criteria for political participation. This growing inclusiveness was facilitated by the various reform acts of the nineteenth century. As Matthew McCormack has argued: 'the story of the British parliamentary reform movement can be told in terms of how reformers gradually came to associate ever-humbler groups of men with "independence", until manhood suffrage made the identification complete'.[13] Whereas only a minority of men met these standards in 1832, subsequent generations of reformers contested, aspired to or appropriated its terms until – by the Third Reform Act of 1884–85 – citizenship was symbolically synonymous with adult masculinity.[14]

Electors were expected to act the part of the 'independent man'. It was here that notions of 'electoral independence' came into play. This was the means by which electors defended local privileges and challenged abuses of power, such as those wielded by dictatorial MPs. This could take the form of voting against the instructions of patrons or 'interests', or by nominating a candidate who was independent of, and therefore opposed to, those interests. Historians have usually associated electoral independence with the pre-1832 'unreformed' political system. A growing body of evidence points to the survival of these eighteenth-century traditions of 'country' patriotism and electoral independence until the end of the nineteenth century.[15] Part of the reason for this was their flexibility and inclusiveness. Originally an anti-party creed, this 'country-party ideology' was subsequently drawn on and adapted by the whole political spectrum.

Only genuinely independent citizens, then, could be entrusted with the franchise. According to the tacit theory of political representation, most Georgians and Victorians conceived of the franchise not as a right but as a trust. Those in possession of the franchise had a responsibility to the wider interests of the community. To those who were devout, their vote was a sacred trust conferred on them by God – to whom they were also answerable.[16] According to this theory, independent men could be trusted to elect 'fit and proper persons' who would honourably discharge the duties of public office in the interests of all. This model of citizenship was thus bound up with one of the fundamental principles of the political system: 'virtual representation'. This held that even those people without the vote were represented 'virtually' by the enfranchised portion of the community.[17] Naturally, it was the perennial complaint of radicals and reformers that 'virtual representation' simply did not work as some electors patently *did* vote for their own selfish interests, hence the charges of 'Old Corruption' (the name given to the idle, tax-eating aristocrats and their placemen, who monopolized control of the political, religious and military establishment) and the need for a wider, more democratic franchise.

Debates about who constituted the political citizen were not only concerned with who could vote, but also with the act of voting. The electoral contest itself was an open affair, with polling usually lasting two days after 1832, and one day after 1835 in the boroughs. Elections were part of the entertainment culture of the day in which the whole local community took part – electors and non-electors, especially in the first half of the nineteenth century. As Frank O'Gorman has shown in his re-creation of electoral culture between 1780 and 1860, the whole campaign from beginning to end (usually spanning a fortnight) was structured by rituals.[18] The commencement of the campaign was marked by the formal entry of the candidates into the constituency to be greeted by an assembled crowd. Many candidates would then conduct a door-to-door canvass – aided by an entourage of the local elite – to court, flatter and possibly bribe potential voters and their families. The campaign was likely to be punctuated by a series of 'treating rituals', such as dinners and breakfasts. The focal point of the contest was the hustings – raised wooden platforms on which compartments or rooms were often erected – usually close to places of civic importance. It was here that candidates made daily speeches and presented themselves for public nomination – a grand civic occasion – by a show of hands,[19] and where electors cast their vote and the interim and final polls were declared. To mark the formal end of the campaign, the winning candidate was 'chaired' around the streets: the victorious – and occasionally the defeated – were literally paraded in a chair as part of a long procession.

The contest from beginning to end called for displays of manly 'independent' behaviour, and could be a very rowdy, even riotous affair. This made the act of voting an ordeal. Voters often had to travel quite long distances to get to the hustings. Also, a measure of physical bravery was often required to get past the drunken mobs and hired thugs who loitered around the hustings. Once the voter had reached the hustings, they had to present themselves to the returning officer and tell them for whom they wished to vote. Even if a polling booth had been erected, it was still of sufficient size to accommodate polling clerks and paid agents of the candidates. Thus, electors were forced to cast their vote in a way that made it visible to others, providing non-electors with an opportunity to ensure that 'virtual representation' was operating. As the vote was held in trust on behalf of the wider community, it was only right and proper that voting should be a *public* act. The votes of individual electors were then subsequently published in a poll book, theoretically available to anyone who wished to scrutinize its contents. One tactic that the visibility of the vote gave rise to was 'exclusive dealing', whereby electors and non-electors would only do business with retailers who shared their political beliefs and voted in accordance with their wishes. Despite being formally denied the vote, the non-elector could be indirectly enfranchised as a consumer, a symbolic empowerment that could be revealed when the masses went shopping (often on Saturday nights), as the following poem from 1852 illustrates:

> Non-Electors Can Vote on A Saturday Night
> Although we are a rabble, an immoral mob,
> Unworthy the notice of a Tea-selling snob,
> And cannot with wealthier neighbours have right,
> We're registered ready for Saturday night.

And when our friend Willans again does appear,
He'll find opposition is banished from here,
For none can withstand the terrible might,
Of Working Men's Votes on a Saturday Night.[20]

In the first half of the nineteenth century, open voting found itself increasingly under attack by the advocates of the secret ballot. 'Official' and, to a lesser extent, 'popular' opinion were divided over the efficacy of secret voting. Opponents of the secret ballot alleged that a vote cast in secrecy in the confines of an enclosed polling booth would be no longer subject to public scrutiny. This, it was feared, would lead to the franchise being exercised for self-interest. Under the shroud of secrecy, electors would be more susceptible to bribery, corruption and dishonesty. In short, in the eyes of its opponents, the secret ballot would be corrosive of the manly, open and demonstrative culture of English citizenship. It would, however, be naïve to presume that such intellectual arguments were the beginning and end of elite objections to the secret ballot: self-interest was also a factor. Supporters were quick to point out that, under the secret ballot, electors would no longer be at the mercy of dictatorial or bribing patrons. In the absence of a poll book, electors would be free to vote as the conscience dictated (a somewhat altruistic expectation). The poll book regime had provided patrons and employers with the means by which to inflict retribution on those who had voted against their wishes. Just how often such retribution was inflicted is unknown.

The secret ballot was finally introduced in 1872, not at the behest of popular demand but, rather, as a necessary evil to prevent growing intimidation and corruption. By this stage, it had become a less controversial issue than it had been in the 1830s, when members of the political elite regarded the secret ballot as the harbinger of democracy.[21] There can be little doubt that the introduction of the secret ballot changed the electoral culture of Victorian Britain. Many of the rituals associated with electioneering went into decline – though they did not disappear everywhere and overnight.

Enfranchising the Citizen, 1832–1885

The nineteenth century used to be regarded as the age in which the British political system underwent a long and gradual process of democratization. The boundaries of the political nation were expanded as electoral citizenship was periodically conferred by the various reform acts. Yet, as the new cultural history of citizenship has revealed, decisions about who to include in the nation as citizens also entailed making decisions about who to exclude. This new history of citizenship has made historians more aware of these exclusions, especially in relation to the franchise.[22] This is part of a wider postmodernist historiography that has challenged the Whiggish view that the nineteenth century became more democratic. In conventional histories of the period, the various reform acts, the rise of party politics and a free press, amongst other developments, were seen as progressive and emancipatory. According to the revisionists, on closer inspection, these reforms turn out to be little more than cynical attempts by the state to stifle what had been a genuinely participatory popular politics.[23] Although definitions of the political citizen became more exacting – theoretically limited to male propertied householders – this has to be balanced with the fact that, during the course of the century, progressively more men qualified for the parliamentary and municipal franchise, even if the expenses and complexities of registration effectively disenfranchised some.[24] Whereas, in 1833, only one adult male in five had the vote in England and Wales (one in eight in Scotland), by 1885 two men in three could vote (three in five in Scotland).[25] In what ways did the major reform acts of the period – the 'Great' Reform Act of 1832; the Second Reform Act of 1867, and the Third Reform Act of 1884–85 – redefine the political citizen?

The 1832 Reform Act used to stand as the great divider between two distinct electoral systems: the 'unreformed', corrupt, closed, deferential and elite-dominated Hanoverian regime; and the 'reformed', participatory, partisan and middle-class led system of Victorian Britain. The Act had two main provisions. First, it enfranchised adult males who occupied (as owners or tenants) property assessed for rating at a minimum of £10 per annum provided that they had been in possession of the property for at least one year, had paid all relevant taxes up to the last three and a half months, and had not been in receipt of poor relief over the previous year. Second, the Act disfranchised 56 elite controlled small boroughs and partially disfranchised a further 30 boroughs by taking one of their seats away. Sixty-three of these seats were redistributed to the industrializing towns. Before 1832, many of these towns (such as Birmingham, Manchester and Sheffield) did not elect their own MPs but were, instead, part of the surrounding county constituencies, which were invariably dominated by the landed interest.

Conventionally, 1832 was interpreted as marking a sizeable transfer of power from the aristocracy to the middle class.[26] Such was the departure introduced by the 1832 Reform Act that it earned the epithet 'great'. This interpretation has been subject to sustained attack by two groups of historians. The first group was the 'tory' revisionists of the 1950s and 1960s, who emphasized the conservative, aristocratic intentions to preserve behind the Reform Act.[27] The second group comprised younger historians writing in the 1980s and 1990s, who presented the 'unreformed' electoral system as being more 'partisan, participatory, and popular'[28] than was once thought. This revisionist literature has largely stripped the 1832 Reform Act of its previously assumed 'greatness'. According to this interpretation, for all the electric atmosphere that surrounded the passage of the Reform Act, when all the dust had settled, the form and content of politics continued much as before. At best, the Reform Act is thought to have accelerated extant processes;[29] at worst, to have retarded them.[30]

Ultimately, the decision of whether to vote for change or continuity when interpreting 1832 depends largely on perspective. High-political accounts focusing on the conservative aims and intentions of those who crafted the Bill, and those studies of popular politics that have examined idioms and rituals (such as corrupt practices and violent behaviour at elections) both before and after 1832, inevitably find that the continuities far outweigh the changes, especially when the focus is on the types of places where one would least expect change – small boroughs being a case in point.[31] By contrast, those historians who have looked at the ways in which the Act was translated into electoral practice, and how it created a national framework for the expression of a more uniform, enduring and widespread partisanship – most notable in the larger boroughs – have rightly emphasized change.[32] Others prefer to split their votes between change and continuity. Hoppen, for instance, notes the decline of electoral violence (a conclusion that has actually been convincingly challenged by Wasserman and Jaggard) but an increase in corruption after 1832.[33]

Nevertheless, when judged from the perspective of promoting active citizenship by means of political participation, the 'down-sizing' of 1832 in revisionist literature has gone much too far. Certainly, it was not as far-reaching as many radicals had hoped – hence the rise of Chartism – but of its dramatic consequences there can be no doubt. First, the expansion of the electorate from 439,200 to 656,000 represented an increase of 49 per cent and, over the next 30 years, the electorate grew by about 60 per cent.[34] Second, there was also a significant increase in voter turnout at general elections after the Reform Act – although, as some historians have pointed out, this trend had been reversed by the 1850s.[35] However, it is noteworthy that the average turnout at general elections between the first and second reform acts was 62.1 per cent; before 1832, turnout was never higher than 40 per cent.[36] Third, areas that were hitherto without separate representation – notably the large industrial towns – now elected MPs to the House of Commons. The abolition of small elite controlled boroughs hardly amounted to a popular loss: they had come to be associated with naked selfish interest that even the most liberal interpretation of virtual representation could no longer justify. Finally, there is little actual evidence to support the argument advanced by some revisionists that the 1832 Reform Act was responsible for the overall contraction of the urban electorate after 1832 – contraction in the sense that the growth rate of the electorate was outstripped by the growth of the adult male population. This led to a relative decline in the proportion of adult males who had the vote. It was not so much the 1832 Reform Act – which actually opened up many new possibilities for electoral participation – rather, it was due mainly to a series of structural factors that were extraneous to, but adversely affected by, the political system created by 1832. Such extraneous factors included: the rapid growth and mobility of the urban population (which presented logistical problems for electoral agents), the growth of cheap working-class housing (which often fell below the £10 qualifying threshold), and residential instability (meaning that many simply did not stay in one place long enough to qualify).[37] It is also probable that this contraction was the 'result of people voluntarily deciding not to participate'.[38] Admittedly, the Reform Act must bear some of the initial responsibility for this. The time and money that was needed to acquire and retain the franchise qualification introduced by the Reform Act undoubtedly deterred many from seeking the vote.[39] However, as Philip Salmon has shown, there was less of a deterrent once the political parties assumed primary responsibility for electoral registration from the mid-1830s.[40]

If the Reform Act purged the 'unreformed system' of some of its most exclusive features, many of the old popular and participatory features remained intact – such as the freeman franchise. This was an ancient voting right that was conferred by chartered boroughs on those connected with an incorporated trade, many of whom were artisans. After 1832, the freeman vote could be acquired either through inheritance (sons of freemen were granted voting rights at the age of 21) or through servitude (a seven-year apprenticeship to a freeman brought the privilege).[41] The 1832 Reform Act only abolished voting rights of all non-resident freemen, future honorary freemen or freemen by marriage. The absence of these limiting conditions before 1832 had allowed corrupt corporations to abuse the right of bestowing freedom to create pliant voters. Neither was the freeman franchise a voting right that was limited to those who did not qualify under the new £10 qualification. As Philip Salmon has shown, in a number of boroughs there were electors who qualified both as £10 householders and as voters by ancient right. Many of these dual-qualifiers opted for the latter voting right as it was 'not dependent upon prompt rate payment or the 1s. registration fee', as was the case with the householder qualification.[42] Borough electorates containing freemen voters could be very democratic – before and after 1832. Although these ancient franchises went into decline after 1832, one should not exaggerate the pace and extent of that decline. The continued existence of the freeman franchise helps to explain why both the 1832 and 1867 Reform Acts did not lead to dramatic expansions of the electorate in older boroughs such as York, where many artisans were already electors.[43]

Those historians who have argued that 1832 acted as a brake to the inclusive and participatory politics of unreformed England have also pointed to the exclusionary gendered implications of the Reform Act. Admittedly, the intention of the legislators who crafted the 1832 Reform Bill was to limit the franchise to 'independent men'. The corollary of this, according to Matthew McCormack, was that 'men who were younger, poorer, non-white (or even just non-English), or homosexual were . . . disadvantaged by the cult of the independent man'.[44] In practice, the franchise was limited to heads of households, who were invariably wealthier, older and married. Nevertheless, it would be disingenuous to imply that the small print of the 1832 Reform Act *systematically* excluded men who did not fit this description. A similar point can be made in relation to women, who were – for the first time – explicitly excluded from the franchise by virtue of it being defined as 'male'.[45] Yet, women had not voted in parliamentary elections for over 150 years (although single and unmarried women did vote occasionally in municipal elections).[46] Either way, as Catherine Hall perceptively observes: 'The naming of the vote as a masculine privilege could only have been necessary if at some level it was felt that this could no longer be assumed'.[47]

One of the indirect consequences of the 1832 Reform Act was to whet the appetite for the reform of local government. If the Reform Act began to peel away some of the rotten layers of borough politics, the 1835 Municipal Corporations Act went to the core by making local government more democratically accountable. This Act replaced 178 closed (that is, self-electing) boroughs with councils to be elected annually by adult males who had been resident ratepayers for three years and had paid up to at least the previous six months' taxes.[48] There was a significant expansion of the municipal electorate in the 1850s due to the introduction of the Small Tenements Rating Act (1850), which permitted the enfranchisement of occupiers who did not pay their rates in person – a further subverting of the axiom that the possession of the franchise was dependent on the personal payment of rates.[49] These democratizing innovations were undoubtedly improvements to the previously haphazard participatory, and frequently inefficient, system of local government that had centred on the parish vestries (administrative bodies based on areas of church administration with minor governing powers made up of local townspeople) and corporations, where they existed.[50] Elections to the vestries and the ways in which they conducted their business might have been more open in theory (if not always in practice) before the Sturges Bourne Acts of 1818 and 1819, and Hobhouse's Act of 1831 made them more 'select'.[51] But more often than not they were either part of the 'Old Corruption' network or else they were the powerless victims of 'Old Corruption' personified in the figures of the local magistrates who were invariably drawn from the landowning classes.[52] Similarly, it was the gentry and established mercantile elites who had dominated the venal corporations that existed prior to the 1835 Municipal Corporations Act.[53] This explains why local elites were often opposed to the Act. To label these new councils as 'ratepayer democracies' would be an exaggeration, not least because the municipal franchise was often more restrictive than that which existed in parliamentary boroughs after 1832. It would be more accurate to describe the new councils as 'settled ratepayer democracies',[54] given that the franchise was conditional on a three-year residence requirement in contrast to the one year that was necessary to qualify for the parliamentary franchise.[55]

What of the Second Reform Act of 1867, passed by Lord Derby and Disraeli's Tory government? On balance, this did more to expand rather than narrow the possibilities of exercising electoral citizenship. Standard historical interpretations present the 1867 Reform Act as the harbinger of mass representative politics. Overall, the Act increased the size of the electorate by 88 per cent. By the time of the 1871 census, 44.7 per cent of adult males possessed the franchise; ten years earlier, it had been a mere 19.7 per cent.[56] The Act introduced household suffrage to adult men who either owned or occupied a house, with the proviso that they had been in possession of the property for at least twelve months. Henceforth, working-class men would constitute a majority of the electorate in many of the larger boroughs. The redistribution clauses were much less dramatic than in 1832. The most important aspects of redistribution were the partial disfranchisement of 38 double-member borough constituencies with populations of less than 10,000 – these lost one of their two MPs – and the granting of a third seat to the largest provincial towns.

Initially, the Conservatives had hedged household suffrage with a series of safeguards: plural voting and 'fancy franchises', as they were termed (effectively more votes for those who were richer); a three-year residential qualification; and the personal payment of rates. This last safeguard would have excluded those large numbers of tenants who paid their rates through their landlord, a practice known as 'compounding'. The franchise was to be further restricted by limiting it to those who occupied distinct separate dwellings where the landlord did not reside – a deliberate attempt to exclude lodgers (invariably young, single men). Disraeli subsequently sacrificed these safeguards in a bid to preserve his party's majority in the House of Commons. The final Act conferred the vote on all rate-paying adult male occupiers and those who lodged in dwellings worth at least £10 a year who had been resident for a minimum of 12 months. The potential number of household voters was drastically increased by Disraeli's approval of the amendment to abolish compounding. The practice of 'compounding' was reintroduced in 1869 on condition it was not to be used as grounds for withholding the franchise. A further 'democratic' breakthrough came with the Parliamentary and Municipal Registration Act of 1878. This permitted the enfranchisement of adult males who occupied a single room in a multiple-occupied house providing it was self-contained, thus potentially converting many lodgers into householders and making it considerably easier to qualify for the vote (the lodger franchise was notoriously difficult to acquire and retain). The effects of the 1869 and 1878 statutes explain, in part, why the borough electorate grew by some 40 per cent *between* the Second and Third Reform Acts.[57]

Consequently, the 1867 Reform Act proved far less exclusionary than its creators had intended. The purpose of the 1867 Reform Bill (as with the bill brought in the previous year by the then Liberal government) was to ensure that a further extension of the franchise would only admit the respectable, independent and self-improving working man who had come to occupy such a prominent position in reforming discourse from the early 1860s. The respectable working man, though, was far from forming a self-evident socio-economic group. Rather, in the context of the reform debates, he was largely an invention of political rhetoric designed to reassure the governing and propertied classes by linguistically separating him from an imagined and feared underclass. The purpose of celebrating his virtues was to allow the government and moderate reformers to steer a safe course between the anti-democratic forces in Parliament and popular democratic excess. The result was a rhetorical sharpening of the emerging distinction between the 'respectable working class' and the underclass, termed by the moderate radical John Bright as the 'residuum'. This rhetorical strategy bore a marked similarity to the Whig's usage of 'middle class' in the debates on the 1832 Reform Bill, which performed the similar heuristic function of steering a safe, middle course between tory reaction and the urban mob.[58] The problem was that, in matters pertaining to electoral registration, such neat linguistic dichotomies were liable to break down.

Little evidence has been found to suggest that the complexities surrounding electoral registration were designed deliberately to restrict the size of the electorate, as argued by some revisionists.[59] It was not so much manipulation as a series of unintended structural factors: the problem of numbers initially overwhelming the system, the lack of assiduousness among officials and party activists, and the dying out of those electors who possessed 'ancient franchises'.[60] For all that the complexities surrounding registration continued to act as a barrier to enfranchisement after 1867, John Davis and Duncan Tanner have shown that registration did not systematically discriminate against the working class: many slum dwellers even managed to make it onto the electoral register. The registration process was apparently rather capricious in the way that it discriminated.[61] It seems that gender and age, rather than class factors, were more likely to influence the levels of enfranchisement: young men of all classes who either lodged or could only afford to rent one or two rooms found it difficult, though not impossible, to qualify for the vote.[62]

In terms of the broader ways in which 1867 redefined political citizenship, the evidence does not universally point in the direction of restriction either. Catherine Hall has argued that the enactment of the Reform Act against the background of Governor Eyre's pre-emptive bloody strike against an imminent rebellion of ex-slaves in Jamaica, the terrorist actions of the Fenians (Irish revolutionaries) on mainland Britain and the non-too distant memory of the Indian Mutiny of 1857, underlined the whiteness of male citizenship. According to Hall, the public debates on the franchise reflected and reinforced the prevailing racial hierarchies in which the English (Anglo-Saxons) were at the top, the Irish halfway down, the Indians a little lower, and Blacks at the bottom.[63] Although some Conservative opponents of enfranchising working men in Britain likened them to the rebellious black ex-slaves, for supporters this juxtaposition heightened the racial affinities between the British propertied classes and the British people. As Gladstone stated, working men were 'our own flesh and blood'.[64] Thus, although a wider imperial frame of reference could draw attention to the hardened racial hierarchy of mid-Victorian Britain, the ultimate effect of this comparison was to facilitate the incorporation of the respectable working man into the pale of the British constitution. Indeed, John Bright drew attention to the numerous colonial instances where English settlers were granted that which was denied to their brethren back in Britain as an argument for extending the franchise:

> Why an Englishman if he goes to the Cape, he can vote; if he goes farther to Australia, to the nascent empires of the New World, he can there vote... It is only in his own country... that he is denied this right which in every other community of Englishmen in the world would be freely accorded to him.[65]

As for the shift towards a more hardened racial hierarchy, this is debatable. As Peter Mandler has argued, Hall's 'placement of the Irish in some half-bestial position between Anglo-Saxons and Africans' cannot 'explain the burgeoning Liberal sympathies for Home Rule' – greater devolved self-government for Ireland. Similarly, Hall's view that biological explanations of African inferiority had largely triumphed by 1867 sits uneasily with the widespread approval for the enfranchisement of black ex-slaves in the United States.[66] It should also be added that one of the reasons why Gladstone and like-minded Liberals claimed to have been converted to a further extension of the franchise in the 1860s was that they had been so impressed with the sacrifice displayed by English cotton workers who, despite suffering from the adverse impact of the American Civil War on their trade and livelihood, stood firm in their support for the North in its crusade against Southern slavery.

What of gendered hierarchies? Once again it is difficult to interpret the Second Reform Act as restrictively defining the political citizen: the consolidation of the masculine political citizen was neither as complete nor incontestable in 1867 as some historians have argued. The revival of parliamentary reform in the mid-1860s was the occasion for the first organized petition for women's suffrage, and the Reform Bill of 1867 provided John Stuart Mill with the opportunity to move an amendment in favour of women's enfranchisement. Jane Rendall has shown how the wording of the Reform Act was interpreted by some as enfranchising women ratepayers, an interpretation that was tested in a concerted campaign at the 1868 general election. It was pointed out that the references to 'man' in the details of the Reform Act technically included women. An Act of 1850 had stipulated that in parliamentary legislation the word 'man' also incorporated women; only the more specific label of 'male person' was limited to men – a label that, with one exception, had not been used in the wording of the 1867 Reform Act. This loophole was subsequently closed by the courts, but not before thousands of women across the country exercised their rights to vote at the 1868 general election.[67] There would be no further extensive parliamentary debates on women's suffrage until the making of the Third Reform Bill in 1884.

The Third Reform Act continues to be overshadowed by its two predecessors. As such, historical knowledge of the ways in which it facilitated or restricted popular participation remains limited compared with that of 1832 and 1867. The Third Reform Act collectively refers to what was actually a package of ten bills. Most significant were the Franchise Bill of 1884 and the Redistribution Act of 1885. The Franchise Act gave the vote to more than one-and-three-quarter million rural electors. This had the effect of increasing the size of the United Kingdom electorate by 72 per cent. Put simply, 1884 did for the rural labourer what 1867 did for the urban artisan. The Redistribution Act was almost revolutionary. The mains terms in England and Wales were: the disfranchisement of 81 small boroughs; the partial disfranchisement of 39 double-member constituencies by taking away one of their two seats; and, with the exception of 22 boroughs that retained their double-member status, the subdivision of all remaining pre-existing multi-member constituencies into single-member seats.[68] Before 1885 there had only been 115 single-member seats in England and Wales; after 1885 this number rose to 446.[69] In total, 132 seats were redistributed in 1885, as against 143 in 1832 and 52 in 1867. The boundary commissioners, who were charged with redrawing the electoral map of the United Kingdom, were to meet three criteria when dividing boroughs and counties: population was to be proximately equalized within the constituent divisions, constituencies were to be geographically compact, and they were to reflect the 'pursuits of the population'.

Based on one reading, the Third Reform Act could be interpreted as regulating and restricting popular participation in the political process. With the enfranchisement of rural householders in 1884, citizenship became further restrictive in gendered terms. Possession of the vote became symbolically synonymous with adult masculinity. As the Liberal MP E. A. Leatham implied, when rejecting a motion to enfranchise women in 1884, this had exclusionary implications: 'It is not because men pay rates or taxes, or own or occupy property, that they have votes, but because they are men.'[70] Thus, as in 1832 and 1867, the intention of the legislators was to exclude not only women but also certain types of men. As Leatham made clear, citizenship should be limited to men 'of the highest type – that is, a man who is independent and free', and, we might add, who was also heterosexual, married and had children.[71]

On the other hand, it could be argued that the Third Reform Act actually subverted the identification between citizenship and independence by enfranchising rural labourers, and by paving the way for a more democratic model of citizenship. While radicals and Liberals tried to convince themselves that rural labourers had become independent men, there was a real worry that many of them would still be under the control of their landlords. Further, the Third Reform Act represented a shift away from the underlying principle of 'virtual representation'. Implicit in the adoption of single-member constituencies was the recognition that 'individuals were politically equal' and, as such, 'notions of proportionality had to inform how their numbers, if not their opinions were represented'.[72] This explains why many contemporaries regarded the Redistribution Act of 1885 as a democratizing measure. The single-member principle, it was argued, would break the tyranny of centralized political associations (which had hitherto ruled over the large boroughs) by dividing, and thus diluting, their power across several constituencies. Finally, the making of the new franchise bill was the occasion for a renewed debate in Parliament and in the country about extending the vote to women, an amendment to that effect being introduced in the House of Commons. These debates registered what would soon become one of the most powerful challenges to the theory of virtual representation. Opponents of women's suffrage drew on the well-worn argument that household suffrage was a 'family vote'. In so doing, they were forced to concede that the head of the household was, in many cases, a woman. Again, this opened an ideological space for the potential enfranchisement of propertied women.[73] In bringing about a shift away from interests and virtual representation towards individuals as the basis for participation in the national political process, the Third Reform Act contained within it the seeds of destruction for the existent model of political citizenship. We will return in the final chapter to assess how far official definitions of the political citizen were subjected to challenge, subversion and expansion between 1832 and 1914. First, it is necessary to look at how the major political movements of the period responded to this model of citizenship.

Chapter 2: Radicalism in the Age of the Chartists

One of the most remarkable political developments during the first half of the nineteenth century was the rise of a more coherent, articulate and organized popular radical movement. This was the heroic age of popular protest, of crowds meeting to demonstrate their collective strength, solidarity and determination to achieve their desired reforms. But what did it mean to be a 'radical' and why were there so many of them in the first half of the nineteenth century? This label denoted either an individual tendency or, more commonly, an association with a particular reforming cause. Most radicals were independent of, and all too frequently in opposition to, the two main political parties but sometimes worked with them to achieve their objectives.

Radicalism is a difficult term to define – indeed, it was a new term during this period (first appearing in the *Times* in 1820), although 'radical' was an established term of identification.[1] However, as will be made clear, there was a discernible radical *movement* during the first half of the nineteenth century, albeit one that assumed many forms and that was often divided in terms of aims, values, tactics, leadership and popular base. What impresses most is the sheer scale of popular radicalism. Somewhere between 100,000 and 250,000 people gathered on Hartshead Moor between Bradford, Huddersfield and Leeds on 15 May 1837 to protest against the New Poor Law of 1834. The second Chartist Petition of 1842 contained no less than 3,317,702 signatures and was more than six miles in length. It was the combustible combination of hunger, hatred and the political diagnosis made by the radicals that accounts for the scale of this popular mobilization. While the chronological focus of this chapter and the next is on the relatively short period between the 1832 Reform Act and the Chartist risings of 1848, both situate this period within the context of the origins and

27

development of the 'radical' tradition, a tradition that dates back to at least the late eighteenth century.

Defining Radicalism

Who were the radicals during this period? There were four radical groupings in the second quarter of the nineteenth century, with some overlap between them. The first of these were the Philosophic Radicals – the Utilitarian followers of Jeremy Bentham such as Joseph Hume and J. A. Roebuck. Their Utilitarian doctrine of the 'greatest happiness of the greatness number' and concern with how the monopoly of government by self-interested groups thwarted the wider public interest along with their attempts to demystify the structures of power lent intellectual weight to the broader radical critique of political and social inequality. The second group were the 'Manchester School' of radicals led by Richard Cobden and, to a lesser extent, John Bright. Identified with the rising economic power of the provincial middle class, these radicals campaigned against aristocratic monopoly. At times, the 'Manchester School' could merge imperceptibly into a third group of radicals who were linked by a commitment to 'moral reform'. Often from deeply religious backgrounds, these radicals (the most prominent being Joseph Sturge) campaigned for a variety of causes: anti-slavery, international peace, temperance, popular education, free trade and parliamentary reform. Representatives of these three groups often made common cause and sometimes tried to use as leverage a fourth group of radicals, the focus of this chapter: the popular radicals.

Popular radicals constituted a loose alliance of extra-parliamentary agitators who campaigned for popular rights. In contrast to the Benthamite radicals (who put their faith in bureaucratic reform) and to the Manchester and 'moral' radicals (who, after 1832, worked mainly for commercial and moral reform), popular radicals laboured more exclusively for extensive parliamentary and social reform. Some were willing to co-operate with those groups who were sympathetic to their cause, but on their own terms. By the early 1830s, it was felt by many radicals that they had all too often been the victims of those who feigned friendship – a fair number of whom were identified with one or more of the other radical groupings outlined above.

Popular radicalism was a movement that campaigned for the rights of the people to be included in the nation as citizens. This necessitated challenging various forms of political and social exclusivity or elitism. As the Chartist *Northern Star* stated in January 1841, the ultimate first principle adhered to by all radicals was: 'The people are the source of all power'.[2] But which 'people'? Notwithstanding radicalism's association with universal manhood suffrage and its cries of 'no taxation without representation', in practice most radicals came to accept – partly for reasons of expediency, partly for patriarchal reasons – that the franchise should be limited to the 'independent man'. Radicals argued that independence and, by extension, political rights were inherent not in property but in the *people* (or, to be more specific, adult men).[3] The danger of enfranchising dependents, such as women and paupers, was that they would be susceptible to bribery, and thereby ultimately reinforce rather than undermine the forces of 'Old Corruption' against which the radicals were battling. Thus, rather than challenge the association between independence and citizenship, radicals tried to redefine that independence in more inclusive terms and aspire to it themselves.[4]

The radical movement had its origins in the last third of the eighteenth century, when reformers began to link a variety of popular grievances with 'the corrupting effects of the concentration of political power'[5] in the hands of the Crown and its aristocratic placemen, who, it was alleged, were overtaxing the nation to pay for their indolent and indulgent lifestyles. The main tactics employed by the radicals were petitioning Parliament and the mass platform: the use of large outdoor public demonstrations to display strength and solidarity as a means to put pressure on the government to concede parliamentary reform. Petitioning similarly reinforced a sense of collective identity and agency.[6]

One crucial, but often overlooked, formative influence in this respect was the anti-slavery movement. For radicals, the abolition of the slave trade (1807) and slavery (1838) confirmed the efficacy of petitioning as a tactic of extra-parliamentary agitation, as well as the organizational rewards of exploiting the potential of material culture to raise revenue and foster a sense of participation by rooting their cause in the everyday life of their members. Chartists and Anti-Corn Law Leaguers, as had the abolitionists, produced a whole range of merchandise – such as food, crockery, clothes, trinkets, stationery and prints – each of which was adorned with emblems, mottos and representations of the leaders of the respective movements.[7]

The radicals also appropriated the arguments, moral outrage and iconography of the anti-slavery movement for their own campaigns.[8] Indeed, by the 1830s radicals were equating the conditions of white English workers with those of Black colonial slaves. It was no coincidence that the tory-radical Richard Oastler drew attention to this parallel in his famous letter to the *Leeds Mercury* of 29 September 1830, in which he exposed the widespread horrors of the factory regime.

Long hours, wretched conditions and cruel exploitation, especially of children, had reduced factory workers to 'a state of slavery, *more horrid* than the victims of that hellish system *"colonial slavery"*'.[9] Who was to blame for this wretched state of affairs? Oastler laid the finger of blame squarely on the avaricious manufacturer. As a result of his interventions and rousing platform oratory, Oastler soon found himself at the head of the campaign for factory reform. The slavery idiom also saturated the rhetoric of the popular campaign against the New Poor Law of 1834, in which Oastler was also involved. This law ended the local practice of administering charitable handouts to able-bodied workers during periods of economic depression. Henceforth, this practice of 'outdoor relief', hitherto widely used in the north of England, was to be replaced by 'indoor relief', meaning that the destitute would be forced to enter workhouses – which, their opponents claimed, reduced inmates to slaves.

Some historians have pointed to examples of radical opposition to the anti-slavery movement. This had less to do with racism per se – although it cannot be denied that some radicals, notably William Cobbett, were virulent racists – and was more to do with priorities. What angered Oastler and radicals such as Cobbett and Henry Hunt, the heroes of the mass platform in the aftermath of the Napoleonic Wars, was the hypocrisy of the middle-class abolitionists whose 'telescopic philanthropy' for colonial slaves apparently blinded them to the plight of the domestic working class. Other historians have gone further and claimed that redirecting the gaze of British society to the oppressed Negro was a deliberate attempt to displace, and distract attention from, domestic forms of slavery.[10] Yet, the evidence does not support this interpretation: the more that the abolitionists drew attention to the evils of colonial slavery, the more the radicals were able to make links with domestic forms of slavery.[11] Some, such as Cobbett, even claimed that the colonial slaves were actually better off than the British working class (due to the 'protection' slavery afforded them); others, such as the Chartist-Socialist Bronterre O'Brien, believed that abolition would merely transform slaves into victims of capitalism, making them 'wage slaves'. Most radicals, though, objected to all forms of slavery, even if their objections began at home.

The essence of the radical argument was that the nation's ills were being caused by the political system. It followed, therefore, that the system would have to be reformed. The radical agenda was increasingly associated with what would become the famous 'six points' of the People's Charter, published on 8 May 1838: manhood suffrage (sometimes universal, sometimes household); annual parliaments (that is, elections every year as a mechanism to make MPs more regularly accountable to their constituents); equal electoral districts (meaning a universal equitable ratio between electors and representatives, thus ending the gross inequality then prevailing – even after 1832); vote by ballot (secret voting to prevent the intimidation and bribery of the electorate); payment for MPs (thus making them disinterested and self-sufficient public servants); and the abolition of the property qualification for MPs (thereby enabling non-propertied citizens to stand for parliament). These points first appeared alongside one another as early as 1777.

Yet, we should not reduce radicalism to these six points; neither should radicalism be regarded as a narrowly focused political movement. Radicals campaigned against various forms of exclusivity. In addition to the franchise, they fought the legal and financial restrictions that the government placed on the press. These were designed to inhibit the development of a popular – and potentially subversive – radical press. To take another example, from the field of literature and the theatre, radicals were also involved in attempts to wrest control of Shakespeare from the elitist literary establishment. They proclaimed him as a proto-radical from a humble background that had eschewed aristocratic courtly culture and had lost no opportunity to attack tyranny and corruption in his plays. As Tony Taylor has shown, this battle for Shakespeare was also part of an attempt by radicals to reclaim the theatre as a popular institution that was not just the preserve of the chattering classes.[12] One of the cultural means by which radicals asserted their opposition to the established order and simultaneously proclaimed their democratic commitment was by challenging and subverting convention: a favourite at radical meetings was to sing their own songs to tunes that were associated with the establishment, such as the national anthem.[13] As these brief examples illustrate, radicalism was a rich and varied movement with a highly developed cultural politics.

In strict definitional terms, 'radical' literally meant 'returning to the roots'. As the Metropolitan radical Francis Place told the electors of Westminster, radicals were concerned to 'root up' and eradicate the causes of corruption.[14] It was commonplace for radicals to liken the corrupt state to an overgrown and unwieldy tree. As Place went on: 'Now the tree of corruption has taken such deep root – its branches have extended themselves so far – that none but an idiot would think of merely lopping off its exuberance, which would only strengthen the tree, and make it strike its roots still deeper'. This is why radicals emphasized 'root *and* branch reform'. The idea of 'returning' to the roots suggests that radicals were restorative in their desire to resurrect the rights of a perceived lost golden age. As Patrick Joyce has argued, this 'had a special resonance for the poor and powerless' as it 'spoke most urgently to those who had felt loss and dispossession' consequent

on the painful transition from the domestic, 'cottage economy' to factory production.[15] This was paradise lost. As we shall see, although
there were some radicals who desired to bring about innovative change,
most were 'restorationists'. It was conservative opponents who did most
to tar radicalism with the brush of destabilizing 'innovation'.[16]

The virtue of this restorative idiom was that it could be used to legitimize the demands of radicalism, even if it did leave them open to the
charge made by the elite of being 'historically illiterate'.[17] Speaking to
a mass meeting of Chartists on Peep Green in the West Riding in 1838,
the fiery tory-radical Joseph Rayner Stephens, echoing William Cobbett, reminded his listeners that they were seeking 'nothing new',[18]
merely the old rights of English freedom enshrined in the Magna
Carta of 1215. This restorative brand of radicalism was concerned
with uncovering historical precedents. For example, the great Chartist
leader Feargus O'Connor argued that a form of universal manhood
suffrage had existed until the reign of Henry VI in the early fifteenth
century. Chartists also pointed out that annual parliaments had been
ordered by statute in 1330 and 1362. The right to hold public meetings
in the open air dated back to the time of the witanagemot (parliament) in Anglo-Saxon England.[19] The popular rights that Stephens and
O'Connor identified – such as the right of free speech, free assembly
and petitioning – flowed from, and were guaranteed by, the English
constitution that had evolved over the centuries. Occasionally, radicals
also drew on precedents, tactics and symbolism associated with classical
republicanism.[20]

The radical appeal to historical precedent often merged with the second definition of radicalism: returning to 'first principles' – that is, to
the original principles that had underpinned the creation of society,
usually traced back to Anglo-Saxon England.[21] The Edinburgh radical W. S. Villiers told a group of Chartists that their 'present movement,
being essentially English, and not having in view any theoretical innovations' merely desired 'a recurrence to the first principles of the original
Saxon Constitution'.[22] As this quote suggests, radicals constructed their
own version of English history, the leitmotif of which was the struggle
of a virtuous and dispossessed people doing battle against tyrannical
and corrupt forces. Many Chartists argued that the popular rights
and forms of popular sovereignty they were campaigning for were
in existence before the Norman Conquest.[23] This somewhat mythi-
cal charmed era of Anglo-Saxon democracy had been vanquished by
'William the Bastard' who, to ensure the survival of the monarchy,
created an aristocratic class to help him rule over the English people.
Together, the monarchs and aristocrats had progressively stripped the
people of their rights and liberties,[24] despite the heroic actions of a

succession of popular crusaders, the most prominent being Wat Tyler, the leader of the peasants' revolt of 1341, and, more ambiguously, Oliver Cromwell as 'the plain man who unmade kings'.[25] To the radicals of the nineteenth century, present-day aristocrats were nothing more than the descendants of the illegitimate Normans.[26] As Robert Hall has argued, the main virtue of appealing to historic precedent and constructing a radical version of the past was that it allowed the radicals 'to counter the contemporary tendency to dismiss democracy as foreign and "unEnglish", and to make a case for the historical legitimacy of their political strategy and democratic programme'.[27] The enemies of radicalism associated theoretical abstractions such as natural rights with the democratic excess of the French Revolution of 1789 and the infant American Republic.

One English radical who had championed the French Revolutionary model of popular sovereignty was Thomas Paine in his immensely popular *Rights of Man*, published in two parts in 1791 and 1792. This became the Bible of British radicalism. For Paine there was no greater folly than to legitimize radical claims by recourse to historical precedent since precedents could be found to legitimize almost anything, including the monopoly of political power in the hands of the few. Similarly, it was erroneous to speak of historic constitutional rights since there was no actual written English constitution, let alone one founded on the principles of popular sovereignty. By contrast, echoing John Locke, Paine argued that man had natural rights by virtue of his existence: his 'Maker' had endowed him with the inalienable rights to life, liberty and property. For Paineite radicals, natural rights and reason, not historic precedent, were the ultimate 'first principles' of radicalism.[28] Having established the rights of *all* men, Paine argued that these natural, equal rights were incompatible with hereditary systems of government as these privileged the monarchy and aristocracy at the expense of the people. 'Expense' was the operative word here, as Paine objected to the expensive and devastating ways in which these privileges were secured: through the colossal business of warfare. Paine argued that it was only the elite who benefited from warfare due to their monopoly on military, diplomatic and colonial appointments. Put simply, more wars meant more appointments. Worst still were those who, at exorbitant rates of interest, had lent money to the government to enable them to sustain the war effort, thereby inflating the National Debt. In Cobbett's writing this assumed a distinctly Antisemitic form: for Cobbett, the quintessential swindling moneylender was the Jewish financier. This gave further ammunition to the assault on 'Old Corruption'.

All this led Paine to advocate representative government in the form of a republic, by which he meant a 'government established and conducted for the interests of the public'.[29] In Part II of the *Rights of Man*, Paine went on to outline his radical egalitarian scheme. This included the abolition of monarchy and aristocracy, and a redistribution of wealth facilitated by a drastic reduction of what he regarded as unnecessary government expenditure (especially on the military) and by a system of progressive taxation in order to provide for the education of children, support for the elderly, relief of poverty, increased salaries for useful public servants and payment for MPs. In a subsequent and even more controversial text, *The Age of Reason*, published in 1794, Paine expanded his radical critique to the superstitious aspects of Christianity, which, he argued, made it an opponent of liberty and progress. Superstition was to be replaced with deistical Christianity, a rational and secular religion that was based on the moral teachings of Christ and that was broadly compatible with a scientific understanding of the world.

Thus, in place of the constitutional narrative, Paine provided radicals with an alternative rational and republican ideology, a tradition that was kept alive down to the mid-nineteenth century by a small group of Metropolitan ultra-radicals. Prominent amongst these were the agrarian reformer Thomas Spence, whose ideas inspired the revolutionary-republican underground, and the freethinking radical Richard Carlile, whose London bookshop on Fleet Street served as a hub for ultra-radicalism. But Paineite radicalism did not establish itself as the dominant ideological strand in nineteenth-century radicalism. One reason for this, as we have seen, was that Paine's ideas were associated with the foreign and unChristian ideas of the French Revolution. Another was that Paine's ideas were also perverted by Carlile's idiosyncratic, introverted, infidel republicanism. Carlile took Paine's rational republicanism to its extremes. He was even more dismissive of historical precedent than Paine: 'I test history by physics', Carlile declared.[30] Carlile's republicanism prioritized self-improvement, education and 'the rooting out of superstition and the restoration of Science to the Church' rather than with mobilizing the masses for political reform. This, Carlile argued, was impractical and would be ineffectual 'until the people were so reformed', by which he meant moral reform.[31] For Carlile, self-reform was the first principle of radicalism.[32]

Nevertheless, although Paineite formulations of natural rights exerted less influence than constitutional historic rights on early nineteenth-century radicalism, the two were by no means mutually exclusive.[33] Paine's influence was plain to see on a number of prominent radicals, especially in the late 1830s and 1840s when there was a renewed interest in Paine. The Chartists W. J. Linton, Henry Vincent and R. G. Gammage were all heavily influenced by Paine's ideas. Most radicals drew on as many arguments and authorities as possible to justify their demands with little sense of any incompatibility. Chartists in the 1830s and 1840s were, in the same breath, still justifying universal manhood suffrage as both a natural, inherent right *and* a privilege guaranteed by the ancient constitution.[34] But what radicals said and did were not always the same, and deliberately so. As James Epstein has illustrated, alongside the verbal invocation of the English constitution radicals often displayed Caps of Liberty, associated in the official public mind with the democratic excess and horrors of the French Revolution.[35]

Similarly, the boundaries separating radicalism based on historic precedent and on natural rights were often blurred. For example, the ancient Anglo-Saxon constitution was thought by some to have enshrined natural rights. The desire to return to 'first principles' could also embody both precedent and natural right. The selection, however, was not always random as the context could determine what it was possible to say. The repressive power of the state circumscribed what radicals could say and do; that is, if they wanted to avoid imprisonment, transportation or even execution – all fates that befell radicals from the 1790s through to the 1840s.[36] So, one can see why radicals justified their demands by recourse to English constitutional precedent rather than to what was perceived as French, revolutionary natural rights. And yet currents of Paineite radicalism survived. The enduring legacy of Paine stemmed from his impassioned attack on privilege and corruption, from his maxim that all adult rational men were entitled to one vote, and one vote only, and from popularization of the right of the people to resist tyrannical rulers on the grounds that the latter had reneged on the consent of the former.

Another ambiguity that permeated radicalism was the co-existence of restorative and progressive elements: this centred on the question of what purpose radical reform was to serve. On the one hand, there were radicals such as Feargus O'Connor, John Fielden and thousands of disaffected artisans who looked back to an egalitarian and harmonious era of popular rights, justice and morality that revolved around family, home and community: this age had finally been destroyed by the rampant forces of industrialization. On the other hand, there were radicals such as the Chartists Bronterre O'Brien, G. J. Harney, William Lovett and Thomas Cooper who rejected what they regarded as a 'rotten and obsolete past' and 'turned their eyes to the future and sought the remedy for past evils in a reconstruction of society which frankly ignored history'.[37] This group of radicals often entertained utopian dreams along socialistic lines, leading some to advocate a positive directing role for the state (notably by nationalization of the land). Others were suspicious of the state and the political system, believing that their goals would be best achieved by forming their own model communities, as was the case with the Owenites, the socialist followers of the paternalist mill owner Robert Owen.[38] A number of short-lived communities were established in Britain, and Owen himself actually established a community in the United States in Indiana. They were to run on cooperative lines in which men *and* women would live and work alongside one another as equals exchanging their products, not in accordance with the arbitrary market price of the capitalist economy but at a price determined by the amount of labour that had gone into making the product. This was known as the 'labour theory of value'.

It would, however, be wrong to presume that all progressive radicals were socialists. Most were not, for 'socialists looked to communal ownership; radicals to individual property rights',[39] although in practice the line between the two was often unclear. Even radicals of the Paineite persuasion were socially and economically individualistic. They desired a fundamental reordering of government in accordance with democratic principles, but there was to be no overhauling of the values and institutions of civil society. Competitive individualism, property and business enterprise were sacrosanct. There was to be equality of opportunity, not social levelling. Here, we begin to see how radicalism could merge with liberalism.

This preoccupation with lost golden ages and popular dispossession explains why many radicals attached great importance to the land, and advocated various policies – allotment schemes, peasant proprietorship, emigration and land nationalization. Whatever the scheme, the purpose was invariably the same: to return the land to its rightful owners, the people. The land, it was argued, had been stolen from them by the Norman invaders and their acolytes. This radical obsession with the land was not necessarily reactionary. As a number of historians have pointed out, the resettling of industrial workers on the land was a practical solution to some of the social problems caused by industrialization, such as overcrowding. Parcelling out land for cultivation supplied workers with the means to liberate themselves from the tyranny of capitalism by giving them control over their own labour.[40] Thus, in its attempts to grapple with contemporary social problems, the agrarian strain in radicalism could be made to serve progressive ends, so illustrating how the line between restorative and progressive radicalism could also be blurred.

Another hazy boundary related to the vexed question of radical strategy and tactics. By the 1830s, many radicals, though by no means all, were content to work within the existing political system, their objective being to widen participation in that system and to make it more accountable and representative of the nation's interests. Thus, radicals employed constitutional means to attain constitutional ends.[41] Mass meetings, petitions and the mobilization of 'members unlimited' through various organizational channels established themselves as the dominant alternative to pre-industrial protest of non-political violence (such as bread riots) and to the conspiratorial tradition of the ultra-radical revolutionary underground dating back to the 1790s. The radicals could sail close to, and sometimes over, the boundaries of constitutional legality – at least, in the eyes of the authorities, which were always ready to contain the radical threat by repressive measures where necessary. Radicals, in particular, exploited this ambiguity, an ambiguity that is lost if an over-exacting distinction between the 'physical' and 'moral' force wings is drawn. 'Physical force' was the label applied to those who were prepared to use violent means to bring about their objectives; 'moral force' to those who favoured reasoned argument and 'moral' example. This dichotomy, usually employed in relation to Chartism, fails to do justice to the subtleties of radical tactics; it also obscures what was, in reality, a continuum of tactical options *within* as well as between the 'physical' and 'moral' force wings.[42] 'Open, intimidating constitutionalism' was the preferred formula for most Chartists. In practice, this amounted to reasoned argument and other methods of unarmed resistance, such as exclusive dealing, backed up with the *threat* of force. As far as the Chartists were concerned, the forcible methods that they threatened were constitutional, such as the historic right of the freeborn Englishman to bear arms. Whether one plumped for physical or moral force, the ultimate objective was the same: to implement the Charter and bring about change, preferably by converting public opinion or intimidating the ruling classes into conceding change, with the use of force if necessary.

One final definitional problem with radicalism concerns the question of whether it was a political or socio-economic movement. Radicalism was, first and foremost, a *political* movement, but one with wide-ranging objectives, suggesting that the political–social dichotomy is also too simplistic. Until the advent of the 'new political history' in the 1980s, historians usually interpreted radicalism as a social protest movement, especially in its Chartist guise.[43] But, as Stedman Jones has demonstrated, even the most cursory analysis of what the Chartists actually said and wrote reveals that political demands were at the centre of Chartism, and of radicalism more generally. These political demands were the essence of the radical tradition. It was a shared commitment to this radical tradition and political programme that made Chartism into a genuinely national movement, albeit one that was decentralized, loosely organized and beset by tensions between local activists and the national leadership.[44] The famous six points of the People's Charter were both a means *and* an end. The obsessive concern with these by the Chartists stemmed both from their belief that they were a natural and/or historic right that was being unlawfully withheld, and in the faith that they vested in the franchise as a vehicle to improve the social and economic position of the masses. The Chartists might have lacked a coherent, fully-worked out and agreed social policy but, as Mark Hovell was forced to concede many years ago, behind the Charter 'lay a vision of social regeneration that alone could remove the terrible evils against which Chartism had revolted'.[45]

For some reformers, radicalism was a social movement with political ends. We have already seen in relation to progressive radicals that many desired a transformation of the social order. Owenite Socialists believed that this would not only precede, but also actually create the conditions for, a thoroughgoing reform of the political system. Without prior social reorganization along co-operative lines, the Owenites argued, political reform would be ineffective. Most radicals disagreed, although by the 1840s a growing number of them were coming round to the view that the masses would have to reform themselves first and thus demonstrate their social fitness for political citizenship. Either way, there were few radicals who rejected politics altogether, and even those who wished to do so were forced periodically to accept its primacy. For example, although trades unionists often expressly discouraged political discussion in their organizations, they were forced to tackle the legal obstacles that stood in the way of effective unionization by means of campaigns for legislative reform and clemency petitions for convicted trades unionists. In addition, the idea of organizing a general strike – ubiquitous during this period – was inherently political, with its aim of realizing 'far-reaching, even revolutionary political and social reform'[46] by establishing a national congress or convention to rival parliament itself. As a trades unionist stated in the *Northern Star* in July 1842, 'nothing short of a participation in the making of the laws by which they were governed, would effectually protect their labour'.[47]

Parliamentary Reform and Chartism

Why, and to what extent, did radicals place so much emphasis on parliamentary reform? As the preceding discussion suggests, not all radicals viewed parliamentary reform as a panacea for the nation's problems. This scepticism was not just confined to Owenite Socialists either. Many radicals regarded parliamentary reform as inadequate by itself or, at the very least, as a means to significantly more important ends. This line of radical thinking did not reject political channels in the same way that Owenites did. Rather than agitate solely for abstract political rights, they campaigned for more direct legislative reform. The movements for the repeal of the 1834 Poor Law, for factory reform, and the campaign for an end to the financial restrictions on newspapers all desired direct legislative reform. It was the failure to achieve direct legislative reform that so often fuelled the demand for parliamentary reform. But this was a frustratingly vicious circle for radicals as illustrated by the Todmorden manufacturer 'Honest' John Fielden, the Radical MP for Oldham (1832–47). Although desirous of manhood suffrage at the time of the 1832 Reform Act, when this failed to materialize Fielden took the practical view that the House of Commons should be given a chance to prove its reforming credentials. Fielden was soon bitterly disappointed with Parliament for the catalogue of betrayals. At the top of his list were the New Poor Law and the failure to secure an adequate measure of factory reform. Since Parliament proved unresponsive and intransigent, in the absence of a concerted popular campaign for parliamentary reform, he turned to the alternative methods of trades unionism and Owenism. But the obstacles faced by these movements, allied to Parliament's growing list of abuses, led Fielden to prioritize the need for manhood suffrage and so he identified, for a time at least, with the Chartists. He subsequently became disillusioned with Chartism and chose to devote most of his reforming energies to factory reform. Fielden's career is not evidence of how erratic radicals were: he was, as were many others, involved simultaneously with these causes, even if the emphasis understandably shifted to suit the context. Rather, Fielden is evidence of the wide-ranging and multi-faceted nature of radicalism, and the pragmatism exhibited by many radicals.[48] It would be wrong, therefore, to exaggerate the enveloping effect of parliamentary reform.

There was another group of dogmatic and doctrinaire radicals who tended to regard this pragmatism, at best, as diversionary and, at worst, as desertion and collaboration. When some Chartists began to redirect their attention to other causes such as temperance, co-operation and education in the early 1840s – further evidence of how radicalism was not just preoccupied with the franchise – Feargus O'Connor denounced these so called 'New Moves' as detracting from the overall goal of securing the enactment of the People's Charter. The more paranoid radicals often saw rival movements in conspiratorial terms: Richard Oastler believed that Chartism, with its goals of abstract political reform, represented a sinister attempt by the manufacturers and their allies to redirect popular unrest away from the Anti-Poor Law campaign.[49] Likewise, there were many Chartists who looked upon the Anti-Corn Law League as a plot to undermine Chartism by diverting attention away from political reform.[50] The Anti-Corn Law League had been established in 1839 to campaign for the abolition of the 1815 Corn Law, which taxed imported grain so as to protect the price of domestically produced wheat – much to the advantage of farmers and ultimately the landowners to whom they paid rent. Aided and abetted by the Tories, many Chartists mounted a counter-conspiracy theory by warning the people that the Anti-Corn Law League was an attempt by the avaricious manufacturers to secure cheaper food so that they could reduce the wages of working men. This, it was argued, explained why the middle class dominated the League.[51] It was also noted that many prominent Leaguers were supporters of the New Poor Law and enemies of factory reform. So, for all that many Chartists were opposed to the Corn Laws, few could bring themselves to co-operate with the Anti-Corn Law League, despite the best efforts of those, such as Thomas Perronet Thompson, who tried to bring both movements together.[52]

But it was not just suspicion and class conflict that kept the two movements apart. There were also ideological differences. Although Chartism and the Anti-Corn Law League shared a common enemy in the form of aristocratic monopoly, they were at loggerheads over what underpinned that monopoly. The Leaguers naturally took the view that it was the Corn Laws: the Chartists, that the Corn Laws were merely an evil manifestation of an underlying monopoly of political power.[53] The Chartists and the Anti-Corn Law League articulated their political ideology in the shared idiom of 'Old Corruption', but they appropriated that idiom in competing and conflicting ways. The question of what exactly 'Old Corruption' entailed, how the various manifestations of it were to be reformed – and in what order – gave rise to serious disagreement and division among radicals. Old Corruption was something of a moving target. This was due, in part, to the widening gap between the shrinking governmental reality of 'Old Corruption' (consequent on various 'economical reforms' introduced between the 1780s and 1840s) and its inflated radical image.[54] Parliamentary reform, therefore, waxed and waned according to the circumstances of the time. This was partly influenced by the state of the economy but, more crucially, by the shifting political context. The Chartist movement itself was subject to such waxing and waning, with peaks in 1839, 1842 and 1848 and troughs in the intervening years when Chartist energies were partly re-directed into other complementary causes – such as temperance, education, land reform, trades unionism, Owenism, the Anti-Corn Law League, foreign affairs and local government. Nonetheless, it cannot be denied that parliamentary reform remained the overriding objective for most radicals between 1832 and 1848.

This still leaves the question of why so many radicals campaigned for parliamentary reform. Why was the franchise coveted by radicals? One of the reasons was that the franchise was widely seen as the badge of citizenship. In radical eyes, to be denied the vote was to be denied one's freedom and even one's human dignity.[55] Those without the vote were no better than slaves and it is no coincidence, as we have seen, that many Chartists drew on a slavery idiom, still fresh in the public's mind from the abolition campaigns, when bemoaning the working man's lack of political rights.[56] Not only was the possession of the franchise the marker of being fully human, it also furnished a mechanism to create an active, vigilant citizenry. For radicals, one of the most important duties of citizenship was the obligation to resist corruption and tyranny, especially political tyranny as this underpinned so many wider abuses. This is why radicals placed so much emphasis on education and the need to make people aware of these abuses – hence the importance attached to repealing the 'taxes on knowledge' (the legal and financial restrictions that the government imposed on the press). Restrictions on knowledge bred ignorance, a condition in which corruption and tyranny thrived. Finally, and perhaps most importantly in the context of the 1830s and 1840s, the radicals believed that the vote was the key to solving the poverty of the masses.

Why did radicals attribute socio-economic distress to political causes? While the origins of this connection could be traced back to the late eighteenth century, it was in the aftermath of the Napoleonic Wars that radicalism began the explicit attribution of a range of socio-economic grievances to 'exclusive law making'.[57] The radicals of the mass platform and the radical press argued that wage reductions, high prices, unemployment and debt were being caused by excessive taxation and by manipulation of the money supply for the sole purpose of enriching the idle and profligate governing elite. The exclusive monopoly of political power by these elites allowed them to tax the unrepresented nation with virtual impunity, especially through indirect taxes on articles of popular consumption, such as corn, that fell disproportionately on the poor. Thus were the masses being denied the full produce of their labour: it was estimated that the productive classes received only one-fifth of their earnings.[58]

It was not just the direct impact of punitive taxation that pressed hard on the masses. Taxes also inflated the price of British goods. This not only made them less competitive in the world market but also limited spending power at home, leading to under-consumption. Consequently, radicals reasoned that the exclusive political power of

the elite needed breaking by making the government more representative and accountable – a means by which to end reckless expenditure
on pensions, sinecures and interest on the National Debt. This, in
turn, would lead to a reduction in taxation and poverty, stimulate the
domestic economy and increase wages.

While this constituted the essence of the radical case for parliamentary reform, radicals were not always agreed on what reform was to
entail. As with the term 'radical', 'parliamentary reform' – and, indeed,
'reform' itself – was also a broad umbrella term that could take on a
number of meanings.[59] As Derek Beales has demonstrated, the word
'reform' was more elusive and was employed far less in the first half of
the nineteenth century than historians have often suggested. When the
word 'Reform' was used, 'and especially if it had a capital R, it almost
invariably meant *parliamentary reform* . . . and people wishing to speak of
other types of reform had to [have] an adjective in front of the word'.[60]
To return more specifically to parliamentary reform, this was not always
synonymous with the six points that we have come to associate with
Chartism. The original 'People's Charter' of May 1838 not only contained the six points but also a whole package of reforms designed
to simplify and standardize electoral procedure.[61] Turning to the earlier agitation for parliamentary reform between 1830 and 1832, it was
evident that moderate (often middle-class) radicals were opposed to
universal manhood suffrage, although some subsequently came round
to the idea. Similarly, by the late 1840s there were even some Chartists
who were willing to accept a more restrictive franchise. These moderate
Chartists, through the National Parliamentary and Financial Reform
Association (established in January 1849) campaigned for a 'Little Charter' of four points: household suffrage, the ballot, triennial parliaments
and a more equal distribution of seats.

These shifting conceptions of parliamentary reform were, to a large
extent, a reflection of the changing goals of the radicals. Prior to
1832, for moderate radicals the primary objective of parliamentary
reform had been to augment the power of the House of Commons with
regard to the executive (that is, the Crown, which at this stage was still
widely viewed as powerful and the pinnacle of 'Old Corruption'). As
such, reform proposals centred on the need to rejuvenate the House
of Commons through shorter parliaments, by reducing the power of
'nomination' boroughs (those controlled by patrons, who were themselves often in the pay of the Crown) and by redistributing seats to the
large boroughs and counties. Such a redistribution of seats, coupled
with a residential franchise would give manufacturing and commercial
interests a more equitable share of representation in the House of
Commons, as demanded by the moderate radicals. After 1832, radical

attention focused more exclusively on the House of Commons itself and on the need to make it more representative of the nation.[62] Yet, one should not exaggerate the extent of this shift as some radicals, arguably those that were most popular, had campaigned for a more representative House of Commons in demanding universal manhood suffrage long before 1832. Neither did radicals cease to fulminate against the Crown after 1832, despite its loss of power.[63] While the 1832 Reform Act did not meet these objectives, they soon reappeared with a renewed and unprecedented sense of urgency in the form of Chartism. Parliament in its present form, Chartists argued, was failing the people. So successful were the Chartists in highlighting the link between socio-economic and political ills that the state eventually responded, but on its own terms and not at the direct bidding of the Chartists: in this respect, the Chartists were victims of their own success.

Chapter 3: The Culture and 'Failure' of Radicalism

For many activists there was more to being a 'radical' than championing popular rights and demanding the six points of the People's Charter. It could also mean subscribing to a set of values, beliefs and practices amounting to a distinct radical lifestyle. For the more zealous and committed, this formed the basis of an alternative culture. The names of some of the organizations, such as the Bradford Chartist Temperance Co-operative Society, give an indication of the breadth of radicalism and the associational culture to which it gave rise.[1] The very act of participating in a movement was part of the radical experience, not only in terms of bringing like-minded people together, but also as a means to create a democratic culture within their organizations as a prelude to creating a democratic society.[2] Radicalism was an ideology *of* change (in both its restorative and progressive, utopian guises) and, by extension, a dynamic movement in which its leaders and supporters had to mobilize *for* change. To preserve what already existed or to amend, rectify and tinker with the existing system, as did the opponents of radicalism, was seemingly far easier to achieve than a drastic reform of that system, let alone building an entirely new system as advocated by some radicals. Of course, the lived experience of being radical was such that many activists were denied this agency by the coercive apparatus of the state, or else it was severely curtailed by the demands and sacrifices that were part of a radical lifestyle. This should be borne in mind when assessing the achievements of the radicals. The purpose of this chapter is to recreate aspects of this radical culture in the years before 1848 by means of a critical discussion of the historiography on the social basis of the movement, the values it promoted and the lifestyle that it entailed. The chapter concludes with an assessment of the ideological and structural constraints that were responsible for weakening the radical movement in the 1840s.

A Class-Based Movement?

Conventionally, radicalism was interpreted as a socio-economic movement, and one that was largely class-based in terms of its objectives and constituency of support. For the urban middle class, according to this interpretation, radicalism (and, subsequently, liberalism) supplied the means to break the interlocking social, economic and political power of the aristocracy that was thwarting their interests. Ideologically, this radicalism drew sustenance from the principles of *laissez-faire* political economy, the essence of which was that the less governments interfered in the economy, the better it functioned. This was anathema to the idea of state-sanctioned special privileges that benefited one interest (the aristocracy) at the expense of others (the middle class). The mantra of middle-class radicalism was freedom – in politics, religion and trade. This radicalism, it was argued, reached its apogee in the Anti-Corn Law League, dominated by the Manchester Manufacturers and led by Richard Cobden. It was no coincidence that, when the agitation against the Corn Laws was at its height, Cobden was forced to admit 'that most of us entered upon this struggle with the belief that we had some distinct class-interest in the question'.[3]

For the working class, by contrast, radicalism represented an assault on the 'middle-class' principles of *laissez-faire* for the ways it appeared to sanction the selfish pursuit of profit and for turning a blind eye to what it regarded as the unavoidable dire social consequences of the 'Industrial Revolution'. To add insult to injury, the selfish manufacturers applauded the Malthusian belief that overpopulation and unemployment was the result of working-class licentiousness and fecklessness, hence the punishing regime of the new workhouses. In retaliation, workers formed trades unions and looked to Parliament to enact legislation that defended traditional rights and customs. This informal moral economy was underpinned by plebeian notions of fairness and social justice, and was encapsulated in slogans such as 'a fair day's wages for a fair day's work'. Joseph Rayner Stephens summed up this plebeian moral economy in the same speech in which he famously defined universal suffrage as 'a knife and fork question':

> every working man in the land had a right to have a good coat to his back, a comfortable aboad [*sic*] in which to shelter himself and his family, a good dinner upon his table, and no more work than

was necessary for keeping him in health, and as much wages for that work as would keep him in plenty, and afford him the enjoyment of all the blessings of life which a reasonable man could desire. (Tremendous Cheers.)[4]

Against the background of economic depression, the introduction of machinery into the workplace and the failure of workers to secure redress by conventional means of protest, they turned to the 'Six Points of the People's Charter'. This pitted the workers against the manufacturers and culminated in Chartism, which for Lenin – writing in 1917 – amounted to 'the first broad, genuinely mass, politically systematic, proletarian-revolutionary movement'.[5] While few historians today would fully subscribe to Lenin's view of Chartism – witness Chartism's constitutional objectives and tactics – many of the movement's most prominent historians, notably John Belchem, James Epstein, Neville Kirk, Paul Pickering and Dorothy Thompson – still interpret radicalism and Chartism as the political expression of a working class that was conscious, in E. P. Thompson's words, of an 'identity of...interests as between themselves, and as against other men'.[6]

Revisionist scholarship has argued that radicalism makes little sense when interpreted through this class-based lens.[7] For example, to see Chartism as 'a reaction of the working class against the Industrial Revolution'[8] is wide of the mark. The pace and nature of industrial change was so uneven, protracted and diverse that the notion of an 'Industrial Revolution' has been called into question.[9] Neither should we assume, as Marxist historians have, a correlation between advanced industrialization and Chartist strength. In 'some of the urban communities which were most completely the product of the industrial expansion', such as Glossop, St Helens and Crewe, Chartism 'was weak or non-existent'.[10] Another variant of the socio-economic interpretation views radicalism, and more specifically Chartism, not as a movement signalling the rise of the modern factory proletariat but, rather, as a reaction on behalf of those declining pre-industrial workers, notably handloom weavers. Certainly, many of these dispossessed workers flocked to the Chartist cause; however, it would be wrong to view radicalism as merely the expression of a dispossessed pre-industrial working class. Radicalism drew support from a much wider social constituency. Further, as Patrick Joyce has shown, radical-liberal visions of lost golden ages were animated not by class but by community,[11] hence the cross-class constituencies of the Anti-Poor Law, Factory and Chartist movements. And notwithstanding tory rhetoric, this was not always the aristocracy and the people united against selfish manufacturers.[12] Turning to the Anti-Corn Law League, class-based tensions certainly existed between the Leaguers and the Chartists; however, it makes little sense to reduce those tensions to class. A series of criss-crossing ideological, strategic and personal tensions kept the two movements, for the most part, at arm's length, to say nothing of the role played by rival conspiratorial myths.[13]

Radicalism was not the spontaneous creation of industrialization and the rise of class-consciousness since there was no obvious and automatic connection between those processes (such as they existed) and a movement seeking political reform. As Stedman Jones has argued, radicalism was the ideology of the politically excluded and spoke to a heterogeneous social constituency.[14] Where possible, most radicals aimed to unite the productive classes in opposition to the idle and parasitical classes – the aristocracy and increasingly the exploitative financier and capitalist. The productive classes included the working class *and* those less wealthy elements within the middle class who were perceived as being non-exploitative and who were themselves victims of punitive taxation. It is instructive to note that the first Chartist Petition of 1839 not only stated 'that the labour of the workman must no longer be deprived of its due reward', it also added 'that the capital of the master must no longer be deprived of its due profit'.[15] Similarly, as the Birmingham radical MP Thomas Attwood told the House of Commons, when introducing the Petition, the members of the middle class with whom the Chartists made common cause were not 'men with small fortunes, and small fundholders or mortgagees, or those who had retired from trade' but 'the productive classes, the merchants, the traders, and the manufacturers'.[16]

Undoubtedly, radicalism *could* take on a class inflection, and it did on a number of occasions after 1832 – notably at the high points of Chartist agitation in 1842 and again in 1848. But more often than not this was a reaction to political exclusion, to a politically derived hostility to liberal political economy, rather than in the Marxist sense of locating working-class alienation within the exploitative means of capitalist production. For most radicals, such economic exploitation was due to the selfish actions of *individuals* whose tyrannical economic power was sanctioned by the state.[17] Even those on the radical fringes – such as the Owenites, who developed theories based on what they regarded as the inherently exploitative nature of the capitalist system – focused not on the mode of production itself as Marx and his followers would do, but on the inequities of exchange and distribution. The demon of iniquitous exchange was the profiteering 'middle man' who bought cheap and sold dear. As such, this attack on parasitical middlemen tended to reinforce, rather than undercut, the radical critique of 'Old Corruption'.[18] This anti-capitalist sentiment seldom translated into revolutionary socialist consciousness.[19] Finally, it seems that even Ernest Jones, the last great leader of Chartism, who was once hailed by historians as one of the first English proto-Marxist socialists – turns out, on closer inspection, to have been little more than a 'restorationist' radical.[20]

In terms of the social composition of the movement, there can be little doubt that radicalism, and especially Chartism, was dominated by the working class. Chartism, though, was not exclusively working class: even in 'class-conscious' Bradford there were shopkeepers and other small property owners who were Chartists.[21] Thus, Chartism was not a working-class political movement with a distinctive anti-capitalist class-based ideology: it was a movement that drew on, but also developed, the radical tradition of parliamentary reform. Neville Kirk dissents from this view and claims that such anti-capitalist ideas, rather than radical ideas of political exclusion, actually constituted the essence of Chartism, at least in terms of the language used by Chartists in the factory districts of Lancashire and Cheshire.[22] This raises the question of the typicality of the north-west. After all, this was a region that was thought to be at the forefront of industrialization and mechanization. Notwithstanding this advanced level of industrialization, it is clear that interclass harmony did exist at various points and in various places in the region as work by others on Bolton and Oldham has shown – work that Kirk does actually acknowledge.[23] Even in militant Ashton-under-Lyne 'there was a constant tension in Chartist politics between class antagonism and a longing for class conciliation'.[24] Either way, it is difficult to accept Kirk's argument that certain Chartists broke out of the traditional radical analysis of attributing economic exploitation to political exclusion by identifying the capitalist system as the root cause of that exploitation. The fact remains that for such a system to exist it had to be sanctioned, however tacitly, by the state. This explains why the Chartists devoted so much attention to reforming the *political* system (all else was derivative), and why they had so much faith in the transforming potential of parliamentary reform. This is not to deny that hostility towards employers either existed or that such hostility could be economic and social as well as political; but most Chartists continued to view the causes of and solution to such hostility as political. As the Elland Chartist Abram Hanson told the thousands of people gathered at the great West Riding Meeting on Hartshead Moor in 1838:

> They were serfs and slaves of those who, possessing the power of law-making, had always the power of extracting the fruits of their industry for the promoting of their own selfish purposes[25]

If the Chartists became more class conscious in the 1840s, then it was due primarily to political divisions between the classes. As Stedman Jones rightly argues, the Chartist rebuff of middle-class offers of co-operation was not evidence of outright opposition to such co-operation; rather, it was to the terms on which it was offered. This accounts for the failure of the Complete Suffrage Union initiative of 1842,[26] when the middle-class delegates accepted the Chartist pro-gramme but insisted that the controversial 'Chartist' label be dropped.

One does not have to subscribe to the class-based interpretation of Chartism to recognize what was novel about the movement. If the content of Chartism was virtually indistinguishable from the radical programme, first articulated in the 1770s, clearly the form was differ-ent. One of the legitimate criticisms of Stedman Jones and his followers made by the latter-day defenders of the class-based interpretation of popular radicalism is that insufficient attention was paid to the chang-ing context and form of that radicalism. First, the Chartists had taken the goal of the 1790s radicals to mobilize 'members unlimited' to unprecedented levels: this was truly a mass popular movement. Second, mobilizing 'members unlimited' made the Chartists a much more visible and threatening public presence than was ever the case with the post-war radicals of the mass platform. That these crowds were composed for the most part of workers is not evidence in itself that radicalism was a class-conscious movement. Third, as made clear by the otherwise contradictory class-based analysis of Dorothy Thompson and the non-class interpretation of Stedman Jones, Chartism was unprecedentedly national in scope.[27] This was the creation of itinerant lecturers, newspa-pers and organizations, which not only spread the Chartist message but also expanded the field of vision of those who were involved by link-ing local grievances to a national framework that prescribed a uniform remedy for those grievances.[28]

Few of the values, ideas and idioms that pervaded radical lan-guage and underpinned radical action were ultimately reducible to class. Whereas radicalism was once thought to be respectable, secu-lar, rationalist, male and class-conscious, the 'new political history' has challenged these assumptions and shown how the culture of radical-ism was far richer and more varied than an exclusive focus on class would suggest. As Iain McCalman's work on the Metropolitan 'radical underworld' has shown, while there might have been an overall shift in the 1820s and 1830s away from the rough and vulgar culture of blas-phemy, sedition, blackmail, pornography and insurrection – hallmarks of Regency radicalism – towards moral respectability, self-improvement and political moderation, that process was neither total nor linear. Similarly, the boundaries between 'respectability' and 'roughness' were not always clear-cut. For example, the seemingly vulgar, bawdy and non-political world of obscene literature that a number of radical publishers were engaged in was 'intended to amuse, shock or disgust readers by exposing the crimes, vices and hypocrisies of the ruling classes'[29] and could be made to serve radical ends by buttressing the attack on 'Old Corruption'. McCalman's work has shown how 'humour, escapism, sex, profit, conviviality, entertainment and saturnalia'[30] could also be political and part of the popular radical experience.

It was not just the radicals of the seedy underworld who politicized sex and gender. Matthew McCormark has shown how mainstream Regency Radicals contrasted the manly citizen patriot with the effeminate and degenerate aristocrat who had been corrupted by luxury and 'unnatural' sexual practices. In the early nineteenth century, some radical leaders, notably Henry Hunt, followed in the footsteps of the 1760s radical libertine John Wilkes and equated active citizenship with an over-active sex life, juxtaposing their virile heterosexuality with the homosexual practices of certain aristocrats (dubbed the Vere Street gang). Such depravity, it was alleged, was symptomatic of the wider femininity of aristocratic corruption and decadence.[31] Yet, by the 1840s, most radicals had disassociated themselves from this bachelor and libertine hyper-masculine culture, and emphasized their fidelity to matrimonial domesticity and temperance as a means to demonstrate their respectability – and, hence, 'fitness' – for the franchise.[32] Those radicals who did not pay lip service to respectability were marginalized: local Chartist associations often refused to grant membership to drunken or immoral men, while other Chartists encouraged men to disassociate themselves from vulgar pleasures such as dog and cock-fighting.[33]

In a related way, other historians have shown how the older historiographical preoccupation with class has obscured the extent to which radicalism shaped, and was shaped by, other categories of social and cultural identity: gender, religion and national identity. As we saw in the last chapter, radical language was explicitly gendered and – with the exception of the Owenite Socialists, who championed sexual equality – tended to 'construct the radical actor, or subject, as male'.[34] To take religion as another example, although many radicals challenged the exclusive political power wielded by the Established Anglican Church and were also hostile to middle-class Nonconformists (who were identified with the tyrannical factory owners or, occasionally, with coercive preachers),[35] this did not make radical politics irreligious. Only a relatively small group of radical artisans were atheists.[36] Most radicals appropriated religion for their own ends.[37] Radicalism, as it emerged in the later eighteenth century, was heavily influenced by the democratic culture of religious Nonconformity, and by Methodism in particular.

That culture had its origins in the civil wars of the seventeenth century and was immortalized in John Bunyan's allegorical novel *Pilgrim's Progress*, published in 1678. This immensely popular book, in addition to the *Rights of Man*, was the other Bible of nineteenth-century popular radicalism.

The role of Methodism in society has been much debated by historians. This debate has revolved around the argument, put forward by Elie Halévy at the turn of the last century, that the conservatizing impact of Methodism prevented the outbreak of revolution in England. Others, pre-eminently Eric Hobsbawm, have taken the opposite view, arguing that it contributed to the radicalization of the working class.[38] E. P. Thompson's more subtle argument is probably closest to the truth: Methodism's contribution to popular radicalism was in spite of itself. As he notes in *The Making of the English Working Class*, theologically, Wesleyan Methodism was quite reactionary. It impressed upon its followers a doctrine of submission (despite its contradictory claim that the souls of Christ's virtuous poor were just as good as middle-class and aristocratic souls).[39] And yet, for all the doctrinal conservatism of official Wesleyanism, the way in which the Methodists organized was very democratic. Congregations were largely self-governing and, from this, the more radical members gained the 'self-confidence and capacity' for political organization. Under the democratizing influence of Paineite radicalism, most of these radical members came to reject the reactionary doctrine of Wesleyanism and seceded, forming their own Methodist churches, notably the Methodist New Connexion in 1797 and the Primitive Methodists in 1806. It was no coincidence that those who seceded in Huddersfield called themselves the 'Tom Paine Methodists'. The Christianity of popular radicalism was based on the principles of social justice preached by the Old Testament Prophets and the doctrine of social equality contained in the New Testament.[40] This radical culture of religious dissent survived into the nineteenth century and did much to shape the form and content of popular radicalism, giving rise to Chartist Churches in the 1830s and 1840s.

But even when organized religion had seemingly little to do with radicalism, and popular politics more generally for that matter, the language and symbolism of political movements were saturated with religious idioms and references. For example, the Anti-Corn Law League drew on Biblical idioms in its propaganda: references to 'the bread of life' and 'Give us this day our daily bread' appeared on banners and membership cards.[41] Many Chartists framed their political programme and opposition to the Establishment in a religious rhetoric that drew heavily on the Bible, and could even go so far as to claim that 'Jesus Christ was the first Chartist'.[42] The singing of hymns was also common practice at Chartist meetings. Radical attempts to construct a 'people's history' on the mass platform and in the press often assumed Biblical proportions and parallels: those excluded from the political nation were the 'Chosen People', the modern day equivalent of the Israelites, who had similarly been despised and persecuted.[43] Radical poetry similarly registered what Miles Taylor terms, in relation to Ernest Jones, as 'primitive Christian theology, and an "olden time" sense of history'.[44]

Another area that has received considerable attention in recent years is the spatial dimension of radicalism. Traditionally, space was conceived by historians as a heuristic device providing the means to investigate radicalism in a particular space – usually in a specific locality. This local case study approach, exemplified by Asa Briggs' edited collection *Chartist Studies*, was concerned mainly with how local structural factors, such as occupational profile, shaped the form and content of radicalism.[45] Historians influenced by the 'new political history' no longer conceive of space as merely constituting a structural backdrop; rather, space is defined in much wider symbolic terms. Consideration is being paid to the ways spaces are imagined communities. Spaces, and the loyalties associated with them, are rightly seen as forming identities in their own right – local, regional, national and imperial identities are all ultimately based on geographical places, however much they are imagined.[46] As with other identities, spatial ones were, and are, no less contested. Radicals constructed their own spatial identities in opposition to official versions. They positioned themselves as the patriotic custodians of the nation's interests and values, notably liberty and freedom, which, they claimed, had been selfishly and carelessly sacrificed by and to 'Old Corruption'. As Hugh Cunningham has shown in relation to the eighteenth century, radical patriotism was a 'tool of opposition' and formed part of radicalism's restorative agenda of returning the nation to its original purity.[47] Radicals challenged the state's exclusive and restrictive definition of the nation to include marginalized groups – the 'people' of England, Wales, Scotland and even the Irish, although it should be added that not all the marginalized flocked to radicalism. Conversely, radicals could also be Anglo-centric. For example, the 'people's history' that the Chartists constructed in opposition to elite versions of the past tended to privilege English traditions and experiences over that of the 'Celtic Fringes'.[48] Nonetheless, it was no coincidence that Feargus O'Connor spoke of 'Imperial Chartism'.[49] As he stated, in an open letter to fellow Chartists in 1842:

> The Charter is intended as our Imperial measure; and see how beautifully its principles have been observed in your constitution. We have two Englishmen, one Irishman, one Scotchman, and one

Welshman, constituting our Executive body. I am very proud to be able thus to arrange you under the banner of Imperial Chartism.[50]

The spatial identities below and above the nation have received relatively little attention by historians. We need to know more about the ways in which popular radicalism tapped into local and regional identities, and about the place of empire within popular radicalism in the first half of the nineteenth century. Historians of popular radicalism are beginning to trace the relationship between these geographical identities and, in particular, how radicals negotiated the competing claims of these identities. Chartism was beset by centre–periphery tensions due to the centrifugal pull of the national leadership and the National Charter Association and the centripetal drag of localities jealous of their independence and resistant to centralization.[51]

The majority of the work on radicalism and space has not really focused on territorial identities at all. Rather, the focus has been on how radicals tried to gain access to space as a means to proclaim their constitutional message in verbal and visual form. This represented an attempt to carve out an alternative popular political sphere that challenged the restrictions of the official public sphere.[52] Limiting and controlling access to public space was one of the main ways that the state attempted to contain the domestic radical threat in the aftermath of the French Revolution. This process of clamping down continued into the nineteenth century, invariably manifesting itself in attempts by the authorities to prevent large numbers of radicals from holding outdoor meetings, often with the aid of troops. As the work of Tony Taylor, James Vernon and James Epstein, amongst others, has shown, the battle for control of public space was a major part of the radical attack on political exclusion.[53] Thus, widening access to the public sphere was not merely about giving people the franchise: democratizing the political system would provide the means to democratize public space.

Where such work on symbolic control of public space becomes less convincing is when used as a defence of the old class-based interpretation of popular radicalism. Feargus O'Connor, ever the consummate showman, wearing fustian clothing (the material out of which the traditional attire of artisans was made) on the occasion of his release from York Gaol in 1841 does not make Chartism a class-conscious movement. To suggest that O'Connor's display of a certain type of fabric 'represented a new-found working-class consciousness in popular radicalism' is reductionist, to say the least.[54] Further, the contests over access to public space and the right to display certain symbols, such as the controversial Cap of Liberty – 'the miserable harbinger of so many murders in France' – were simply about that: it was the subversive *political* meaning that worried the (very paranoid) authorities. They were the ones who chose to see the Cap as an ensign of mob rule. Clearly, the radicals were being deliberately provocative in displaying the Cap, but it would be wrong to assume that it universally symbolized class conflict for radicals. Again, it seems that this association was particularly marked in the north-west in the aftermath of the Napoleonic Wars. As Epstein shows, the Cap of Liberty was originally associated with Ancient Rome: the cap was given to slaves who had won their freedom by performing services for the state. The Cap was thus a passport to citizenship.[55]

To take another example, Dorothy Thompson has argued, in relation to the strikes of 1842, that it was the class composition of Chartism that panicked the authorities, not what was said. She makes the interesting observation that the pre-eminently middle-class Anti-Corn Law League ran the Chartists pretty close in its use of violent language. In spite of this, she notes that, while hundreds of Chartists were imprisoned, no Leaguers were arrested.[56] John Belchem has made similar arguments, concluding that: 'It was context, not content, that gave the radical mass platform its remarkable resonance and purchase.'[57] That context, argues Belchem, was class conflict. The fact remains that, contrary to the claims of Thompson and Belchem, the language in terms of the objectives and tactics of radicalism *was* important; careful attention to it reveals that radicalism is not reducible to monolithic middle- and working-class ideologies. Granted, the core political analyses of all the radical movements were similar, based on a critique of 'Old Corruption' (although, as already observed, that was a contested concept). But the vehemence with which the Chartists articulated that critique and the threatening manner in which it was proclaimed were far more extreme than the Anti-Corn Law League. If the elite and propertied classes ultimately interpreted radicalism as a dangerous working-class movement that was bent on spoliation and revolution, then this had more to do with the paranoid minds of the political and social elite than with the radicals themselves. The medium had not quite become the message.[58]

The Radical Ordeal

One aspect that historians have always been sensitive towards is the lived experience of radicalism. This ranged from the rich associational culture surrounding the movement to the sufferings and sacrifices that individuals and groups made to further the cause. Many radicals endured the cruel hardship of imprisonment, and even transportation, such as the Tolpuddle Martyrs (who had done little more than form an agricultural trades union and swear an oath to that effect), and the ringleaders of the Chartist rising at Newport in 1839, the latter initially having been sentenced to death. The dire conditions of prison life inflicted a heavy toll on the health of those who, like Ernest Jones, did not enjoy the relative comfort of other imprisoned radicals such as Richard Oastler and Feargus O'Connor. The physical and mental ordeals of a radical life outside of prison could also be punishing. The incessant battles fought by O'Connor, especially over the legality of the Land Plan, which had been designed to create land communities of smallholders, undoubtedly contributed to the deterioration of his mental health in later life. He was finally admitted to an asylum in June 1852.

It was no coincidence that suffering, terror and horror were such dominant themes in radical literature, especially poetry, for much of this period. The suffering that was captured in radical literature, some of which was actually composed in prison, was evidence of the continuing literary influence of romanticism on radical writers, hence the popularity of Byron and Shelley. After all, the emotive object of romanticism was suffering humanity (often at the hands of tyrannical aristocrats). Its melodramatic evocation of contrasts – such as good and evil (again symbolized by the aristocratic seducer unmasked by the tenacious radical) – provided radicals with 'a kind of language of feeling'.[59] Romanticism, with its pastoral celebration of nature and Arcadian England, also lent force to the 'restorationist' strain within radicalism and buttressed the critique of rapacious industrialization and stultifying utilitarianism, followers of the latter, it was argued, tried to reduce human happiness to a mechanical formula.[60] The obsessive concern of the Utilitarians with order, classification and symmetry was anathema to the romantic spirit. Above all, romanticism was taken up with gusto by the suffering 'gentleman radical' who had voluntarily renounced his own class and wealth to do battle on behalf of the people. The politician as romantic-hero was a guise assumed by a succession of radicals: Hunt, Oastler, Stephens, O'Connor and Ernest Jones.[61]

Suffering, however, was not only the preserve of radical leaders; suffering humanity meant precisely that. There was no shortage of victims in the radical crowd: the dispossessed handloom weaver; the enslaved factory worker, to say nothing of those men, women and children who had experienced the dehumanizing workhouse. When it came to exposing the torture and cruelties endured by factory operatives and those that had been forced into the workhouses, the Romantic idiom took a distinctly gothic turn in the language and images of the Anti-Poor Law and factory reformers.[62] True to the gothic genre, Oastler and his band of reformers were bent on unmasking the factory tyrants. The Factory and Anti-Poor Law movements gave rise to a frenetic crowd politics: factory owners and those charged with implementing the New Poor Law (often the same people) were burnt in effigy and subjected to verbal and physical assault.

Thus, radical identity went far beyond an ability to recite the catechisms of the movement's political programme. Radicalism was, for better and for worse, a way of life. It was at this level that the movement was at its most coherent. One of the reasons for this was the crossover of personnel and overlap between the various organizations and causes. This was most evident in relation to ultra-radicalism, where the desire to live a holistic radical life necessitated support for various reforms and possibly the rejection of orthodox lifestyles. This could include the adoption of unorthodox medical practices and beliefs (such as phrenology and homeopathy), vegetarianism, teetotalism and advocacy of birth control, female equality and free love. These corporeal dimensions were constitutive of radicalism and represented an attempt to live a democratic life. As James Gregory has argued, the adoption of such practices constituted an act of independence – part of the freethinking mentality that refused to accept orthodoxy uncritically.[63]

A number of the mainstream movements also illustrate the interconnectedness of radicalism. To take one such example, it has been argued, by radicals at the time and subsequently by historians, that the movement for factory reform gave birth to the Anti-Poor Law campaign, which was in turn absorbed by Chartism. 'Had there been no New Poor Law', one contemporary noted, 'the name of Chartist would never have been heard'.[64] Indeed, much of the popular outrage, platform invective and the recourse to methods of physical force associated with these movements were carried over into Chartism.

There were other similar metamorphic relationships: the Association of Working Men to procure a Cheap and Honest Press became the London Working Men's Association, the organization that drew up and first published the six points of the 'People's Charter'.[65] More generally, as Edward Royle has argued:

> Members of political unions, vendors of the unstamped press, trades unionists, members of Short-Time Committees (for an eight- or ten-hour day), and opponents of the poor law were not different people ... the same people were involved in all these activities and were thinking of them as parts of a whole.[66]

The Owenites, and to a lesser extent the Chartists, came close to establishing an 'alternative culture' for their members – alternative in the sense of being separate from, and to some extent in opposition to, the dominant culture of society. Owenites and Chartists did not merely form local groups, but gave 'expression to the cultural side of their radical commitment'[67] by providing a range of recreational, educational and religious activities such as lectures, debates, parties and dinners. These movements also formed their own schools, chapels, co-operative stores, burial clubs and temperance societies; they even composed their own songs, novels and poetry. This culture reached its zenith in the Chartist movement, which, in Paul Pickering's words, produced its own 'informal economy' through exclusive dealing and co-operative retailing.[68] While serving practical functions, such as providing movements with funds and a living for some of its members (especially for those who found it impossible to gain employment due to their radical activities), this associational culture engendered a radical identity and continuous commitment to the cause by providing a sense of community, fraternity and progress. Signing and organizing petitions, and reading and singing radical poetry and songs were other 'means of strengthening resolve in adversity' and fostering an associational culture.[69] Malcolm Chase has captured the range of the typical Chartist lifestyle:

The new-born child of Chartist parents might be received into the movement at a special ceremony presided over by one of its leaders, and possibly given his name. Subsequently they might attend a Chartist Sunday School or have a subscription to the Chartist Land Plan taken out on their behalf. Meanwhile the parents would be immersed in the political and social life of the local branch of the National Charter Association, maybe the father was also in one of its trade localities and the mother in a Female Chartist Association. They might shop at a Chartist joint stock provision (i.e. co-operative) store. If a ratepayer, the father might be able to support Chartist candidates in local elections; if teetotal, the family could enlist in a Chartist Temperance Association. Prints of Chartist leaders would adorn the home and spare pence subscribed to support Chartist prisoners and their families. The family's main source of national news would be a Chartist weekly paper, usually the *Northern Star*. Male Chartists might join a clandestine group for arms drill. And men and women would participate in the great nocturnal mass meetings[70]

How successful were Chartists and Owenites in establishing an alternative culture? For all that the Chartists provided an impressive array of activities and met the various needs of its supporters, the most that can be said is that the movement provided what political scientists have termed a politics of social integration: a movement characterized by permanent organization permeating all aspects of their members' lives. In contrast to Owenism (which did attempt to create an ideal community – the 'New Moral World' – by rejecting the dominant cultural values of competition, individualism and patriarchy), most Chartists, if not necessarily subscribing to these values wholeheartedly, were, at the very least, resigned to them. However, this is not to suggest that creating an alternative culture should be viewed as the litmus test of a movement's success. After all, Owenism was a very small movement compared to Chartism: the catch-22 of political movements that create alternative cultures is that they cut themselves off, and become alienated from, wider society. This made Owenism appear sect-like (especially with its rejection of Orthodox Christianity) and remote from the everyday concerns of the people. The same could not be said of Chartism, or some of the other popular movements. Paradoxically, though, it could be argued that these other popular movements were no more successful than Owenism in achieving their objectives. This, in turn, raises the final question of why radicals so often failed to achieve their objectives.

Radical 'Failings'

The question of radical failure is one that anticipates the historical debates on the transition from the independent and confrontational politics of the Chartist era to the relatively harmonious and compromising politics of mid-Victorian popular Liberalism, discussed in Chapters 4 and 5. It is necessary, however, to conclude with an assessment of radicalism's achievements during the first half of the nineteenth century. In assessing those achievements, one needs to be clear about what criteria are being used and which groups are being assessed. To return to the distinct groupings of radicals that were used in the introduction of Chapter 2, both the Benthamite and Manchester radicals appear to have been considerably more successful than the popular radicals in achieving their objectives. The range of bureaucratic reforms (principally the 1834 New Poor Law, the 1829 and 1839 Metropolitan Police Acts, and the 1848 Public Health Act) and the commercial legislation that was responsible for dismantling the *ancien régime* and establishing the *laissez-faire* doctrines of political economy (such as the repeal of the Corn Laws) can all be cited as examples of success for the Benthamites and Manchester radicals. While historians might debate

the extent to which these reforms were either successes or the result
of extra-parliamentary agitation, the fact remains that the tangible
achievements of the popular radicals appear less impressive. Indeed,
the only notable success came in the shape of the 1847 Factory Act.
This finally established a ten-hour day for women and children in textile factories, but even this fell short of what many radicals had hoped
for. A qualified victory it might have been, but it was a victory for popular radicalism: not only was the Act largely the work of John Fielden,
but the extra-parliamentary agitation that he headed played a crucial role in facilitating the passage of the Ten Hours Bill through the
House of Commons.[71] As for the other popular radical movements,
successes were not forthcoming: restrictions still hampered both the
press and trades unions (although advances had been made); the New
Poor Law had not been repealed; for all that Owenism was a genuinely
counter-cultural movement, it had amounted to very little; and, most
importantly of all, the 'People's Charter' was not the law of the land.
How are we to account for these 'failures'?

Historians have tended to focus on either the internal weaknesses of
the radical movement or on the external obstacles that they faced –
usually in the form of state repression. Neither are these explanations
mutually exclusive: the divisions within the radical movement made it
all the more difficult to surmount the various obstacles. These ranged
from the problems that the radicals faced in the mobilization of 'members unlimited' – working people often lacked the time and money to
devote themselves to the 'cause' – while apathy or transient support,
the forces of popular Conservatism, and the coercive and conciliatory
power of the state all conspired against the movement. Radicals had
to contend with what was universally regarded as an unjust legal system that was biased towards the rich. As voiced by the 1790s radical
William Godwin, speaking through one of his characters in his novel
Caleb Williams: 'law was better adapted for a weapon of tyranny in the
hands of the rich, than for a shield to protect the humbler part of
the community'. More specifically, the law also proved to be a significant barrier to effective mobilization. The coercive power of the state,
backed up by special constables drawn from the middle class, undoubtedly played a significant part in containing the Chartist threat in 1848,
as did the judiciary. As John Saville has shown, the central authorities
appeared calm, resolute and calculating in their decision to delay the
arrest of the radical ringleaders until middle-class public opinion had
been sufficiently frightened.[72] Despite the appearance of masterly state
control, there is no doubt that the Chartists genuinely alarmed the government in 1848 as many Chartists up and down the country began
arming and drilling. The state identified the Chartists with the same

forces that were responsible for continental revolutionary upheavals. This identification seemed to be confirmed by those Chartists who made common cause with the Irish Confederates, who were sowing the revolutionary nationalist seeds of post-famine discontent in Ireland and amongst the Irish in England. In reality, although many Chartists drew inspiration from their European counterparts in 1848, few desired a continental-style revolution.[73] Perhaps most damaging of all was that Chartism had become tainted in the public eye by its association with the wave of riots, disorder and crime that swept across London in 1848. The Chartists were guilty by association, thereby further playing into the hands of the state.[74] The improved efficiency of the police after 1848, allied to the greater control exercised by municipal authorities over public space (often by simply building on land previously used for open air meetings), further undermined the efficacy of the mass platform as a radical strategy. This encouraged the movement of radicalism 'indoors'; that is, when radicals were fortunate enough to be given access to venues, of which most were in the control of the civic elite.[75]

What of the failings of the radicals? It has been argued that the radicals were so divided amongst themselves in terms of ideology, policy, strategy and personal rivalries that failure was virtually a foregone conclusion. Nowhere was this more evident than in relation to the Chartist movement, beset as it was by endless divisions. Other historians have argued that the failure of radicalism went deeper than these divisions. It was not that radicals lacked a vision of what a transformed society would be like after political reform; rather, there were competing visions over what constituted the ideal society and polity. 'I have never desired', O'Connor admitted, 'a too close investigation into the various results likely to sprint from Universal Suffrage, and for this reason; one section of society would object to one measure, and another to another measure.'[76] To make matters worse they were also divided over how to achieve their objectives. The ignominious divisions and setbacks that bedevilled Chartism illustrate this: should they resort to 'ulterior measures' if Parliament refused to grant the Charter? What 'ulterior measures' should be employed, and in what order: a general strike, a widespread withdrawal of savings to precipitate the financial collapse of the state, boycotting taxes, exclusive dealing, or mass arming?

In hindsight, perhaps the real failing of radicalism stemmed from the limited ideological challenge that it posed. It was no coincidence that many radicals were qualified monarchists. They often identified monarchs with 'Old Corruption' and objected to the excessive cost of the royal household, but many could also conceive of a popular and positive role for those sagacious monarchs who championed the interests of the people. As Paul Pickering has recently shown, many Chartists were

willing to build their campaign around Queen Victoria (especially after
Parliament had rejected their petitions), whom Ernest Jones described
as 'the last authority to which they could appeal'.[77] The extent to which
this stance was merely shrewd and opportunistic legitimizing is unclear.
Other radicals simply regarded the monarchy as a benign, almost irrelevant force that was largely ceremonial and would eventually die out
of its own accord. Either way, few radicals made the leap from anti-
monarchism to avowed republicanism; those that did often lacked a
vision of what a republic would entail, let alone how it would be brought
about.[78] Not only were most radicals content to work within the existing
political and social framework – to employ constitutional means for constitutional ends – they also found themselves working within a reformist
paradigm that contained the seeds of its own destruction. According
to this argument, by employing the constitutionalist idiom the radicals
played into the hands of the state. The reliance on historic precedent to
legitimize their demands was always a double-edged sword, since it was
based on such a partisan and contested reading of the past. Similarly,
the radicals could be accused of placing too much emphasis on the vote
as a means to an end. Once it became clear that 'ends' such as factory
reform could be achieved within the existing political framework, the
radical critique of a negligent and biased state was undermined. This
forced radicalism into an ideological cul-de-sac.[79]

There can be little doubt that the new reforming initiatives shown
by the state took the wind out of the Chartist sails, but to argue that
the radicals had got it wrong by focusing on the political origins of
socio-economic grievances is not only ahistorical and condescending,
it is also simplistic. The radicals had diagnosed the causes of popular grievances in broad terms and were fully alive to the interlocking
political, social and economic roots of those grievances, even if that did
not amount to a proto-Marxist class-consciousness. The Chartists took
the view, which was surely correct, that gaining more control over the
political sphere was essential if they were to stand a chance of successfully addressing popular grievances. The Chartists were only too aware
of how the social and economic power of their oppressors was underpinned by political power. In this respect, the Chartists did not 'fail': the
state became more responsive to popular grievances. Granted, the state
responded largely on its own terms, and not at the direct bidding of the
Chartists (which it could not be seen to do). But it was Chartism – and,
more broadly, radicalism – that had dramatically drawn attention to
state-sanctioned iniquities and had, therefore, put reform of the state
on the political agenda in the first place. Finally, the Chartists might
have been proved wrong in believing that the state was incapable of
reforming itself without being democratized; however, it would have

been naïve of the Chartists to have presumed otherwise. Without the threat of democratization at the back of the minds of the political elite, the state would never have reformed itself in the way it did. The evolution of a 'disinterested' approach to government, by not legislating for the benefit of one class at the expense of another – the touchstone of mid-century political stability – was precisely the result for which the Chartists had been agitating. In this respect, the radicals played a significant part in bringing about the 'Age of Equipoise', the subject of the next chapter.

Chapter 4: The Making of Mid-Victorian Popular Liberalism

In contrast to the tumultuous 1830s and 1840s, the mid-Victorian decades were politically and socially tranquil. If the early Victorian period was the age of protest, the mid-Victorian era was the 'Age of Equipoise': stability, co-operation, conciliation and compromise replaced unrest, division, conflict and intransigence.[1] Politically, this stability manifested itself in the rise of popular Liberalism, based on a coalition of former Chartists and moderate reformers who agreed to sink their differences and come together in support of the Liberal party and the principles that were identified with a new set of popular tribunes. One tribune in particular towered above the rest: Mr. Gladstone (Prime Minister 1868–74, 1880–85, 1886 and 1892–94). This chapter and Chapter 5 explore the extent to which Liberals and radicals were able to coalesce under the banner of Liberalism between 1848 and 1880, and analyse the reasons for this. Traditionally, this period was largely written-off by labour historians, as it represented a hiatus in the making of the working class – a process that ended dramatically with the 'failure' of Chartism in 1848 and one that was only resumed in the 1880s with the revival of socialism. Frederick Engels gave expression to this view in 1890, when he wrote that the English proletariat had just awoken 'from its forty years winter sleep'.[2] Yet, the mid-Victorian decades were not quite the sedate and slumbering years that Engels suggested, and neither had the working class been reduced, in the words of Karl Marx, to 'nothing more than the tail of the great Liberal Party'.[3]

The Mechanics of Mid-Century Stability

Why did the confrontational politics of the Chartist period give way to the relative harmonious and compromising politics of moderate

reformism? Why were relations between Liberals and radicals characterized more by co-operation than conflict after 1848? These questions
were central to the Marxist inspired historiography of the 1960s and
1970s: the juxtaposition of the early and mid-Victorian decades presented these historians with the uncomfortable question of why, having
come so close to achieving its revolutionary destiny in the 1830s and
1840s, did the working class subsequently abandon its historical mission and reconcile itself to the established order? A range of consolatory
explanations was advanced to explain this 'false consciousness', most
of which highlighted the socio-economic, materialistic foundations of
mid-century stability. Against the background of economic recovery
in the late 1840s and the boom conditions of the 1850s, social tensions began to lessen as cyclical unemployment began to decrease and
real wages began to rise, thus limiting the appeal of a radical politics based on 'hunger and hatred'.[4] Further, as the economy began
to improve and stabilize, the capitalists were able – by mechanization
and rationalization – to gain control of the productive process, thereby
undermining the authority and autonomy of the traditional craft elite.
In place of the autonomous craftsman, the employers created an elite
stratum of workers in their own image by paying them higher wages,
co-opting them into the management process by giving them super-
visory roles over the rest of the workforce.[5] This 'labour aristocracy'
now had a stake in the capitalist order, which transformed them from
ardent Chartists and militant trades unionists into a cautious and politically moderate group concerned, primarily, with the defence of their
privileged position. As these labour aristocrats possessed the most skills
and resources, they exercised an influential position over the rest of the
working class. Their newly acquired conservatism thus checked the revolutionary impulses of the wider working class.[6] While some historians
argued for the need to define this 'labour aristocracy' more expansively to include the persistence of traditional craftsmen who retained
their privileges and debated just how well-paid, secure and collabora-
tionist they were,[7] most were agreed that the emergence of this stratum
was symptomatic of the growth of differences and divisions within the
working class – in terms of skill, income, values, gender and ethnicity.
These divisions acted as a further barrier to unified, radical political
action.

Under the combined impact of the failure of Chartism as a radical strategy, the rise of prosperity and a new willingness to work for
gradual, piecemeal reform of the existing system due to the more
accommodating stance of the state and propertied classes, many workers began to turn their attention away from radicalism. Their attention
was now devoted to religious, educational, provident and recreational

institutions and activities. Prominent among these were co-operative, friendly and temperance societies and even trades unions, each of which came to champion the values of self-help, respectability, self-improvement and self-reliance. These institutions and values, it is argued, were instruments of middle-class social control or 'moral imperialism', consciously disseminated as a means to transform the working class in their own image.[8]

The subordination and incorporation of the working class was further reinforced by factory paternalism, an explanation for mid-century stability outlined most comprehensively by Patrick Joyce. Joyce argued that the transference of control over the productive process from workers to employers, consequent on the rise of the factory and its disciplining and patriarchal regime, eroded the hitherto privileged status of skilled labour. This, in turn, made factory workers more vulnerable and dependent on their employers. Family members often worked alongside one another under the immediate supervision of the male head. Patriarchal authority extended all the way up to the factory owner himself, who was the father of his workforce and of the community in which his factory dominated. In the single-industry towns – ubiquitous in the textile districts of the north-west – the factory was the central and common institution in the lives of working people. The same people worked, lived and socialized alongside one another. The dependency of the workers on the factory owner, when fertilized by the paternalistic practices of 'enlightened' middle-class industrialists, created a deferential workforce and community. This paternalism involved holding social events, providing recreational and educational facilities, and, in some instances, building self-contained model industrial communities, such as existed at Saltaire, Bourneville and Port Sunlight. Factory paternalists, so the argument went, were able to influence the political loyalties of their workforce, thus further explaining why popular politics was integrated into formal partisan, elite-led politics. These communal bonds were reinforced by a shared religious affiliation, facilitated by the building of churches and chapels in which employer and employee worshipped alongside one another. Religion – or, to be more accurate, religious and sectarian conflict – was especially potent when it could be used to strengthen this partisanship. In the north-west textile towns, many of the factory paternalists were Tory and Anglican. With the help of the Anglican clergy, they were able to fashion a popular Conservatism based on a crude appeal to the economic self-interest and religious/ethnic sentiments of the native worker against puritanical Liberal Nonconformist employers and Irish Catholic immigrants who were saturating the labour market. These mutually reinforcing political, religious, ethnic and territorial conflicts channelled and neutralized the grievances of the factory workers by distracting them from criticizing their employers and the capitalist system more generally.[9] Here, then, were the structural foundations of mid-century stability: a nexus of economic, social and ideological factors was advanced as explanation for the transition from the turbulent 1830s and 1840s to the mid-Victorian 'Age of Equipoise'.

There were, of course, nuanced versions, different combinations and prioritizations of these factors but, in broad terms, they can all be labelled as 'socio-structural'. For example, Neville Kirk emphasizes the 'emergence of a restabilized and dynamic capitalism'. This led to 'substantial improvement in material conditions', which 'greatly enhanced the scope for class manoeuvre, for concessions and initiatives towards labour "from above"'. Further, 'the advancement of sections of the working class within the system' convinced 'workers of the new-found viability of the capitalist system', which workers were, in any case, too divided along cultural and ethnic lines to mount an effective challenge.[10]

These more nuanced socio-structural interpretations anticipated many of the more stridently revisionist interpretations of mid-Victorian social and political stability that have emerged since the late 1980s. An older body of scholarship, much of it written by economic historians, demonstrated that there was no automatic correlation between the state of the economy and the popularity of radicalism. Several events point to the limitations of economically reductionist interpretations of popular politics: the collapse of Chartism in 1842, amidst continued poverty and unemployment, and its revival in 1848 against the background of economic improvement, to say nothing of the lack of radical revival in the face of the severe economic crisis of 1857 and the Cotton Famine of the 1860s. This limitation is further illustrated by the continued existence of working-class poverty in some occupations and regions during the so-called 'Age of Equipoise'.[11] As for working-class fragmentation and the 'labour aristocracy' thesis, these are hardly satisfactory explanations for the growth of moderate reformism, given that such fragmentation and status differentials had existed in the 1830s and 1840s. Neither can the growth of reformism be reduced to the emergence of a relatively prosperous, respectable and politically moderate 'labour aristocracy'. First, it is difficult to define who actually belonged to the labour aristocracy and to agree on the determining criteria. Second, it is highly reductionist to suggest that economic privilege automatically translated into political moderation and class harmony (which, in some instances, it clearly did not) and that it is possible to 'read-off' the political behaviour of the entire working class from a particular stratum.

We also need to be careful not to confuse causes with consequences of stability. Political stability, based on co-operation and compromise between Liberals and radicals, used to be seen as the outcome of the growth of a more cautious and moderate labour movement. But this is not a satisfactory explanation either. As mentioned, many labour activists, who had previously been Chartists, turned away from political solutions and party politics in the 1850s and 1860s altogether, channelling their efforts into co-operatives, friendly societies and trades unions. Now, the fact that many ex-Chartists turned their backs on formal politics might account, to some extent, for the political stability of these years by virtue of their absence, but it cannot explain why many of those radical activists who remained convinced of the efficacy of political solutions attempted to co-operate, where possible, with the Liberal party (or the Tory party, for that matter). Neither can it account for why increasing numbers of working men began to vote for the Liberal and Conservative parties, especially after 1867.

This brings us to the problems with factory paternalism. A number of structural constraints inhibited its development or weakened its impact – even in the textile towns of the north-west, few of which were dominated by a single industry, let alone a single employer. More generally, many northern factory owners lacked the necessary profits to indulge in sustained paternalistic practices. As for the larger towns and cities, even Joyce was forced to concede that industrial diversity, social heterogeneity and 'the anomic character of the urban environment' precluded the development of 'meaningful personal relationships between masters and workpeople', especially given the high-rate of employee turnover and frequent changes in proprietorship.[12] In terms of the political loyalties of factory workforces, they were more than capable of asserting their independence from, and opposition to, their employers, even when they were of the same religion.[13] This independence and opposition was, in fact, evidence of the wider social and political conflict that broke out in these supposedly harmonious factory communities. Taken together, this conflict was not on the scale of the 1830s and 1840s, but there can be little doubt that the 'Age of Equipoise' was regularly punctuated by episodes of intense industrial conflict.[14]

To reduce the working class to being passive victims of middle-class social control is to deny the working class any individual and collective agency. As Peter Bailey has shown, working-class involvement in 'middle-class' institutions and their attachment to 'middle-class' values was conditioned by strategic and tactical considerations, as was the case between Liberals and radicals. This often involved a good deal of shrewd 'respectable' role-playing as the working class realized that certain values, beliefs and codes of conduct were required at certain times and in certain places, such as in court.[15] This role-playing was evident in popular politics: while dialect and rowdy behaviour was more characteristic of street politics, 'respectable' language and orderly behaviour was more evident at indoor political and trades union meetings; although the boundary between the two could be blurred by print.[16]

Further, values such as respectability and self-help could issue from *within* working-class culture and be appropriated by the working class as a means to assert their independence from, and equality with, their middle-class 'betters'. Notwithstanding the overall shift towards cross-class co-operation, based in part on the commitment to apparent shared values such as respectability and independence, these values could still assume distinctive class connotations, even if they did not give rise to class conflict. For example, many working-class men and women still prided themselves on their individual and collective independence, autonomy and commitment to democratic beliefs and practices, all of which belies the assumption of widespread working-class deference.[17] Further, it has become clearer that the so-called 'self-help' institutions, such as co-operatives and mechanics institutes, were far from being depoliticized or innately Liberal organizations. On Tyneside, some of these self-help institutions were part of a wider radical network that looked to the 'militant democracy' of Joseph Cowen and not the mainstream Liberalism of the Newcastle Liberal establishment.[18] Finally, and perhaps most importantly, as Martin Hewitt has shown in his study of mid-century stability in Manchester, overt attempts by middle-class reformers to regulate working-class lives 'were met almost universally with suspicion and hostility'.[19] And what was true in Manchester was true elsewhere. More often than not, initiatives that reeked of bourgeois respectability were shunned, subverted or hijacked; and this was reflected in politics.[20] Consequently, these socio-structural factors can only be made to explain so much. A more satisfactory explanation of mid-century political stability is to be found by focusing on the political process itself and, specifically, on the active role the Liberal party played in constructing a broad-based coalition of supporters.

Liberty, Retrenchment and Reform

The Liberal party used to be seen as a largely incoherent and contradictory group of reformers, each preoccupied with their own 'fad'. Precarious and transient unity was only achieved when the party's leaders were able to rally the ad hoc group of reformers behind a transcending issue, such as Gladstone's support for the disestablishment of the Irish Church in 1868.[21] In recent years, popular and parliamentary Liberalism has emerged as a more coherent political movement, especially in terms of its ideology.[22] Consequently, it is no longer possible to view the Liberal party as little more than a set of irreconcilable faddists with no coherent ideology, animated only by their periodic opposition to Conservatism and fickle love affair with Mr. Gladstone. So popular was this programme, that Liberalism was the most geographically dispersed, and arguably the most socially heterogeneous, of all the popular movements of the nineteenth century. The party succeeded in harmonizing a wide variety of interests and social groups from all over the United Kingdom, with the rank and file being dominated by 'a mixture of independent artisans, small employers and tradesmen, and organized workers'.[23] Although the precise geographical distribution of popular Liberalism fluctuated during the nineteenth century, this was truly a *British* political movement that drew substantial support from across the four nations.[24] Yet, their electoral support was not evenly spread throughout the United Kingdom. The electoral heartland of popular Liberalism in the mid-Victorian years was to be found in the north, the midlands and increasingly in Scotland and Wales.

What did it mean to be a Liberal? As one would expect, the idea of liberty was central to this ideology; this was a rallying cry around which a broad spectrum of reformers was able to unify. As with radicalism, Liberalism was grounded in a particular view of English history. The crucial difference was that the Liberals, rather than look back to a vanquished golden age, viewed the past in a similar way to their Whig aristocratic allies: as the progressive unfolding of liberty in its triumph over arbitrary rule and religious intolerance. While the Whigs focused more on the 'Glorious Revolution' of 1688, which had established a mixed constitution in which power was to be shared between Crown and parliament, the Liberals looked more to the preceding Civil War period and, particularly, to the heroic battles of Cromwell and his supporters against political tyranny and religious intolerance.[25]

By the nineteenth century, liberty – at its most abstract – translated into support for 'civil and religious liberty, for all men and for all countries'.[26] More specifically, civil liberty meant that all people, regardless of their status or beliefs, should be equal in the eyes of the law. This overlapped with religious liberty. As the Liberal *Weekly Times* put in 1867, 'where divers [sic] religions co-exist in the same community, none should be petted and none coerced'.[27] Thus many Liberals, though by no means all, were opposed to the existence of an 'officially' established state church. This led to calls for the 'disestablishment' of the Anglican Church – that is, the formal separation of church and state – by ending such egregious privileges as the exclusive right of the Anglican bishops to sit in the House of Lords; the right of the Church (as the self-proclaimed 'National Church') to levy compulsory rates on the people, irrespective of whether they were Anglicans; and to the dominance it exercised in the sphere of education. Nonconformists spearheaded this campaign through the Anti-State Church Association, established in 1844. This was transformed into the Liberation Society in 1853. Although, when it came to the Anglican Church and moral issues such as temperance, Nonconformity (especially its militant wing) could be a thorn in the side of the more cautious and conservative stance of Liberal governments, it did nonetheless constitute the electoral backbone of popular Liberalism. The moral sensibilities of Nonconformity provided much of the Liberal party's reforming zeal and organizational dynamic,[28] a dynamic that Gladstone was to harness so effectively in his moral crusades. Indeed, much of the enthusiasm of popular Liberalism stemmed from the melodramatic, religious rhetoric that was employed by popular Liberals on the public platform and in the press, the resonances of which went far beyond the devout.[29]

The war between Church and Chapel did not just focus on the national political arena. Arguably, it was at its most intense at the local level. This stemmed largely from the legal right of the Church to levy a compulsory rate on the community for the maintenance and running costs of what its defenders argued was the 'National Church'. This right was challenged – and, in some cases, overturned – by Nonconformists at vestry meetings and by contesting the elections to the office of churchwarden. This battle was finally won in 1868 when church rates were formally abolished, the levying of which had been one of the last remaining significant powers of the vestry. Thereafter, the war continued in other parochial and township institutions (notably the School Board after 1870) and in the council chamber.[30] But this was not just a 'middle-class' Liberal battle. Opposition to the Established Church was also advocated by radicals (many of whom were Nonconformists and secularists), who viewed the Church as one of the pillars of 'Old Corruption'. As the *Labourer's Union Chronicle* told its readers:

> The Church not only has itself a large interest in land, but it is in close alliance with the great landowners of the country. It is the rich man's friend, but in the great struggle in which labour finds itself pitted against wealth, this Church, which will kindly patronize the contented serf, is fast proving itself to be the poor man's foe.[31]

One of the linking threads between middle-class Liberals and working-class radicals was a democratic and egalitarian ethos derived from the culture of religious Dissent (or Nonconformity, as it was increasingly referred to from the 1840s). In contrast to the Church of England and Roman Catholicism, most Nonconformists emphasized the importance of lay participation in church government and individual interpretation of the Bible, which gave Liberalism a radical edge by making Nonconformists 'non-deferential', and even subversive. They were also possessed of a heightened sense of morality, righteousness and confidence. Thus, Liberals and radicals demanded that, at home and abroad, government be conducted along ethical and humanitarian lines. Many were able to find common ground in support of free trade, continental Liberal-nationalist movements and in the cause of the democratic North against the slaveholding and aristocratic South during the American Civil War in the 1860s.

Notions of liberty also informed Liberal views about the role of government. Liberalism was based on the belief that individuals and groups should be free to pursue their interests, provided they did not harm others, without unnecessary interference from the state. This was one reason why Liberals and radicals placed such a high premium on values such as manly independence, self-reliance and self-help. Government interference, it was feared, would sap these characteristics and produce a servile population that was over-reliant on state patronage and handouts. The role of government, beyond providing order and stability, was to preside over a disinterested state that did not identify with or reward specific interests at the expense of others.[32] Motivated by the need to reinvigorate the legitimacy of elite government and by pragmatic and moral considerations, the governments of the mid-Victorian years – especially those dominated by Whigs and Liberals – sought to position themselves, to an unprecedented degree, as the disinterested custodians of the national interest.[33] This was achieved by ending the remaining financial restrictions on the press (spearheaded by Cobden), lowering taxes, abolishing duties on items of popular consumption, some of the privileges of the Anglican Church (such as Church rates and disestablishment of the Irish Church), and removing civil disabilities that discriminated against Nonconformists, Catholics and Jews.

For popular Liberals, the ultimate symbol of the state's disinterestedness was its commitment to free trade. This went far beyond the seemingly narrow materialistic view of securing cheap food for the masses. The repeal of the Corn Laws in 1846 and the subsequent abolition of various duties were part of the process by which the state disassociated itself from particular (selfish) interests. This was linked to a growing belief that it was not the state's responsibility to provide for the welfare of the community. That was the job of voluntary self-governing organizations (such as co-operatives) – the space and scope for which was increasing because the state was retreating. Liberty thus created the conditions for the growth of a vibrant and inclusive civil society: the voluntary organization of collective action in pursuit of shared interests. In turn, this fostered a sense of civic duty and communal responsibility.[34]

This commitment to liberty can be seen as the positive expression of a more fundamental underlying negative principle: opposition to privilege. More than any other political movement, Liberalism eschewed class politics and sought to unite, though not always successfully, the productive classes (those who worked by hand and by brain) in opposition to the idle and selfish classes. Anti-privilege and opposition to class politics were the overarching principles of Liberalism, especially in relation to 'vested' interests such as the monarchy, the landed monopoly, the Anglican Church, self-electing local corporations and colonial trading monopolies. For Liberals and radicals, retrenchment provided a powerful weapon to combat these privileges, many of which were paid for by the state and, by extension, the taxpayer. To Richard Cobden – echoing James Mill and Tom Paine before him – expenditure on the National Debt, the army and navy, and the Civil List had 'for the real object the granting of out-door relief for the younger sons, poor relations, and favourites of the aristocracy' and, in return, gave the people 'nothing except debts, taxes, obligations and bad trade'.[35] The solution was a drastic reduction in state expenditure. In turn, this would reduce taxes, stimulate trade and industry, and increase wages. The popularity of Richard Cobden in the 1840s and 1850s, and that of John Bright and Gladstone in the 1860s, rested largely on their commitment to low and more equitable taxation, free trade and cheap food (the 'free breakfast table'), and to their articulation of these demands in the language of moral entitlement. To take the example of Gladstone – arguably the most popular of these three tribunes – his services to the masses were listed as follows by the radical John Watts in 1865:

> His early sacrifices and distinguished services in the promotion of free trade; his equalization of direct taxation, making wealthy men of Ireland pay the income-tax, by widening the contributions to it in England, and by subjecting real property to the succession duties; [and] his completion of the removing of the taxes on knowledge[36]

As this list of legislative achievements implies, Liberals and radicals did not oppose government intervention per se. It was quite acceptable to use legislative means to combat privilege, especially when that privilege derived from political sources. Nevertheless, it was not only in this negative sense that Liberals and radicals accepted the need for state intervention. They could also conceive of a positive role for the state and make exceptions to the *laissez-faire* rule in the areas of education, poor relief, public services, the limitations on the hours of labour and the regulation of conditions of work. These exceptions were justified on the grounds that maxims such as *laissez-faire*, as John Stuart Mill argued, had to be applied with 'regard to times, places and circumstances'. It was accepted that *laissez-faire* had to be qualified in practice by 'Christian concerns to preserve the life, health and morality of the workers'.[37] Of course, arguments based on morality could also be used to justify state intervention to stamp out *im*morality such as drunkenness – a vice that many Nonconformists wished to see curbed through various legislative means.

Thus, the power of the state could be used, temporarily, as a corrective to recreate liberty and freedom. Where government control was necessary, 'it was imperative that "the people" were given political control of the government machine, to ensure that only the "right" kind of intervention took place'.[38] So, when Gladstone's first government introduced a national system of state education in 1870 it was to be administered and controlled locally by elected School Boards. Participation in these local institutions, either as electors or as elected representatives, also fostered active citizenship. Indeed, debates about citizenship were central to Liberalism. For Liberals and radicals, the alpha-omega of citizenship was independence. Only independent men had the capacity for 'enlightened disinterestedness'. Social responsibility, moral seriousness and personal accomplishment were the stock ingredients of active citizenship, especially for Nonconformists, who were acutely aware of the 'Christian duties of citizenship': the obligation to participate in public life, as electors and representatives, and to elevate its moral tone.[39] The ideal society envisaged by Liberals and radicals was self-regulating and composed of independent small-scale producers, in which citizens co-operated with one another on equal terms. This accounts for the Liberal and radical preoccupation with the land and in facilitating wider ownership and, thereby, wider citizenship. Limited progress was made in this sphere through the freehold land societies in the late 1840s and 1850s: members paid a monthly subscription, which would then be pooled to purchase tracts of land. These would be divided into freehold plots, assigned to individual members, and were of sufficient value to entitle the owner to the forty-shilling freehold franchise – an ancient voting right that existed in county constituencies. One of the main purposes of these societies was to widen property ownership and break the aristocratic monopoly on land, thus bringing about free trade in land.[40] For most radicals, widening ownership was more practical and desirable than land nationalization (the compulsory acquisition of land by the state and the parcelling of it out on an equal basis). Liberals and most radicals agreed that there was to be equality of opportunity, not social equality: 'It was not a society from which differences in status or wealth had been eliminated but one where these were based on differences in effort and enterprise, rather than privilege.'[41]

Nowhere was this preoccupation with independence and character more evident than in relation to the franchise. The disinterested maturity that Liberals sought would be guaranteed by limiting the franchise to male householders.[42] This question of fitness was intimately bound up in notions of 'character': a multi-faceted concept that 'included industry, energy, self-help and self-discipline, thrift, honesty, integrity, devotion to duty, and manliness in the face of difficulty'.[43] This had implications for political entitlement, since 'character' was an accessible notion, potentially open to all, irrespective of birth. On the other hand, these virtues were not universal in the eyes of Liberals; they had to be learned (hence the importance of education for many Liberals) or earned through hard work, consistently demonstrated through participation in voluntary organizations such as co-operatives, and then – and only then – would political entitlement follow.[44] Liberalism, therefore, was far from being democratic. To many radicals, these Liberal criteria seemed elitist and this helps to explain why Liberals and radicals often disagreed over what constituted fitness and who should be enfranchised, the former usually favouring a more restrictive definition, or, if possible, to avoid franchise extension altogether.[45]

As these divisions over the franchise imply, when it came to translating Liberal ideology into practice, differences and divisions emerged within the Liberal coalition. Biagini highlights the ways in which the cries of 'Liberty, Retrenchment and Reform' mobilized diverse constituencies of electoral support for the Liberal party. Indeed, the very elasticity and capaciousness of these cries, which assumed many different contextual forms, helps to explain why so many different individuals and interests supported the Liberal party. It was relatively easy to champion abstract rights such as religious freedom, individual liberty, equality below the law, the rights of oppressed minorities on the continent, and to be in favour of 'reform' (whatever that meant). On the other hand, when it came to specifics, these watchwords could just as easily divide as unite the disparate band of Liberals and radicals in terms of how they were to be defined, prioritized and achieved.

There were tensions about how to 'define and defend liberty'.[46] For all the Liberal rhetoric on civil liberty and equality before the law, there continued to be a widespread view amongst radicals that one law existed for the rich and another for the people, and that the Liberal

party was complicit in perpetuating these injustices. This sense of popular injustice was acutely felt in relation to trades unions, as it was
widely believed that the law was biased in favour of employers, many of
whom just so happened to be Liberal manufacturers. While Gladstone's
first government extended legal protection to the unions through the
Trades Union Act of 1871, this was accompanied by another act that
made picketing illegal, 'the one activity considered by union members
as fundamental to successful strike action'.[47] One can see why some
working-class radicals and trades unionists were susceptible to Tory
propaganda that the Liberal party was the employers' party. The rapacious and tyrannical elites that radicals were fighting against could, on
those occasions when the 'tyranny of capital' was at issue, be extended to
include the manufacturers and commercial plutocrats that dominated
the Liberal party in urban Britain.

Although radicals were often to the fore in demanding legislative
protection for certain vulnerable groups such as factory workers and
trades unionists, it would be wrong to assume that they were in favour
of widespread state intervention. Indeed, radicals could be far more
libertarian than Liberals, as evidenced by their hostility both to the
centralization of state power and towards temperance legislation, Sab-
batarianism (those who believed that Sunday, in accordance with the
Fourth Commandment, should be kept free of work) and compulsory
vaccination.[48] On these issues, radicals often made common cause with
tories rather than Liberals. The Liberals, especially Nonconformists,
were usually to the fore in supporting legislative intervention in these
spheres on the grounds that wider public interests and morals needed
protecting. Biagini draws attention to the ways radicals drew on Liberal
ideology – based on the old Whig cry of 'equality before the law' – and
appropriated it to their own ends as a means to emphasize the affinities
between radicals and Liberals.[49] Quite so, but one should also note how
disaffected these radicals were with the mainstream Liberal party. Even
when it came to religious liberty, Liberals and radicals often disagreed.
While radicals tended to be overtly hostile to an Established Church,
the powerful minority of Anglicans within the Liberal party, and even
some Nonconformists, believed that an Established Church was not
only essential for promoting morality in the public political sphere,
but was also crucial in fostering religious freedom and toleration by
subjecting clerics to the rule of law.[50]

As for the contentious issue of franchise extension and parliamentary reform, we have already seen that Liberals and radicals all too
frequently found themselves at loggerheads. For Biagini, democratization 'was the really all-embracing issue for popular Liberals' and
popular commitment to franchise extension was the most conspicuous

issue that 'illustrates the continuity between Chartism and working-class Liberalism'.[51] While radicals and advanced Liberals might have worked for democratization, moderate Liberals and Whigs were deeply fearful of moves in this direction. For these moderate Liberals, the all-embracing issue was how to restrain democratic excess – the tyranny of the majority – through safeguards such as education, the ballot and representation of minorities. It is worth emphasizing that such moderate Liberals were not confined to the parliamentary backbenchers, but were also to be found in great numbers out in the constituencies. These moderate Liberals were usually the ones in control of local Liberal Associations, much to the chagrin of the radicals.[52]

This brings us to the question of why popular radicals campaigned for the Reform Bill 1867 when it was based on the limited principle of household suffrage. Had the radicals come round to the limited conception of political citizenship advanced by Gladstone and Bright, in which the franchise was seen as a privilege to be conferred on those respectable, independent, taxpaying men who were heads of households? Arguably, this was not because many radicals had abandoned their attachment to the *principle* of manhood suffrage, muted cries for which soon re-emerged after 1867 in any case. After all, the Reform League – the radical organization established in 1865 to campaign for franchise extension – was committed from the outset to *manhood* suffrage as the following resolution shows:

That the League having been formed for the purpose of advocating the extension of the franchise on the basis of manhood, cannot consistently, countenance, approve, or support the effort of individuals, or associations, who seek the extension of the franchise on the diametrically opposite and unjust principle, of a property qualification.[53]

Admittedly, this seemingly resolute statement actually left the Reform League with some room for manoeuvre. What is clear is that radicals continued to vest the right of the franchise in persons (and, more specifically, adult men) and not property. At the very least, they conceived of property as residing in the person in the form of labour or in issuing from the person in the form of dependents – their wives and children. That the Reform League came round to the more limited proposals of the Tory government's 1867 Reform Act – which effectively created a registered, residential manhood suffrage (vested more in property than in the person) – was due more to their tactical finesse and realistic appraisal of what could be achieved from the high-political firmament at Westminster than to an abandonment of their commitment to the principle of manhood suffrage: Biagini is forced to concede that among plebeian reformers the cry of 'manhood suffrage' was the most ubiquitous.[54]

On the other hand, the 1867 Reform Act hardly represented a wholesale defeat for the Reform League. After all, manhood suffrage had been introduced, albeit with the limiting condition of household residence, hence the generally favourable reaction to the final Bill – at least, in the immediate aftermath. The Tory 1867 Reform Bill was far more 'radical' than the Liberal government's bill of 1866. This had been too extreme for the renegade anti-democratic parliamentary Liberals who voted against the bill, but not radical enough for the Reform League. Although the eventual realization of this had more to do with Disraeli's opportunism in the House of Commons, the extra-parliamentary agitation by the Reform League made it clear that a more substantial measure of franchise extension was required.[55] As such, these popular demonstrations throughout the country were not simply about vindicating the 'moral character' of the people against allegations by Tories and the Adullamite Liberals against the charge that they were unfit for citizenship.[56] This convinced a growing number of previously timid Liberals who had wanted to hedge household suffrage with a rental or rateable qualification to throw in their lot with the Reform League. As Derek Fraser notes: 'In Leeds, Manchester, and many other towns, the Reform League was a political force to be taken seriously' during the suffrage campaigns of 1867 and in the subsequent general election.[57]

The crucial difference in radical politics in 1867 from 1839, 1842 and 1848 was that the 'instalment men', as Feargus O'Connor had once derisively dubbed them, now held sway. This position was illustrated by one of the members of the Reform League executive, one that would become the leading light of independent radicalism in the 1870s and 1880s: the secularist and republican Charles Bradlaugh. As he told one radical meeting at the time of the Reform Bill, while he favoured universal suffrage as a natural right

> if he could not get all that he asked for, rather than have nothing, and thus leave matters in the bad state in which he found them, he would take what ameliorations he could get without ceasing to aim at ultimately winning the whole.[58]

Perhaps few would have shared Bradlaugh's Paineite view that the franchise was a natural right, but many more demanded it as a historic right, the birthright of the 'freeborn Englishman', as the acme of full citizenship and as a means to secure wider social and economic justice – all arguments that an increasing number of Liberals had come to accept.[59] The American Civil War and the North's campaign against slavery were instrumental in rekindling popular interest in parliamentary reform, and the advocates of the latter linked their cause with that of the American abolitionists. Men without votes, it was argued, were little more than slaves, and those who refused to give working men the vote were as tyrannical as the Southern slave-owners in the United States. True to the disparate and heterogeneous nature of the radical tradition, radicals deployed a range of arguments to justify a further extension of the franchise. For example, radicals often conflated arguments based on Paineite notions of natural rights with arguments based on the cry of 'no taxation without representation'. But even the Chartists had drawn on a range of arguments and had never solely claimed the franchise as an 'inalienable' natural right, the purpose of which was exactly the same in the 1840s as it was in the 1860s: to persuade as many people as possible to support their demands by drawing on as many supporting arguments as possible. When Liberals such as John Bright and Gladstone started speaking in the mid-1860s of the 'moral right' of every citizen 'not presumably incapacitated by some consideration of personal unfitness',[60] most radicals welcomed this as a new argument that could be added to their existing stock. If the leaders of the Reform League went to great lengths to claim that it sought entry into the political nation for independent and respectable working men, then this was primarily a rhetoric strategy to allay the fears of the political elite and demonstrate to them that working men were fit for the franchise.

Either way, given the complexities that surrounded the operation of the borough franchise after 1867, most notably in terms of defining what actually constituted a household,[61] it is hardly surprising that many radicals were soon disappointed with the working of the Act. These complexities soon gave rise to a renewed demand for a simplistic franchise on the basis of manhood. The campaign to extend the franchise to the counties, which again drew on a range of arguments, simmered away in the 1870s, spearheaded by the miners and rural radicals, but in the absence of high-political support and urban apathy (many working-class radicals now enjoyed the franchise), it would not bear fruit until 1884 – precipitated, once again, by high-political manoeuvring. Also, if agricultural labourers and most of the miners focused their agitation on extending household suffrage to the counties, surely this could be justified as having the greatest likelihood of being granted by the government, given the precedent established by the 1867 Reform Act. If the cry for 'manhood suffrage' largely disappeared after 1884, this was because it was no longer practical politics. The granting of household suffrage had taken the sting out of the agitation, but it was far from being 'highly acceptable'[62] to the subaltern classes, some of whom were disfranchised due to the complexities of electoral registration law. While Liberals and radicals could co-operate and make common cause, as Chapter 5 demonstrates, this was a far cry from Biagini's assertion that: 'In the popular mind, Chartism, Liberalism and democracy seemed to have become completely identified.'[63]

Chapter 5: Post-Chartist Radicalism and the (Un)making of Popular Liberalism

The transition from the confrontational and independent radical politics of Chartism to the relatively harmonious, compromising cross-class politics of Gladstonian Liberalism has given rise to an extensive and often confusing historical debate. Much of that confusion stems from a failure to define the terms of the debate satisfactorily. This definitional imprecision has its origins in the period itself. Ambiguity surrounds the shifting nomenclature of the popular movements and their members – Chartists, radicals, Liberals, reformers. Even more difficult to pinpoint are the boundaries between these groupings. Were Chartists merely radicals by another name, as Feargus O'Connor believed? Or was Chartism an aberration of radicalism, a view that was propagated by former disillusioned Chartists such as R. G. Gammage? At what point did 'moral force' Chartists become Liberals? What was the relationship between the popular radicals and the group of parliamentary radicals known as the 'reform party' in the House of Commons? There are also ambiguities surrounding chronology. When, why and to what extent did radicalism decline after 1848? Was the rise of popular Liberalism based on the incorporation of radicalism, or did the Liberal party merely fill the gap *after* the collapse of Chartism?

The purpose of this chapter is to clarify the terms of this historical debate and provide an account of the nature and extent of popular support for the Liberal party in the mid-Victorian decades. The outlines of the argument can be sketched in the following terms. The evolution of popular politics from Chartism to Gladstonian Liberalism was neither smooth nor complete. The Liberal party – inside and, especially, outside of Parliament – was ultimately a coalition of reformers who maintained their own distinct identities, and this was particularly true of the radicals. While the balance of forces might have been in favour of co-operation under the umbrella of Gladstonian Liberalism, some revisionist scholarship has tended either to exaggerate the success of popular Liberalism and its containment of radicalism or else it has failed to appreciate the extent to which Liberals and radicals continued to be divided by ideas. Indeed, radical frustration within the Liberal coalition had the periodic effect of reinvigorating an independent radical politics.

Out of Chartism, into Liberalism

One of the major contributions of the 'new political history' has been its attempt to rethink the conventional chronologies of the nineteenth century.[1] According to this new interpretation, popular Liberalism had its origins in the late eighteenth century. It was a product of the broad ideas associated with the 'Age of Reason' (notably the rationalism of the Enlightenment) and the 'Age of Revolutions' by championing the cause of liberty, equality and fraternity (although Liberals tended to distance themselves from equality). This popular Liberalism gathered pace from the late eighteenth century and began to translate into popular support for the Liberal party not, as was traditionally assumed, in the late 1850s but, rather, in the 1830s. This parallels revisionist work on the parliamentary Liberal party. In conventional accounts, the Liberal party's formal existence dated from the momentous meeting at the 'Willis Rooms' on 6 June 1859 when Whigs, Liberals and radicals came together, broadly in support of Polish independence, Italian unification and the North in the American Civil War. There was also a general feeling that a further instalment of parliamentary reform might be possible. For John Vincent, what was truly remarkable about this was not the formation of a distinctive parliamentary Liberal party in 1859, but 'the adoption of that Parliamentary party by the rank and file' in the 1850s and 1860s. Vincent argued that four main factors were responsible for the creation of this popular Liberalism: the growth of the provincial press (stimulated by the removal of the 'taxes on knowledge'), the rise of militant Nonconformity, the moderate and reformist goals of the skilled working class, and the charismatic politics of John Bright and Gladstone.[2]

Some of these factors certainly contributed to the *growth* of popular Liberalism in the 1850s and 1860s, but they were not responsible for its emergence, much less *the* cause. What Vincent and those historians that followed in his footsteps failed to recognize was that this process was hardly remarkable or novel: a recognizable Liberal party had been in existence, both in parliament and out in the constituencies, since the 1830s, as the work of Jon Parry, Joseph Coohill and Philip Salmon has recently shown.[3] Others have rejected this new chronology, which pushes the formation of the Liberal party back into the 1830s by virtue of the divisions between Whigs, Liberals, reformers and radicals in parliament.[4] Yet, as Jon Parry has rightly argued, to point to divisions within the parliamentary Liberal party in the 1830s and 1840s as evidence for the absence of a coherent and unified party is disingenuous. The Liberal party would always be a coalition of reformers, beset by periodic division, long before – and even during – Gladstone's leadership of the party.[5] The fact that a relatively coherent parliamentary Liberal party existed was part cause and consequence of the local registration societies that were set up in the wake of 1832. The Liberals, however, were neither as quick off the mark as the Tories, nor as effective. The Liberals were hampered by an overly centralized structure; divisions between local Whigs, Liberals and radicals; a somewhat disinterested approach to electoral registration (some took the lofty view that it was wrong to deprive political opponents of the franchise, which made some Liberals reluctant to make partisan objections in the annual revision courts); and by the failure of the Liberals to cultivate a political culture of organizational sociability to rival the Tories.[6]

Pushing the origins of the Liberal party further back in time adds grist to the mill of those revisionist historians who have argued that a coherent and genuinely 'popular' radical Liberalism dominated the agenda of reform politics from the time of John Wilkes in the late 1760s through to the rise of Labour in the early twentieth century. To these historians, the lynchpin of this radical Liberalism was opposition to political exclusion (various forms of 'Old Corruption'), which united the productive classes against idle parasitical elites. This led to calls for 'open government and the rule of law, for freedom from intervention both at home and abroad, and for individual liberty and community-centred democracy.'[7] This political diagnosis of socio-economic evils was the linking thread between Chartism, Gladstonian Liberalism and the Labour party. For Biagini and Reid, this explains why 'those who were originally called Chartists, were afterwards called Liberal and Labour activists'.[8] Thus, according to this interpretation, the transition from Chartism into Gladstonian Liberalism was a relatively seamless, linear and inevitable development – evidence of the hegemonic status exercised by this radical Liberalism.

Several variants exist of this 'continuity thesis', in terms of both causation and chronology. In relation to the causation, a debate exists about the reasons *why* Liberals and radicals were able to work together in the mid-Victorian years. Biagini argues for a rationalist interpretation of popular Liberalism: Liberals and radicals were linked by a shared, if problematic, cerebral commitment to 'liberty, retrenchment and reform'. Even the charismatic politics of Bright and Gladstone were underpinned by rational considerations. Joyce, on the other hand, places far more emphasis on the emotional loyalties generated by the romantic language of these popular tribunes who bound the masses to Liberalism by symbolically empowering them as the moral arbiters of the nation. The emissary of this politics was the 'gentleman radical', hero-politicians in the romantic mould – personified in radicalism by Feargus O'Connor and Ernest Jones, and then recast from the 1850s in the moral populism of John Bright and Gladstone.[9] For these tribunes, it was precisely the lack of wealth and pretensions of the masses that made them so virtuous in contrast to the selfish and unjust propertied classes.[10] Leaving aside the question of the very real differences in the politics and style of O'Connor and Jones on the one hand, and Bright and Gladstone on the other,[11] one wonders just how empowering it really was to be labelled as virtuous; no doubt such rhetoric *cemented* popular Liberalism, but it was not the cause. Biagini's rationalist interpretation is more plausible as an explanation, as opposed to a description, of popular Liberalism, despite its presentation of that Liberalism as largely consensual.

Turning to the issue of chronology, Biagini and Joyce are broadly in agreement: both of them are advocates of an unalloyed continuity in radicalism in the 'long' nineteenth century from Wilkes to Labour. Gareth Stedman Jones, Miles Taylor and Jon Lawrence do not share this chronology.[12] Stedman Jones argues for what might be termed a truncated form of radical continuity, which ran from the 1760s through to 1848. Notwithstanding his argument that Chartism represented a continuation of an older eighteenth-century radical tradition, Stedman Jones identifies a major caesura in radicalism in the 1840s, when its critique of the socially negligent view of the state was undermined by the state's willingness to reform itself – what happened to radicalism thereafter is less evident.[13] Miles Taylor's work on parliamentary radicalism provides one possible answer to this.[14] He has argued that Chartism itself represented a break with this radical tradition, a tradition that Taylor rightly sees as being more protean than Stedman Jones, Biagini and Reid, and Joyce. For Taylor, Chartism represented a largely disparate, incoherent and militant extra-parliamentary movement that hijacked the moderate and focused programme for parliamentary reform espoused by radicals in parliament after 1832. Once Chartism had exhausted itself, its mass following 'began to diminish, and the leadership began to be reabsorbed back into the less militant radical politics from which it had emerged in the mid-1830s'.[15]

As Taylor's work highlights, there is a danger of reducing the 'currents of radicalism' school to a monolithic account of radical continuity as its various members have advanced different forms of continuity, and even discontinuity in some cases. This can be seen in various contributions to *Currents of Radicalism*, a collection of essays edited by Biagini and Reid, each telling against the hegemonic status of radical Liberalism. This radical Liberalism was clearly unable to contain these discordant outbreaks of independent radicalism.[16]

Nevertheless, in explaining the transition from Chartism into Liberalism in such ways, Biagini and Reid, Joyce and Taylor have, in fact, reverted to a very old argument advanced by disillusioned radicals such as R. G. Gammage in the immediate aftermath of Chartism's collapse in 1848: that O'Connorite Chartism – with its stress on independence and 'physical force', and its socially conservative and backward-looking vision – was, at best, an outgrowth or, at worst, an aberration, of radicalism.[17] Seen from this perspective, it was the 'moral force' Chartists who were the true heirs to the radical tradition, a tradition that had many affinities with Liberalism. Moral force Chartists and Liberals were able to coalesce around shared values such as individualism, respectability, self-improvement and self-reliance, and work for 'liberty, retrenchment and reform' by rational discussion and means. If only the O'Connorite mainstream had been willing to see the error of their ways and adopt 'sensible Chartism', as Thomas Perronet Thompson dubbed the moral force Chartists with whom he sympathized and wished to broker an alliance with other reformers, they would have achieved all that they desired and more.[18] Once O'Connorite Chartism had collapsed, Liberals of the type personified by John Bright and Richard Cobden and moderate radicals such as Robert Lowery and William Lovett were able to co-operate and make real progress. This interpretation was subsequently taken up by the Fabian Socialists in the late nineteenth century to validate their own gradualist and educational approach to improving society.[19]

Once again, this is an interpretation derived from hindsight; and one that plays down the tensions and contradictions that existed between popular Liberalism and radicalism. First, a good deal of confusion surrounds the relationship between Liberals and radicals in the 1830s and 1840s, and the respective coherence of those two groupings. This confusion and lack of coherence is further evidence against the hegemonic status of radical Liberalism. As we have seen, a relatively coherent Liberal party certainly existed in the 1830s but, in terms of its overall popularity (electors and non-electors), it was a rather narrow movement with its support base limited largely to the urban middle class.[20] As for the 'radical' reformers in parliament after 1832, with a few notable exceptions such as Thomas Perronet Thompson, most of them were largely divorced from the world of popular radicalism, they 'lacked organization and leadership',[21] and the number who consistently voted in favour of radical causes was small. For the most part, these were dismissed by popular radicals as 'Sham Radicals', 'rotten Whigs' and 'Malthusian Radicals'.[22] So, Liberalism might have been a more coherent movement than radicalism, but it was nowhere near as popular. Second, even if the boundaries between the two movements were not always clear, two distinct movements undoubtedly existed. Indeed, the popularity of radicalism was in part due to the hostility towards the Whigs and their middle-class Liberal accomplices, who had betrayed the people, especially over reform and the New Poor Law. There were real ideological divisions separating these two movements. As Theodore Koditschek frames it, radicalism 'questioned the liberal's very authenticity' by 'demanding the immediate enactment of the kind of progressive democracy that liberalism had already theoretically proclaimed'.[23] Urban Liberals were rather complacent in the 1830s and were, in the words of the Bradford radical Peter Bussey, 'indifferent to the people's rights'.[24] As far as radicals such as Bussey were concerned, it was high time for the Liberals to make good on their ideological promises. What concern existed was with the manner, rather than the condition, in which the working class lived – hence the priority of moral reform. This, in turn, helps to explain the rise of the tory-radical alliance and the subsequent growth of Chartism. Third, if radicals did not necessarily oppose capitalism per se, they did single out exploitative individual capitalists for criticism. Thus, in the industrial heartlands, co-operation between Liberals and radicals was contingent on harmonious employer–employee relations. This explains why Liberal manufacturers of John Fielden's stamp, men who worked for genuine radical reform, were popular with radicals. But Fielden, with his respect for the moral economy of the workers (the right to vote, the right to join a union and the right to secure employment) was the exception in the 1830s and 1840s.[25] One only needs to compare Fielden with the far more typical stance adopted by John Bright, who was an outspoken opponent of the Ten Hours movement and trades unions.[26] Fourth, although 'moral force' Chartists were not the weak-kneed reformers that O'Connor made them out to be (many were committed to the principles of co-operative socialism), to write off O'Connorite Chartism as conservative (or to dismiss O'Connor personally as a tory-radical) is to underestimate the popularity of the restorative, pastoral and individualistic brand of radicalism that he personified.[27] That there were many affinities between tory-radicalism and O'Connorite Chartism is hardly surprising, given that the latter was in many respects a continuation of the former, and it is no coincidence that the heartland of both was in the West Riding of Yorkshire. Finally, what the advocates of continuity obscure, above all, is the way in which the acute social and political tensions of the 1830s and 1840s jolted urban Liberals out of their complacency and taught both Liberals and radicals the virtues of moderation, co-operation, flexibility and tactical finesse. The moderate, mainstream movement for parliamentary reform about which Miles Taylor has written only became moderate and mainstream *after* the traumas of the 1830s and 1840s – at least, for popular radicals.

On the Liberal side, the rise of Chartism had dramatically drawn attention to the plight of the working class, and this induced the more advanced middle-class Liberals, especially those who had been involved in the anti-slavery movement (such as Joseph Sturge and W. E. Forster), to co-operate with moderate Chartists. In the first instance, this co-operation came to fruition in 1842 with the short-lived Complete Suffrage Movement. Yet, these overtures and the subsequent 'New Move' ultimately failed to prevent the re-emergence of militant Chartism in 1848, a militancy that overshadowed and stifled the immediate efforts of moderate ventures around that time (such as the People's Charter Union, the People's League and the National Parliamentary and Financial Reform Association). As these social tensions began to worsen and descend into violence in May and June 1848, as was the case in Forster's Bradford, Liberals such as Forster (who had hitherto been sympathetic) felt that there was no choice but to unleash the forces of state repression on the Chartists. As Cobden noted rather indignantly: 'The Charter has been so dragged in the mud, & so often thrust in our faces, at the point of the pike, that the middle class cannot be brought to look at it with calmness or toleration.'[28] Historians have often pointed to the mass enlisting of the middle class as special constables as evidence of the rally of the propertied classes to the defence of the established order. Certainly, many did enlist, including Forster, but it seems that there was a general reluctance to volunteer in some towns – evidence, in part, of middle class sympathies for Chartism.[29] Either way, the acute social tensions revealed by the Chartist risings of 1848 had pricked the conscience of the urban middle class and convinced many of their leaders that social conditions would have to be improved if a return to unrest was to be prevented. This social conscience manifested itself in the rise of the idiosyncratic and short-lived Christian Socialist movement (which sought to adapt the co-operative labour schemes of the French Socialist Louis Blanc to English soil). More tangibly, this social conscience was one of the motivating factors behind the decision to inaugurate programmes of municipal reform, a marked feature in mid-Victorian towns, even though it was gradual, limited and begrudging in some cases.

This reforming pulse was quickened by the rise of a distinctly Non-conformist civic gospel, articulated in the 1840s and 1850s by a group of prominent Nonconformist ministers. According to this gospel, for those who were able it was a Christian obligation to participate in public life and to address the social problems of the day. Urban Liberals realized that it was in the immediate locale where the harsher edges of political economy needed to be blunted and smoothed. The rise of this softened Liberalism was evidence of the growing view amongst Liberals that social distress was not necessarily the result of individual moral failing; the harsh urban environment was increasingly held responsible, hence the need for municipal public health initiatives. This became practical politics after the democratization of the municipal franchise in the 1850s. Previously, the electorate had been dominated by the penny-pinching shopocracy whose demands for low taxes had prevented the improvement of local amenities. There was now more of an electoral incentive for town councils to stamp out the 'disruption, deprivation, disease and death' that inflicted a heavy toll on the urban working class, many of whom desired municipal reform.[30] As this list of urban problems suggests, a presumption that this softened Liberalism was entirely altruistic, or even motivated solely by expectations of electoral advantage, would be a mistake. Outbreaks of disease, such as cholera, and fears of contamination prompted urban elites into legislative action. Thus did urban Liberals become less dogmatic in their commitment to the strictures of political economy, and show themselves willing to make exceptions to the principle of *laissez-faire*.[31] As early as 1848, the Liberal *Bradford Observer*, once the stern and unbending voice of political economy, conceded that 'the laws of political economy by their natural operation, do not always direct the industry of the country in the channels which lead to the greatest amount of national happiness'.[32] More cynically, there were those advanced Liberals who had come round to the view that the only way to achieve some of their own objectives was to enlist the support of the radicals and the masses. The militant Nonconformist Edward Miall adopted this strategy, believing that enfranchised workers would be staunch allies in his campaign to disestablish the Church of England.[33] Whatever the motives, there can be little doubt that a growing number of urban Liberals and the national leadership began to pay more attention to the plight of the masses and made more effort to include and empower them.[34]

Growing numbers of radicals were also coming round to the idea of moderate reform and the need to co-operate with middle-class Liberals, although it took others like Ernest Jones longer to accept compromise. Some – Bronterre O'Brien and George Julian Harney, for example – remained opposed to compromise in their objectives and carried over their ultra-radicalism into causes such as socialism and republicanism. But, of those Chartists who remained activists, by the 1860s many had become 'instalment men'. As Robert Cooper explained to the Newcastle radical Joseph Cowan, 'Let us work for an instalment, as a means of securing a larger instalment, until the whole is gained.' Cooper saw no inconsistency or abandonment of principle in advocating this strategy, as it was the one most likely to result in success. Gradual reform, he argued, would set the elite's mind at rest and induce middle-class Liberals to co-operate with working-class radicals. For Cooper, past experience had taught him that 'every great measure, political or social, has only been carried by the joint action of the two classes'.[35] The dialectic of compromise and co-operation produced, on behalf of radicals and the labour movement, 'a narrowing of aims, a growing concern less with the oppressive and exploitative features of the system as a whole than with specific features of oppression and the ways in which the policies of gradualism and limited reform would assuredly remove such features'.[36] As Liberals were forced to blunt the harsher edges of political economy, so radicals became more reconciled to its existence. Above all, Chartism as a particular strategy, based on the mass platform, had failed to achieve radical objectives. It made sense, therefore, for radicals to reassess their strategic and tactical options. Seen from this perspective, there is no need to resort to theoretically exacting Marxist models, such as the 'labour aristocracy' thesis, to explain why the working class failed to develop a revolutionary consciousness (whatever that might mean). Rather, as Martin Hewitt has argued, the growth of working-class reformism 'was not the result of a failure to comprehend the circumstances in which the working class found themselves, but rather the consequence of a realistic assessment of changing social, economic and political conditions'.[37]

Out of Liberalism, into Radicalism?

A growing body of post-revisionist work has revealed the painful and violent transition from Chartism into Liberalism, a process that was fraught with tension and liable to break down. To present this transition as seamless, consensual and inevitable, and as the product of a shared ideological tradition, is to replicate 'the prejudices and political purposes of Victorian Whig-Liberal discourse itself',[38] by showing 'Liberal culture as an untroubled entity... and celebrating an untroubled Gladstonian Age of Equipoise'.[39] Indeed, there is something almost 'official' about this vision of popular Liberalism, a vision seen through the rose-tinted lens of Gladstone; one that often seems quite removed from the rowdy, interactive world of popular platform politics. This is more a vision of William's People than the 'People's William'. This consensual portrait has its origins in the latter-day careers of those Chartists who eventually threw in their lot with the Gladstonian Liberal party. These ex-Chartists deliberately played down their radical pasts as a means to legitimize their Liberal credentials and to emphasize the populist antecedents of the Liberal party.[40] While it would be disingenuous to suggest that conflict and division were the dominant characteristics of mid-Victorian popular reform politics, attention should be paid, as Tony Taylor notes, to the 'agendas that continued to divide Chartism and Liberalism' and to 'the hard process of negotiation' that brought Liberals and radicals together.[41]

This underlines the extent to which the Liberal party was a coalition of reformers, whose relationship with one another would always be determined by strategic and tactical considerations. This uneasy coalition of reformers was kept together by ongoing negotiation and compromise, in terms of strategy and tactics, if not necessarily in terms of objectives. In contrast to Biagini's portrait of a largely untroubled Liberal coalition, Margot Finn's work on post-Chartist radicalism illustrates some of the points of tension and division that existed between Liberals and radicals in the 1850s, albeit from a perspective that exaggerates the class-based nature of these divisions. Traditionally, historians pointed to the ways in which Liberals and radicals were able to unite in support of the liberties of European peoples. The continental masses were the victims of continental autocratic expansionism, either in the domestic sphere as downtrodden subjects (as was periodically the case in France, Germany and Italy) or as the foreign victims of imperial rule and aggrandisement (as in Hungary, Italy and Poland). But, as Finn shows, continental revolts and popular movements could just as easily divide as unite the coalition of reformers, not least because there was a tendency to refract continental developments through filters that revealed the conflicting domestic priorities of Liberals and radicals. Liberals tended to champion civil and religious liberties, national independence, political economy and voluntary association. Radicals were more preoccupied with popular sovereignty and urged the continental revolutionaries to demand that their state acknowledge its social (and often social*ist*) responsibilities towards its citizens and protect the rights of labour – responsibilities that made Liberals, at best, deeply uncomfortable.[42] Again, at the abstract level, reformers of all hues could wave the flag of Liberal-nationalism; however, bubbling beneath the surface was often an antagonistic politics that continued to divide the reformers. Then there was the vexed question of what role – if any – the British government should play in aiding these continental popular movements. Pacifistic Liberals of Cobden and Bright's stamp were opposed to intervention, while radical sympathy for the oppressed translated into demands for military intervention – a fissure that was dramatically revealed by the Crimean War in the mid-1850s. Continental developments therefore – in the shape of the 1848 revolutions and the Polish, Hungarian and Italian nationalist movements of the 1850s and 1860s – played a part in sustaining an independent style of popular radicalism that celebrated an international radical fraternity. This radicalism was disseminated and organized by the press and a rich associational, ceremonial culture of processions, dinners and meetings held in honour of revolutionary figures such as the Hungarian nationalist Louis Kossuth, the French Socialist Louis Blanc and the Italian nationalist Giuseppe Garibaldi.

Finn's subtle portrait recaptures some of the vicissitudes of Liberal-radical relations after 1848. The problem with Finn's account is that she underplays the ongoing tensions and strategic considerations that continued to shape the Liberal coalition *after* the 1860s. She argues that the radicals and Liberals began to gravitate towards one another from the late 1850s and, by the late 1860s, had largely fused together: 'For as working-class radicals moved to the centre, middle-class Liberals moved to the left, first questioning and then discarding the rigid adherence to received dogmas of political economy'.[43] This leads Finn to argue that the 'New Liberalism' (a shorthand term for state-sponsored welfare reforms) associated with the Edwardian Liberal party actually had its origins in the 1860s and 1870s. On closer inspection, however, there seems to be little evidence of this. Political economy, although less dogmatically adhered to after the 1840s, was still in the ascendant in the 1860s and 1870s. There was also little interest in state-sponsored social reforms.[44] Further, we might note how the fusion she speaks of was, as John Vincent noted in a different context, like 'a badly set limb' – prone to fracture when the process of negotiation and compromise broke down, as it so often did out in the constituencies in the 1860s and 1870s.[45] Liberals and radicals could be divided amongst themselves, let alone from each other. The division between the constitutional and extreme wings of the republican movement in the early 1870s was one such example of this splintering within radicalism.

At the level of popular politics, this fracturing was evident by the periodic resurgence of independent radicalism between the 1850s and 1880s that manifested itself in a variety of guises: latter-day Chartism, labour militancy (which spilled over into radical suffrage politics as trades unions fought to end the legal restrictions hampering them), republican and secularist radicalism, rival Liberal candidatures in the constituencies and, latterly, socialism. It makes little sense to reduce this independent radicalism to a barometer of underlying class conflict within the Liberal coalition. As in the Chartist era, Liberal-radical divisions were, first and foremost, *political* and concerned issues of ideological difference. Similarly, when class tensions were apparent, they were politically derived (as was the case with conflicts over the extension of the franchise in the mid-1860s) or politically focused (as demonstrated by the calls of some radicals for independent political representation for the working class). In a direct echo of their Chartist forebears, the Reform League maintained that the political exclusion of the working class was the main cause of class conflict.[46]

In terms of geographical concentration, this independent radicalism was most evident, and most continuous, in London between the 1850s and 1880s. As Tony Taylor has shown, a constellation of structural and environmental factors enabled Chartism to survive in London long after it had collapsed elsewhere.[47] London is probably one of the few places where it is possible to discern a continuous radical tradition that cuts across the mid-Victorian divide, but not a tradition that would fit into the 'currents of radicalism' school. One of the main institutional repositories of this tradition was the dozen or so metropolitan radical clubs. These radical clubs represented a counter-cultural 'world of anti-hierarchical egalitarianism',[48] and many of those who frequented them (mainly artisans) kept alive the socialistic Chartism of Bronterre O'Brien in the underworld of Soho, and supplied the leadership and activist core of various radical movements during these decades. These included the First International Workingmen's Association (the first avowedly Marxist labour organization, established in 1864), the Reform League demonstrations of 1866–67, the republican movement of the early 1870s, the Manhood Suffrage League in the mid-1870s, the campaign in support of Charles Bradlaugh in the early 1880s, and the Trafalgar Square demonstrations against unemployment in 1887 and the Government's attempt to prevent public meetings being held there.[49] The metropolitan radical clubs were also at the forefront of the socialist revival in the 1880s, which would, in turn, play its part in the establishment of independent labour politics.

But this independent radicalism was not only a metropolitan movement: it could also survive, and periodically flourish, at a national level. National periodicals and newspapers – notably the widely circulating *Reynolds's Newspaper* and the *National Reformer* – continued to fulminate against 'Old Corruption' and disseminate Chartist, republican, secularist and even socialist politics.[50] These newspapers played an important part in mobilizing a radicalism that was often at odds with mainstream Liberalism, especially in the 1850s.[51] The gothic idioms of romanticism that had characterized early Victorian radicalism could still be found in mid-Victorian radical rhetoric, as the following attack on the monarchy by *Reynolds's Newspaper* in 1868 illustrates: 'Royal, clerical and aristocratic lechers are all at one-time sucking at the veins of the people and vampire-like, drawing their life-blood.'[52] The melodramatic, sensational exposé of royal and aristocratic misdemeanours were similarly ubiquitous in the radical press. This radicalism did not always translate into discrete, coherent movements and, in some cases, it might not have amounted to much more than a gut opposition to privilege, but its expression could represent an 'attempt to outflank liberalism'.[53]

Furthermore, even when popular Gladstonianism was at its zenith in the 1870s and 1880s, the popular Liberal coalition could fracture in the provinces (especially in the absence of a strong Tory opposition). This was revealed at the 1874 general election when a number of independent radicals contested seats against Liberals. Loyalty to Gladstone, it seems, did not preclude opposition to the Liberal party and, very occasionally, loyalty to the Liberal party did not preclude opposition to Gladstone. The dynamics of electoral politics in Leeds provides a good example of these Liberal-radical tensions. At the general election of 1874, the sitting Liberal MPs were challenged by Dr. Frederick Lees, who stood as a latter-day Chartist (which overshadowed his position as a temperance fanatic). At the 1880 general election, the Leeds Liberal Association was so divided and unable to agree on a second candidate that they nominated Gladstone. A small group of ultra-radicals led by the republican John De Morgan objected to the dictatorial actions of the Association in nominating Gladstone, whom they regarded as an unsuitable candidate due to his previously poor record as a constituency MP.[54]

There remained a powerful radical current of suspicion, and even outright opposition, to dictatorial Liberal elites. This situation was paradoxically reinforced from the 1870s, when many local Liberal Associations reconstituted themselves, broadly along the lines of the Birmingham Liberal Association, known as the 'Caucus', established in 1867. As critics noted at the time, despite its professed aim of democratizing party organization by opening up membership to all who professed Liberal principles and by implementing an integrated pyramidal structure with the local wards at the bottom and a general committee at the top, power in the 'Caucus' model remained deeply hierarchical. Granted, the 'Caucus' model played a positive role in mobilizing electoral support for the Gladstonian Liberal party in many of the constituencies where it was adopted. It kept MPs in closer contact with their constituents and provided some radicals with an entry into Liberal politics. On the other hand, the 'Caucus' model could be unpopular with the radicals who resented the formalized chains of command that it put in place – and often into the hands of dictatorial elites who, in some cases, not only tried to impose their authority on local radicals, but also on MPs. Those MPs who placed a high premium on their independence and/or remained committed to the importance of a direct relationship with their constituents over the heads of the Caucus were hounded, censured and even deselected in some cases. W. E. Forster at Bradford and Joseph Cowen at Newcastle fought long, bitter and, ultimately, unsuccessful campaigns against the dictation of their respective caucuses.[55] Thus, for the politicized sections of organized labour and disaffected radicals there was an alternative, albeit less charged, 'current of radicalism' than that delineated by Biagini and his followers. Nowhere are these independent currents better illustrated than in the career of 'Iconoclast', the formidable Charles Bradlaugh.[56]

Committed to rationality, atheism and republicanism, Bradlaugh was the foremost and most forthright exponent of Paineite radicalism in the mid-Victorian years. Many facets of the traditional radical platform crystallized around him. His first encounters with radicalism were most probably at the open-air meetings at Victoria Park in London and, subsequently, through contact with a group of secularists that were determined to purge the state and organized society of religion, and secure equal freedom of thought for all. Bradlaugh's entrée into radical activism was occasioned by the metropolitan campaigns for the right to hold meetings in public places. The attempts by the state to prohibit demonstrations in public places united the various radicals who used these spaces into a broader campaign for the broader issue of rights of assembly and demonstration. In this respect, they kept alive the spirit of the mass platform and metropolitan Chartism, and fuelled popular hostility towards government (both Tory *and* Liberal) and the police.[57] Bradlaugh first came to the public's attention through his complaints about the brutality that the police had used against crowds protesting against the legislative proposals to restrict Sunday trading in July 1855. Testament to the continuing impact of continental affairs on mid-Victorian radicalism, Bradlaugh achieved further notoriety in 1858 through his defence of Felice Orsini, the Italian revolutionary who had tried to assassinate Napoleon III – the new autocratic *bête-noire* of English radicals. By the early 1860s, Bradlaugh had emerged as the determined leader of the secularist movement, displacing the more cautious George Jacob Holyoake in the process.

The popular campaigns for the rights of public access that Bradlaugh had been involved with also fed into the Reform League demonstrations, which reached fever pitch with the Hyde Park riots of 1866. Indeed, the Reform League had its origins in a campaign for the right of public assembly, the occasion being the break-up by the police of a meeting protesting against the then government's curtailment of Garibaldi's visit.[58] Bradlaugh was a member of the executive committee of the League, and was in favour of manhood suffrage; his disillusionment with the 1867 Reform Act fuelled his republicanism and secularism. By the late 1870s, he had emerged as one of the main national voices of independent radicalism due to his editorship of the *National Reformer* (the organ of the secularist movement) and through his commanding oratory, along with his position as President of the National Secular Society and his association with the moderate wing of the republican movement in the 1870s. Yet, there was always more to Bradlaugh and the independent radicalism that he headed than his outspoken atheism and republicanism, as demonstrated by his insistence that the *National Reformer* should not only concern itself with secularism. Even the republicanism that he espoused, like that of many others, was part of a wider critique of privilege that viewed the monarchy as part of the remnants of 'Old Corruption' and antithetical to meritocracy. This radicalism not only appealed to the relatively small band of committed secularists and republicans, many of whom were skilled artisans, but also to those who were disappointed with the 1867 Reform Act and the subsequent concord that was struck between the Reform League and Gladstonian Liberalism. During the mid-Victorian decades, the secularist and republican movements continued in the earlier vein of the Chartists and Owenites by providing their members with a culture of debating classes, lectures, singing classes, tea parties and concerts.[59]

Bradlaugh was also at the forefront of the latter-day campaigns for the repeal of taxes on knowledge and freedom of expression, dramatically symbolized by his publication of *The Fruits of Philosophy*, a birth-control manual by Charles Knowlton. Bradlaugh and his co-publisher, Annie Besant, were prosecuted for obscenity and initially found guilty – that is, until Bradlaugh exploited a legal loophole and, in the process, won a victory for the cause of freedom of publication. Testament to Bradlaugh's uneasy relationship with the Liberal party and mainstream Liberalism was his repeated failure to gain election for the borough of Northampton between 1868 and 1880, the year in which he was finally elected. It would, however, be another six years before Bradlaugh was allowed to take his seat in the House of Commons. Taking a seat in the House of Commons was conditional on swearing an oath – before God. As an atheist, Bradlaugh believed it was hypocritical to swear an oath of allegiance to God and so requested that he be allowed to affirm rather than swear an oath. This was a right granted to certain Dissenters in which the words 'I swear' were replaced with 'I solemnly, sincerely, and truly declare and affirm', and the reference to

'So help me God' was also dropped.[60] When this was denied, Bradlaugh asked to take the oath; this was also refused, until 1886, on the grounds that he had previously declared it to be meaningless to him. It was not until 1888 that he finally secured the right to affirm. In the meantime, he was effectively denied the right of taking his seat – meaning that the seat was declared vacant, thus necessitating a by-election. However, the constituents of Northampton kept re-electing him (in 1881, 1882, 1884 and 1885), thus creating something of a constitutional crisis: and so began the notorious 'Bradlaugh Case'. As Edward Royle has argued, the battle for Northampton's constitutional rights to elect an MP of its choice transformed Bradlaugh into a popular tribune and made him the indisputable leader of radicalism.[61] Bradlaugh's 'direct and effective' oratory came into its own as he toured the country whipping up popular support.

There were parallels here with the sensational Tichborne Campaign that had begun in 1867 and was still simmering away in the 1880s, even though this was not an explicitly political movement.[62] The Bradlaugh and Tichborne cases gave rise to two of the three largest popular movements between the collapse of Chartism and the rise of Labour (the other being the Reform League), turning their respective figureheads into popular tribunes, with thousands signing petitions in support of their claims. A material culture grew up around these movements. For example, Bradlaugh's celebrity status was soon turned to commercial profit through the production of mugs, pots and razors. The Tichborne Campaign was the farcical and melodramatic legal case of restoring the property of a long lost aristocrat by the name of Sir Roger Tichborne to a poor butcher called Tomas Castro from Australia (originally from the East End of London) who claimed to be Sir Roger. It is doubtful that Castro was, in fact, Tichborne. Yet, ultimately, this mattered very little, especially after the establishment appeared to close ranks against him. When that happened, he became the underdog. For Tichborne's supporters, as with Bradlaugh's, this campaign was about defending popular rights against a seemingly corrupt, bigoted and intolerant political establishment – the latest incarnations of 'Old Corruption'. Bradlaugh was fighting against injustice, against the establishment's blatant flouting of the law in its refusal to let him take his seat on account of his atheism, republicanism and advocacy of birth control. What right, Bradlaugh and his supporters asked, did the House of Commons have to overturn the democratically expressed wishes of the electors of Northampton? This left him with no choice but to appeal to the people, the ultimate court of appeal. Both Bradlaugh and Tichborne demanded 'fair play'. As the supporters of John Wilkes, Henry Hunt and Feargus O'Connor before them, the Tichbornites and the

Bradlaughites drew on the extra-parliamentary, constitutional tradition of the mass platform by organizing monster demonstrations and petitions – further evidence that this tradition survived the demise of Chartism.[63]

Although radicals and Liberals came together in support of Bradlaugh, they did so for different reasons. Radicals tended to emphasize the populist dimensions of the campaign – the masses against the classes, fair play and popular rights; the Liberals focused on the legal and religious aspects of the case. Indeed, the dilemma for those Liberals who objected to Bradlaugh due to his republicanism, atheism and advocacy of birth control, was that his 'case' raised issues that went to the very heart of Liberal ideology: civil and religious liberty, toleration, equality before the law, and the constitutional rights of electors and their representatives. While some Liberals were sympathetic to Bradlaugh's case others were not, and radicals were quick to point to the hypocrisy of those who belonged to a party that supposedly defended religious toleration and equality before the law. Not for the first time were radicals asking Liberalism to deliver on its ideological promises. The radicalism personified by Bradlaugh was, at the very least, in advance of mainstream Liberalism (on issues such as parliamentary, constitutional and land reform) and, at most, openly critical – especially when it came to rooting out the remnants of 'Old Corruption'.

If outbreaks of independent forms of radicalism represented the exception rather than the norm after the fall of Chartism, this was because the Liberal party was finally taking the radical agenda seriously. It was no coincidence that these outbreaks became more regular and, ultimately, more permanent when radicals once again felt sidelined. The result of that sidelining would be the establishment of an independent labour party.

Chapter 6: Rethinking the 'Transformation' of Popular Conservatism

If popular Conservatism is defined as electoral support for the Conservative party, then it formally came into existence in 1830. This was the year in which the term 'Conservative' was first used in English political language as the new name for the old Tory party. The Conservative party was in a perilous state at the moment of its birth. The granting of full political and civil liberties to both Protestant Dissenters in 1828 and Roman Catholics in 1829, along with the passage of the 1832 Reform Act, greatly weakened the Anglican and aristocratic edifice of the English constitution, the integrity of which the Tories had sworn to preserve. There is an irony in dating the formal existence of popular Conservatism from 1830, as it was the old Tory party's resistance to popular politics in the shape of parliamentary reform that was responsible, in part, for the coalescing of Tories and conservative Whigs into the new Conservative party. Despite this decidedly *un*popular birth, the party soon established itself as one of the most successful and popular political parties of the modern world. The Tories were in office, either on their own or as part of a coalition, for nearly 58 years of the nineteenth century.

And yet, the Conservative party was, for so long, the stranger at the rich historiographical feasts of nineteenth-century popular politics. For many historians, the electoral success of the Conservative party was unremarkable and largely attributable to the enduring power of the propertied classes, whose privileged existence the party was pledged to maintain. What 'popular' – or, more specifically, working-class – Conservatism existed was usually dismissed as a form of political deviancy, the product of apathy or lower class deference.[1] To many of the left-leaning historians of popular politics writing in the 1960s through to the early 1980s, the issues of real historical substance

97

clustered around radicalism, Liberalism and the rise of Labour. When historians did pay attention to Conservatism, it was usually in the small 'c' sense of the term – defined as a traditional, defensive, introverted and fatalistic mindset – and how this largely depoliticized outlook inhibited the development of a genuinely class-conscious, socialist working class.[2] This conservative outlook could, under circumstances such as extreme poverty and ethnic tensions, translate into popular Conservatism.[3] However, this was not deemed worthy of serious historical attention. Thus, as late as 1985, Martin Pugh could still comment that: 'Popular Conservatism remains a somewhat elusive and under-studied phenomenon.'[4]

By the early 1990s, a combination of factors had forced popular Conservatism onto the historical agenda. The continuing electoral success of Thatcher's Conservative party – which clearly rested, in part, on widespread working-class support, the collapse of Communism and the related challenge to class-based interpretations of present and past politics – had the combined effect of establishing popular Conservatism as a topic of serious historical inquiry. Consequently, since the early 1990s historians of nineteenth- and early twentieth-century popular politics have devoted an unprecedented amount of attention to the Conservative party, focusing specifically on the party's electoral support and, more broadly, on the relationship between the party and British society. This chapter resumes the narrative of popular political development by looking at the electoral fortunes of the Conservative party between 1832 and 1914, arguing that conventional historical narratives of the 'transformation of late Victorian Conservatism', which focused on the party's meteoric electoral rise after 1867, have obscured the party's (albeit more limited) electoral success before 1867. It shows how these narratives have underestimated the limits to, and fragility of, the late-Victorian Conservative party's electoral dominance. In doing so, the chapter also calls into question the stark historiographical juxtaposition between the late Victorian Tory hegemony and the so-called Edwardian 'crisis of Conservatism', when the party was kept from power: it is argued that the extent of this 'crisis' has been much exaggerated.

The Electoral Politics of Urban Conservatism

That narratives of transformation have dominated interpretations of the late Victorian Conservative party is hardly surprising.[5] The party was in government for some 20 years after 1886, except for a brief period when the Liberals returned to power between 1892 and 1895. The Conservative electoral ascendancy reached its apogee with the

general election of 1900, when the party won its second victory in succession and became the first government since 1865 to win a second
term. The Conservatives had won three of the four general elections
held after 1885 (in 1886, 1895 and 1900). This transformation appears
all the more dramatic when set against the relatively poor electoral performance of mid-Victorian Conservatism. Between the general elections
of 1832 and 1880, the Tories won a majority of seats in the House
of Commons only on two occasions (in 1841 and 1874). Nevertheless, one should not underestimate the extent of popular Conservatism
prior to 1886. Taking the period of Conservative electoral dominance
between 1886 and 1900, the Tories won 49 per cent of the popular
vote; yet, in the allegedly lean early and mid-Victorian years, the party
still averaged 41 per cent between 1832 and 1885, albeit on a more
restricted franchise before 1867. What stands out is the underlying
stability of support for the Conservatives in the period 1832 to 1910:
during which time the Tory popular vote averaged 43 per cent.[6]

Neither should one underestimate the *breadth* of popular Conservatism prior to 1886. While the party's electoral support was concentrated in the English counties and small boroughs, invariably
dominated by agricultural interests, there were few boroughs of any
size without a tory interest during this period. In the 1830s and
1840s, urban Conservatism was concentrated in the more established
towns such as Bristol, Hull, Leeds, Liverpool, Newcastle and York. In
these older boroughs, the tory interest centred on a core group of
Anglican merchants, professionals and manufacturers, who had exercised a virtual monopoly on the closed (that is, self-electing) local
corporations before 1835. Thus, in the late eighteenth and early nineteenth centuries, the Dissenting merchants and manufacturers found
themselves excluded from participating in the public affairs of many
boroughs. It was this political exclusion (both at local and national
level) that gave rise to the nascent 'Whig-Liberal' and 'Tory' political
connections.[7] The rising tide of reform in the first 30 years of the nineteenth century, spearheaded by an alliance of whig landowners and
urban Dissenters, forged a defensive tory interest amongst the mer-
chant oligarchies. The extent and depth of this partisanship received
a substantial fillip in those boroughs affected by the 1835 Municipal
Corporations Act, which introduced annual elections. Although the
Tories were ousted from municipal power in many places, they refused
to accept defeat and began regularly to contest municipal elections.

In contrast to urban Liberalism, which tended to attract relatively
new industrialists who had recently made their fortunes, tory merchants
and manufacturers were usually more established: their wealth dated
back a generation or two.[8] Urban Conservatism in the early nineteenth

century was usually a more powerful force in those boroughs that had either a weak aristocratic presence, as in Leeds, or where the distinction between rural and urban elites was less clear-cut, as in some of the Lancashire boroughs. In both scenarios, the urban middle class were less conscious of being in conflict with the landed interest.[9] By contrast, when there was an aristocratic presence – but one that had a limited, or non-existent, urban support-base – any interference in urban affairs tended to unify the middle class in support of the Liberal party, as in Sheffield.[10] In the absence of that interference, or in those areas where there was more co-operation between urban and rural elites, the middle class were likely to be more divided amongst themselves. This gave rise to powerful Liberal *and* Tory groupings.

For traditional urban tory elites, it was all the more imperative to win over the urban middle classes, since the 1832 Reform Act had enfranchised many of the latter as £10 householders for the first time. Yet, urban Conservatism was not entirely a middle-class affair during the 1830s and 1840s, as demonstrated by the proliferation of 'Operative Conservative' Associations, which were aimed at the working class.[11] Many tories were sympathetic to a number of popular causes; notably, factory reform – and even trades unionism, which won the party working-class support.[12] This sympathy was born of a genuine anxiety amongst urban tory elites, many of whom believed that industrialization was spiralling out of control and needed to be regulated and restrained. To the established tory elites, the parvenu and unscrupulous Liberal, Nonconformist manufacturers, whose sole concern was profit, were responsible for 'factory slavery' and urban squalor. Richard Oastler, the Tory leader of the factory movement, unleashed a series of vituperative attacks on the 'brawling, praying, canting Dissenters...Messrs. Get-All, Keep-All, Grasp-All...Lie-Well, Swear-Well, Scratch-Em and Company'.[13] These irresponsible elites were destroying the social fabric that bound communities together. This explains why urban tories formed tactical alliances with radicals, thus giving birth to the strange and brief affair of tory-radicalism.

Tory-radicalism has been dismissed by historians of high politics as a movement remote from the concerns of Sir Robert Peel, party leader from 1834 to 1846, and his new Conservatism of moderate and cautious reform.[14] Out in the constituencies, especially in the north, matters were different. Tory-radicalism did much to shape the form and content of popular Conservatism, even if it did not directly contribute to the party's electoral victories.[15] Tory-radicalism is a rather elusive concept but, broadly defined, it refers to the coming together of tories and radicals in opposition to the unrestrained forces of industrialization and its harmful and disruptive social consequences. This tory-radical alliance crystallized around support for factory legislation (primarily to restrict working hours) and opposition to the New Poor Law of 1834. For tories and radicals, the campaign for factory reform and opposition to the New Poor Law were related issues. One of the reasons for yoking them together was that they demonstrated the hypocrisy of the Whig-Liberals, who were reluctant to restrict the hours of labour in the factories but had no problem interfering with the dispensing of poor relief.

Such was the strength of this working-class Conservatism that it did much to shape the ideology and policies of the burgeoning Chartism movement, particularly in Lancashire and Yorkshire. As historians have long recognized, there was more than a hint of toryism in Feargus O'Connor's politics, a politics that was heavily influenced by the ideology and rhetoric of the tory-radicals Richard Oastler and the ex-Methodist preacher Joseph Rayner Stephens. Further, the tory antecedents of northern Chartism also help to explain why, in the aftermath of the movement's disintegration, a significant minority of former Chartists made the transition not into the Gladstonian Liberal party but, rather, into the Conservative party of Lord Derby (party leader, 1846–68) and, subsequently, Benjamin Disraeli, who led the party from 1868 until his death in 1881.[16] This was most evident in those areas with strong 'tory-radical' traditions, such as in Lancashire and, to a lesser extent, in the West Riding, especially when Tory candidates made attempts to position themselves as latter-day advocates of that tradition. Rayner Stephens continued to attract popular support in and around Ashton-under-Lyne in the 1860s and 1870s for his continuing harangues against Liberal political economy, capitalism and the Poor Law.[17] Similarly, Tories such as W. R. Callendar in Manchester and William Wheelhouse in Leeds donned the mantle of Oastler in the 1860s and 1870s.[18] This latter-day 'tory-radicalism' was rooted in a criticism of the 'harsh, parsimonious and hypocritical Manchester School economic doctrines',[19] and translated into support for a further extension of the factory acts, trades unionism and the customary pleasures of the masses that were under threat from censorious reforming Liberal Nonconformists.

For a party associated with privilege and inequality, the Conservative party had made impressive electoral gains in the period after the 1832 Reform Act, culminating with the 1841 general election. In the aftermath of Peel's decision to repeal the Corn Laws in 1846 – which split the Conservative party into protectionists (the 222 MPs who opposed Peel) and Peelites (the 120 MPs who supported Peel) – problems of leadership, policy, strategy and organization bedevilled the party. The status of protection itself was also ambiguous, being soft-pedalled at the 1847

general election so as to (unsuccessfully) entice the re-engaged Peelites
back into the Tory party. Protectionism remained the official creed of
the party until it was finally jettisoned in 1852, having been discred-
ited for its perceived impracticality and electoral unpopularity. The free
traders had won the economic argument – for the time being, at least.
Thus, following the split over the Corn Laws, the party found itself confined to the electoral doldrums. Many local Conservative organizations
were casualties of the split over repeal, with some going into decline.

And yet, for a party decimated by Peel's apostasy, there was a remarkable underlying stability in the party's electoral support for many of
the mid-Victorian years: only in the late 1850s did it fall considerably
below 40 per cent (to 33 per cent in 1857). Nevertheless, stability had
been recovered by the time of the 1868 general election and the Tory
share of the vote continued to hover around 40 per cent until 1886. In
the 1850s and 1860s, 'there were probably about as many Conservative
voters as Whigs and Peelites, but they did not succeed in electing as
many MPs',[20] one of the reasons being that the electoral system under-
represented rural areas and big towns – that is, areas with substantial
pockets of tory interests. Further, narratives of late-Victorian Conservative transformation are unduly Anglo-centric and have little wider
applicability. Admittedly, Scotland proved to be infertile soil for the
Conservative party for much of this period: only in the late 1880s and
1890s was there a discernible growth in Scottish popular Conservatism.
Even then this was largely due to the alliance with the Liberal Unionists after 1886 – those Liberals who opposed Gladstone's policy of Irish
Home Rule and made common cause with the Tories.[21] By contrast,
in Ireland and Wales the party enjoyed considerable electoral support
between the 1830s and 1870s. For example, in Wales the Tories won
more seats than the Liberals at seven of the nine general elections held
between the First and Second Reform Acts.[22] Between 1832 and 1865,
the Conservatives averaged 55 per cent of the popular vote in Wales
and 40 per cent in Ireland. It was only in the later nineteenth century
that the Conservative party became the party of England.[23]

Although the Tories were confined to the electoral doldrums in many
of the new industrial centres such as in Birmingham and Sheffield during the mid-Victorian decades, this was not the case in older boroughs
such as Bristol, Coventry, Grantham, Leeds, Norwich, Southampton
and York. There would be no dramatic 'transformation of Conservatism' in these places during the last decades of the nineteenth century
as there would be in some of the biggest towns. In some of these older
urban centres and in Ireland and Wales, the electoral apogee of popular
Conservatism was reached in the mid-Victorian years.[24] For all the fears
surrounding the 'leap in the dark' into the democratic abyss following

the 1867 Reform Act and, despite losing the 1868 general election to the Liberal party, the Tories still won 38.4 per cent of the popular vote. This was only 1.4 per cent less than their share at the 1865 general election. Given that the number of electors voting Conservative had increased from some 346,000 in 1865 to 903,000 in 1868, it is clear that the 1867 Reform Act had enfranchised a significant amount of popular Conservatism, and not just in Lancashire.

If the existence of popular Conservatism serves to highlight the limits to the early and mid-Victorian Liberal hegemony, the opposite was true in the late Victorian period when the Tories dominated government. While Disraeli went on to win the 1874 general election, from the vantage point of the 1880 general election, when the Tories were resoundingly defeated by Gladstone and the Liberals' indictment of the Conservative government's foreign and imperial policy, the Conservative party did not look set for a period of electoral dominance. In the aftermath of Disraeli's death in 1881, the party was again beset by problems of leadership, party unity, organization and the perceived disintegration of Conservative values. Worse still, the party was further disadvantaged by the Franchise Act of 1884, which gave the vote to more than one-and-three-quarter million rural electors, thus democratizating the hitherto Tory dominated county constituencies. This created an electorate composed for the most part of those without property whose support, following the legislative clampdown on corruption and treating at elections in 1883, could no longer be 'bought'. These problems culminated in the Conservative party's defeat at the 1885 general election.

The environment in which late Victorian Tories were forced to operate was seemingly less hospitable than the mid-Victorian years. Economic depression, growing public awareness of acute poverty, renewed threats to the Established Church, nationalism in Ireland, socialist agitation and the growth of trades unionism, all threatened the fabric of the existing order. Even the 'trump' electioneering cards of patriotism and imperialism, which the Tories went to great lengths to secure in the 1880s and 1890s, were far from being unproblematic assets.[25] Neither did the Conservative party have a monopoly on these assets. As new studies have demonstrated, they were contestable concepts.[26] For example, while the Tories were at pains to identify themselves with the material and spiritual benefits of empire, this did not always reap electoral dividends. During periods of protracted foreign and imperial conflict involving Britain, the Tories, when in power, were vulnerable to the Liberal charge that they represented the 'self-promoting, selfish and violent tendencies of the new imperialism, based on conquest, appropriation and exploitation',[27] charges that were never far from the mind of Liberal Nonconformists.

The biggest threat of all to the Tories was that of democratization. For all the hysteria that the 1832 Reform Act had unleashed, the Tories had been able to take some comfort in the knowledge that the franchise was still largely restricted to the owners of property. This was not the case after the 1867 and 1884 Reform Acts. Small wonder that Lord Salisbury, who had emerged as the new leader of the party by 1885, concluded in 1882 that 'It will be interesting to be the last of the Conservatives.'[28] Although Salisbury would preside over the Conservative electoral ascendancy in the 1880s and 1890s, he never ceased to be amazed by the party's election victories, and nowhere more so than in suburban 'villadom': the large tracts of residential housing found on the urban fringes of towns and cities.

Villadom was once thought to be the electoral heartland of late-Victorian Conservatism.[29] Yet, as recent work has demonstrated, villadom was the exclusive preserve of neither the Conservative party nor the middle class.[30] There was also a great deal of what might be termed 'villa Liberalism', itself a reflection of the social and political diversity of late Victorian suburbia, and of the middle class more generally.[31] This is not to suggest that there were no middle-class defections from the Liberal party to the Conservatives during the later Victorian years (due to the growing anxiety of propertied opinion towards a radicalized Liberalism – which, at least to the paranoid tory mind, was infringing the rights of private property. Rather, it suggests that historians have exaggerated the scale of these defections. The continuing political divisions within the propertied classes illustrate how difficult it was for the Conservative party to unify and satisfy all propertied interests simultaneously. In part, this stemmed from the persistence and legacy of politico-religious conflict, between Tory Anglicanism and Liberal Nonconformity. It was also shaped by occupational and status differentials within the propertied classes, giving rise to a secondary division based on geographical location. Although both the Conservative and Liberal parties drew support from all classes and locations in late Victorian Britain, the most solid support for Conservatism 'came from the service economy of the south-east of England', at the head of which were the Metropolitan 'gentlemanly capitalists' whose wealth was based on 'an amalgam of rentier money, service employment and the remnants of landed society'.[32] By contrast, the Liberal party remained a more provincial political movement, dominated by manufacturers from the midlands and the north who had made their fortunes in textiles, iron and steel, shipbuilding and coalmining. In sum, these political, religious and occupational differences were mutually reinforcing: it was no coincidence that the Anglican Church was much stronger in the south than in the north, and that the upper, longer-established middle class was disproportionately Anglican.[33]

Thus, one can understand why, from the perspective of the national party leadership, the years of electoral ascendancy seemed to be built on insecure foundations. Although the Tories began to do well in constituencies in which they had previously been marginalized, this was not uniformly the case. Some boroughs and counties did not become bastions of Conservatism and only registered the nationwide Conservative advance in muted form, as was the case in Leeds, Manchester and Nottingham. In these constituencies, the Tories were only too aware of the fragility of their electoral position.[34] On the other hand, there can be no doubt that the party made impressive gains in many boroughs and counties, often in rather surprising places. For example, the West Riding was thought to be a Liberal stronghold between 1885 and 1910. Certainly, the Liberals were the overall dominant electoral force, but there were significant pockets of popular Conservatism throughout the region, often sufficiently concentrated to produce regular Tory majorities. Perhaps more surprising is that, across the 38 constituencies that comprised the West Riding, the Conservatives averaged 42 per cent of the popular vote between 1885 and 1910. In areas where the Tories were in the ascendant, a localized vision of optimism and confidence existed that was far removed from the pessimism and anxiety of the national leadership, who were only too aware of the party's precarious electoral dominance, underlined by their reliance for parliamentary majorities on the support of their Liberal Unionist allies. Only at the general elections of 1886 and 1900 did the Tories manage to secure a popular mandate with, respectively, 51.4 and 50.3 per cent of the popular vote. This hardly amounted to dominance, let alone hegemony.

And yet, this precarious dominance was not just a reflection of the limits to the party's popularity: what historians have seldom recognized is that the Tories were, on occasions, victims of the electoral system. Contrary to the assumptions of electoral sociology, Conservatives were often disadvantaged by the proliferation of single-member constituencies, introduced by the Redistribution Act of 1885. It has often been assumed that these liberated the hitherto swamped islands of Conservative support in large urban areas by separating them off from contaminating, overwhelmingly Liberal, working-class areas. A statistical analysis of the impact of single-member seats on Tory electoral fortunes has, in fact, revealed that they did not produce long-term benefits for the party.[35] This was because the electoral support base of urban Conservatism was not as geographically concentrated as many historians have often assumed, as Lord Salisbury was only too aware.[36]

Having won 334 seats in the 'Khaki' election of 1900, when they swept back to power on a wave of patriotic and imperialistic sentiment in response to the Boer War, the fragility of the Conservative electoral ascendancy was exposed at the 1906 general election, when the Tories were reduced to a mere 157 seats. The party would not win another general election outright until 1922. This collapse in the party's electoral support even extended into hitherto Tory bastions such as the north-west. Having won 56 of the 71 seats in the region at the 1900 general election, the party was reduced to a rump of 16 after the 1906 'Liberal landslide'.[37] In the two general elections of 1910, the Conservatives recovered some lost ground across the nation, but they were still unable to dislodge their opponents from power. The problems facing the Conservative party were so acute and seemingly insurmountable that some historians have interpreted this as nothing less than a 'crisis of Conservatism'. Economic decline (in the shape of agricultural and industrial depression), the threat of imperial disintegration (dramatically underlined by the protracted Boer War and the renewed threat of Irish Home Rule), the growth of international rivalry, along with the difficulties in adjusting to mass politics, were all causing alarm within governing circles, and nowhere more so than in the Conservative party. The Liberal landslide at the 1906 general election was symptomatic of the Conservative party's inability to respond effectively to these problems. Ewen Green has argued that the party's defeat stemmed in large part from the widespread collapse of working-class Conservatism. The situation did not improve between 1906 and 1910, when the Tories were 'faced with a more disturbing phenomenon: a broader, positive working-class movement in favour of Socialism', which was 'both a symptom and cause of a widespread collapse of working-class Conservatism' as 'Labour made most of its gains, in terms of both seats and votes, in old working-class Conservative districts'.[38]

So acute was this 'crisis of Conservatism' that the party sought out a radical solution in the shape of tariff reform, a policy of imposing taxes on foreign imported goods (except those from the empire) as a means with which to protect the British economy from foreign competition. In the hands of its Liberal Unionist architect, Joseph Chamberlain, tariff reform had initially been conceived in 1903 as a strategy for promoting imperial unity, although there had been suggestions that it could serve broader domestic purposes. In the aftermath of 1906, tariff reform grew into a multi-faceted policy, designed to act as a panacea for a raft of domestic, foreign and imperial problems. Tariffs would not only protect British industry – and, by extension, employment – by making foreign goods more expensive than native products, but also the revenue they generated could be used to fund state-sponsored social reform and subsidize ailing domestic industries, such as agriculture. In addition, the allied policy of 'imperial preference', whereby Britain and its colonies would waive tariffs on each other's imports, would foster imperial unity. Thus, tariff reform would supply the Conservative party with a constructive policy that would appeal to, and unite, urban and rural propertied interests, and win back working-class voters by protecting their jobs and introducing social reform.

Yet, somewhat paradoxically, this seemingly well-conceived and integrated policy added fuel to the flames of crisis. When Joseph Chamberlain raised the flag of tariff reform in 1903, it split the party into warring factions. Tariff reformers were pitted against free traders who feared that such a policy would involve taxing imported foodstuffs, in particular cheap corn, and risk placing an intolerable financial burden on the working class, allowing the Liberals to mount a defence of the people's food by raising the old battle cry of 'free trade versus protection'. This is exactly what happened at the 1906 general election, with catastrophic electoral consequences for the Tories. To make matters worse, the internal battle lines in the run-up to the 1906 general election were not clear-cut due to the ambiguous stance on tariff reform of the Tory leader, Arthur Balfour, and much of the party. This sent out mixed messages to the electorate, leaving the less discriminating elements far more susceptible to Liberal propaganda on the moral and economic imperatives of defending the 'free breakfast table'. Despite the Conservative party presenting a more united front in support of tariff reform, and presenting it in a more clear and positive light to the electorate at the two general elections of 1910, the 'crisis' continued unabated.

The political temperature at Westminster was even higher. The general election of January 1910 was meant to break the constitutional deadlock that had arisen on account of the House of Lords' rejection of Lloyd George's 1909 budget. This 'constitutional crisis' centred on the nature of the budget. Conventionally, there was a tacit understanding that the House of Lords would not reject financial measures on the grounds that they did not represent tax payers, hence the Government's indignation when it was rejected. The Lords, however, claimed that Lloyd George's budget was, in reality, a political measure. The Lords were also adamant that the Liberal Government did not have a mandate to introduce such a far-reaching measure (since it had not been mentioned at the 1906 general election). By rejecting Lloyd George's budget, the Lords maintained that they were merely fulfilling their constitutional role in forcing the Liberal Government to seek electoral approval for their policies. This enabled the Liberals to fight two general elections on the traditional issues of 'peers versus people' and, once again, 'free trade versus protection'. The electorate returned a hung parliament. When inter-party negotiations failed to end the constitutional deadlock, a second general election was held in December 1910 – the result: a hung parliament. The Tory defence of the House of Lords and the alternative of tariff reform (indirect taxation) to the Liberal budget of 1909 (with its direct taxation of wealth) had failed to dislodge the Liberals from power.

Thereafter, the crisis worsened. The 1911 Parliament Act emasculated the House of Lords by ending its right to veto legislation indefinitely – a longstanding indispensable part of the Tory party's armoury in frustrating the reforming agendas of Liberal governments. This now paved the way for the Liberal Government to grant Irish Home Rule: the price it had to pay for the loyalty of the Irish MPs who held the balance of power in the House of Commons. The failure of the Tories to wrest power from their opponents, allied to the spectre of Irish Home Rule, resulted in further frustration and despair to the extent that mainstream Conservatism began to fracture. This frustration was one of the main driving forces behind the establishment of a whole range of radical right-wing pressure groups in the Edwardian period, such as the Anti-Socialist Union (1908) and the Budget Protest League (1909). Those that were already established grew in popularity – the Navy League (1895) and the Tariff Reform League (1903). The 'legion of leagues' and 'revolt from the right' were symptomatic of the failure of the Conservative party to mount an effective challenge to the Liberal Government. The rise of the radical right was instrumental in bringing about Balfour's resignation and his replacement by Andrew Bonar Law as leader of the Conservative party in 1911.

In the years before the First World War, the Conservative party lacked direction, was divided over tariff reform, social reform and how to deal with Ireland. In electoral terms, the party's prospects did not look good for the anticipated general election of 1915, faced as it was by what Green calls 'an unprecedentedly cohesive anti-Conservative bloc' in the form of the 'progressive alliance': the cross-class co-operation between the Liberal and Labour parties. Green concludes that 'when the Great War broke out . . . there were few signs that the party was in a position to break out of this enclave'.[39] It was only the rallying experiences of the First World War, together with the Tory's partial return to power through the continuation of the wartime coalition government with the Lloyd George Liberals, that rehabilitated the Tory party and divided their opponents.

It would be fanciful to suppose that the Conservative party was in a healthy position in the Edwardian years. Yet, the notion of a 'crisis of Conservatism' goes too far, and can be refuted on a number of levels. First, although Green is correct to draw attention to the problems facing the late-Victorian Conservative party, to suggest that the Edwardian crisis had its origins in the party's complacency and inertness underestimates both the party's dynamism and success, especially at the local level, in responding to those problems. In electoral terms, the party's performance between 1906 and 1914 was far from dismal. The defeat at the 1906 general election was not that universally catastrophic – the party received 43.4 per cent of the popular vote, a share that was sufficient to produce a Conservative majority at a number of future general elections.[40] In addition, although the Liberals polled some 300,000 more votes than the Tories, it should be noted that the Tories actually polled some 775,000 more votes in 1906 than they had in 1900, on a *higher* turnout and augmented electoral register. This was hardly testament to the widespread collapse of popular Conservatism.

There can be little doubt that the party improved its electoral position at the general election held in January 1910. In that election, the Tories increased their share of the popular vote to 46.8 per cent (falling to 46.6 per cent in the December election). Even the 1906 Liberal avalanche in the north-west had been halted and, to a large extent, reversed by December 1910: the Conservatives held 32 seats; the Liberal and Labour parties 38.[41] What kept the Tories from power at Westminster was the alliance between Liberal, Labour and Irish Nationalist MPs. Unprecedented this alliance might have been; cohesive it was certainly not. There is little evidence to suggest that the progressive alliance outside of parliament was indicative of a new and reinvigorated political left, with the Liberal and Labour parties drawing closer together in either ideological or electoral terms. The Labour party was planning to contest a large number of seats at the next general election, and independent of the Liberals. This would have led to divisions on the political left and produced a swathe of three-cornered contests in many constituencies – much to the anticipated benefit of the Conservative party. Indeed, the Liberals were already experiencing stiff competition from the Tories for the working-class vote *before* Labour proved to be a major contender. In this respect, the origins of progressive Liberalism, and the subsequent rationale for an alliance with Labour, stemmed from the very strength of popular Conservatism, especially in Lancashire.[42]

As for Labour making inroads into working-class Tory support, the evidence is not as clear-cut as Green suggests. Jon Lawrence's work on Wolverhampton, and his wider statistical analysis of industrial constituencies that experienced Conservative–Labour contests, shows that Labour was able to make *some* inroads into popular Conservatism with the caveat that 'before the Great War, Labour always remained vulnerable to a genuinely popular Tory candidate'.[43] Furthermore, the fact that the burgeoning Labour party was shaped just as much by a conservative political tradition as by a radical and socialist political tradition is surely evidence of the continued vitality of popular Conservatism.[44] By the time war broke out, the Conservatives had 287 MPs, 30 more than the Liberals (due to a series of by-election victories) and were fast approaching the combined strength of the Liberal and Labour parties. The Conservatives might have been anxious about the expected general election of 1915: this is understandable in light of their defeat at the three previous general elections. And yet, the omens were good for the Tories. Local government election results confirm this. As Chris Cook comments: 'by 1913, the Conservatives had rarely been stronger in the Councils of the land, or indeed more poised for success in the forthcoming election'.[45] Once again, this was apparent in areas thought to be Liberal strongholds, as in West Yorkshire. By 1913, the Tories had established themselves as the largest party in several of the region's council chambers, including Leeds and Bradford. In neighbouring Huddersfield, the party secured an overall majority on the council for the first time since the town had been incorporated in 1868. Thus, it is interesting to note that, in a region that has long been held up as the example *par excellence* of Labour's pre-war triumph over Liberalism, 'from the Liberal perspective it was not Labour but the Conservatives who posed the central threat to their control of local government'.[46] As Chapter 7 will show, such was the extent of popular support for the Conservative party throughout this period, that it challenges many of the traditional historiographical assumptions about popular Conservatism.

Chapter 7: Defining and Debating Popular Conservatism

The electoral success of the Conservative party used to be dismissed as accidental, or else it was seen as the result of anti-democratic strategizing. According to this 'negative' interpretation of popular Conservatism, the Tories were largely the passive beneficiaries of deference; religious, ethnic and class tensions; or of patriotic and imperial sentiment, and their opponent's weaknesses.[1] In addition, it was noted how the Tories went to great lengths to 'avoid rather than confront the mass electorate'.[2] Few historians would now accept, in the wake of the critique of 'electoral sociology' and the 'new political history', that popular Conservatism can be viewed as the product of elite manipulation or reduced to the expression of underlying socio-economic structures, such as class.[3] As Francis and Zweiniger-Bargielowska have argued, the problem with subjecting the history of the British Conservative party to a class analysis is that it has 'always had difficulty in explaining how a party led by landed aristocrats and the bourgeoisie has sustained a dominant position in an emerging parliamentary democracy in which the majority of the electorate were working class.'[4] This chapter offers a critique of the 'negative' and sociological model of popular Conservatism. It shows just how active, creative and integrative the Conservative party was in the face of democratization, and how aspects of Conservative ideology resonated with popular audiences.

Popular Conservatism or Anti-Liberalism?

In conventional historical interpretations the rise of popular Conservatism was often correlated with socio-economic change, such as the sharpening of class tensions in the late Victorian period, or with changes in workplace relations in the northern factory towns in the mid-Victorian years. The latter, according to Patrick Joyce, facilitated the construction of factory paternalism, especially in the supposedly Tory dominated textile districts of Lancashire and the West Riding. Employee deference to the factory owner, especially the easy-going tory paternalist, was reinforced by the latter's deference to popular pleasures such as cockfighting and football. When it came to politics and elections, deferential workers voted at the behest of their patrons, most of whom, Joyce argued, were Tories in the Lancashire Cotton Towns.[5] As discussed in Chapter 6, factory paternalism has emerged as an impoverished explanatory model for mid-century stability, which, in turn, has challenged the deferential model of voting behaviour. In factory towns, political loyalties were far more dynamic, fluid, issue-based and individualistic than this deferential model allowed. Factory owners could not take the political loyalties of their workforce for granted. As Vee Barbary has shown in a reassessment of factory politics, based on a case study of Bury, 'the politics of employers had little influence over those of their workforces'.[6] Voters had to be actively courted, socialized and educated – hence the importance placed on issues, organization and platform politics. Certainly, paternalism, philanthropy and civic virtue were stock ingredients in making a communitarian style of populist politics, but they did not automatically translate into electoral success. Indeed, such social and economic capital could be an electoral liability for those local elites who had reputations of being either 'bad employers' or 'self-promoters'.[7] On the other hand, when urban elites compounded this capital with a populist style and supported popular policies, electoral success usually followed.

Similarly, revisionist work on late Victorian suburbia has demonstrated that villa toryism was not the political expression of a socially homogeneous, innately conservative, suburban middle class. Originally intended as a derisive phrase that mocked the pretensions of the suburban middle class,[8] many historians have elevated villa toryism into a shorthand term to describe the processes by which the Conservative party (accidentally) consolidated its hold over the suburban middle class in the late nineteenth century. In this reading, the rise of villa toryism – regarded as anti-Liberal rather than pro-Conservative – was thought to be the inevitable outcome of the transition to class-based voting, facilitated by the Redistribution Act of 1885. Lord Salisbury's preference for the widespread adoption of single-member seats was interpreted as a deliberate attempt to create the electoral framework under which villa toryism could flourish.[9] According to this interpretation, this pre-existing, innately Conservative constituency of support simply needed organizing and symbolic recognition by the party leadership. This symbolic recognition came in 1884, when Salisbury conceded minor organizational powers from the party's aristocratic Central Office to the National Union of Conservative and Constitutional Associations. This latter body was being used as a vehicle for advancing the 'Tory Democratic' agenda of provincial middle-class tory elites, who felt that their interests were being ignored and their services unrewarded by the party's aristocratic leadership.

As historians of popular politics have begun to focus more attention on the suburbs, it has become clear that this 'sociological' interpretation cannot be sustained. First, it pays no attention to the timing, or to the extent, of the middle-class defection to Conservatism. As discussed in Chapter 6, a great deal of villa Liberalism existed in the suburbs. Second, the Redistribution Act of 1885 not only failed, in any significant way, to isolate middle-class suburban pockets from less socially exclusive districts – a lack of isolation that only became more marked with the passage of time due to working-class suburbanization[10] – but also found little favour among many Conservatives, who doubted the efficacy of single-member seats.[11] Third, the Conservative party itself did not look exclusively to the villas for electoral salvation, which, in any case, were neither a self-mobilizing nor a self-sufficient constituency of electoral support. Indeed, Salisbury was too much of a pessimist to pin the electoral hopes of the Conservative party on the villas, and he advanced single-member constituencies as a last resort, primarily as a tactic to improve the party's position in the countryside, not in the towns.[12]

As for Tory Democracy, the historiographical preoccupation with its organizational dimensions, focusing as its does on disgruntled urban tory elites, has exaggerated the middle-class bias of late-Victorian popular Conservatism.[13] In its original and widest formulation, Tory Democracy denoted 'the recurring attempt of nineteenth-century Conservatives to link their party in parliament with the "working-classes"'.[14] Yet, discussions of the social constituency of Tory Democracy have far too often resolved themselves into an either/or dichotomy: was it middle class or working class? As far as the central party organizer J. E. Gorst and urban tory elites such as Arthur Forwood were concerned, this was a false dichotomy. From their perspective, 'Tory Democracy' was an umbrella term denoting a multi-faceted strategy for reform. They campaigned for more constructive and reformist legislation at both national and municipal level as a means to cement their own popularity with the working class – who dominated their constituencies, and of whose electoral importance they were only too aware.[15] These urban tory elites were increasingly conscious of the pivotal position they occupied in the constituencies as the people with the organizational power to integrate the working class into the Conservative party.

Consequently, they wanted the national party leadership to recognize their importance through honours and promotions. Tory Democracy might have had 'more to do with the Toryism of democracy than the democracy of Toryism',[16] in the sense that its promoters had no desire for universal manhood suffrage or social levelling. However, Tory Democracy did represent a 'commitment to making politics more representative'.[17]

The lack of Conservative hegemony among middle-class voters underlined the electoral importance of the working class, who comprised between two thirds and three quarters of the post-1884 electorate.[18] Revisionist work has overturned many of the ahistorical and reductionist sociological models that were invented to explain (away) working-class Conservatism. For example, it is now clear that working-class Tories did not occupy atypical positions within the class structure. As Jon Lawrence has shown in relation to Wolverhampton, 'working-class Conservative activists frequently performed exactly the same jobs, in the same factories, as their working-class Liberal or Socialist opponents'. Lawrence makes a related point that the party's support 'came from poor and prosperous workers alike'.[19] Neither is it possible to assume, as was once the case, that those workers who voted Tory had a limited understanding of their economic interests. In those areas with industries that were suffering from foreign competition (such as the Bradford wool trade) or were dependent on armaments contracts (as were some of the Sheffield steel works) voting Tory represented the height of economic self-interest.

Yet, these old models have cast a long shadow over the study of working-class Conservatism. Only in the negative sense of attempting to stem the rise of mass politics is the party thought to have been active, either by resorting to tactics such as restricting the size of the electorate or by exploiting religious and ethnic prejudices.[20] Those historians who have subscribed to this interpretation have argued that the party's success was based on low turnout at general elections, keeping as many potential voters off the electoral register, Liberal abstentions from voting, weak Liberal organization and resistance to Liberal proposals. Marc Brodie's study of Conservatism in the East End of London is the most recent and extended restatement of this 'negative' interpretation.[21]

What these class-based and negative interpretations cannot explain is why so many workers voted Conservative. They have less to say about the reasons for Conservatism's popularity, and more about the continued weaknesses of Liberalism until 1914, weaknesses that have been greatly exaggerated.[22] The negative spin placed on the role of the Conservative party's organization can only be made to explain so much – as, indeed, can organization more generally. By contrast, new studies have shown just how active, constructive and integrative the Tories were, both on the public platform and in the press.[23] The party's attitude towards religion and ethnicity illustrates this. In some places the Conservative party sought to temper the denominational and sectarian prejudices of its militant members. As C. S. Ford has argued in relation to south-east Lancashire, an area that was previously thought to be the epitome of a sectarian Conservatism: 'the Conservative party was concerned to widen its base and not to be associated by the electorate exclusively with the Church of England'.[24] For example, the popular tory-radical Joseph Rayner Stephens tried to quell sectarian tensions in Ashton-Under-Lyne in the late 1860s; and it seems that Rayner Stephens represented a significant body of wider tory opinion that was concerned to distance itself from the rabid Protestantism then being whipped up by William Murphy, agent of the Protestant Electoral Union.[25] In areas where there were concentrated pockets of Irish immigrants, as was the case in Liverpool, it was previously argued that the Conservative party fomented Protestant 'Orange' prejudices and crafted a xenophobic politics of Englishness in opposition to the Irish Catholic 'other'.[26] Although the Conservatives might have benefited from these latent prejudices, even in Liverpool (the city of sectarianism *par excellence*) one local study has concluded that: 'It is surprisingly difficult to locate any explicit appeal to sectarian identities within the formal political discourse of Liverpool Conservatism during the late nineteenth century.' Indeed, the Liverpool tory populist Archibald Salvidge had the Orange Order expelled from the formal Conservative party organization.[27] Certainly, the Tory party could usually count on the support of Anglicans by the late nineteenth century and benefit from the powerful organizational resources of the Church of England. But, with the exception of a handful of Anglican and Protestant zealots, many Tories wore their religion rather lightly, partly out of fear of limiting their electoral appeal. Even when it came to the Irish and Jews, the Conservative party could be inclusive, which might have reflected the fact these groups were often more socially, economically and even culturally integrated than traditional stereotypes have suggested.[28] It also reflected shrewd Tory electoral calculation as a growing number of the more established immigrant groups and their descendants were finding their way on to the electoral registers.

However, perhaps the main reason why many Tories wore their religion lightly was due to the 'greater relaxedness, indeed laxity, of Anglicanism when compared with the dissenting sects'.[29] This ethos pervaded the culture of popular Conservatism. This translated into the party's defence of – and even patronage and participation in – the vulgar pleasures of the masses. For example, local tories were prominent in the financing and running of numerous football and cricket clubs. Few populist Conservatives lost an opportunity to excite the fears of the masses that Liberal Nonconformists, given half a chance, would censor enjoyment. As one hyperbolic Conservative activist warned the electors of Lincolnshire: 'if they did not support the Unionists the faddists would close the music halls, stop horse-racing, and would gladly put a veto on football matches'.[30] Yet, this was far from being entirely the product of tory hyperbole: for example, in the midlands the Liberal *Midland Free Press* refused to print information on horse racing. Even more censorious were the steps taken in the 1890s by the Liberal controlled Leicester town council, which 'blacked-out' the racing and gambling news from the pages of the newspapers in the public library.[31]

The thrust of revisionist work, therefore, constructs a positive view of the Conservative party that impresses by its ability to use politics and ritual to socialize the masses (through fetes, picnics, teas, garden parties and excursions); by its indulgence of 'manly' pleasures (such as defending the working man's right to a pint of beer, thus highlighting the importance of gendered, as opposed to class-based, identities); by its promotion of state-sponsored social reform; and by its unrivalled ability to politicize the link between patriotism, imperialism and everyday concerns.[32] As for the party employing anti-democratic stratagems to control popular politics, little evidence has been found to confirm the view that Tory agents deliberately sought to restrict the size of electorates by raising more objections than claims at the annual revision courts. Further, various statistical analyses of general election results between 1885 and 1910 have revealed that there was no significant inverse correlation between turnout and the Conservative share of the poll, as originally argued by James Cornford.[33] Put simply, it was far from being uniformly the case that Tory candidates did better when less people voted.

Ultimately, the success of the Conservative party was dependent upon its ability to knit together different strands of popular Conservatism on the platform and in the political press, and to straddle diverse constituencies of electoral support – from villadom to the manufacturing districts. As noted by historians long ago, organization – and, in particular, a culture of sociability – was instrumental in mobilizing popular Conservatism. What has only become clear in the light of recent work is that many of these organizational developments occurred much earlier than was once thought. In the aftermath of the 1832 Reform Act, there was a widespread fear in propertied circles of the radicalism that had been unleashed. One means of containing that radicalism was to integrate the masses into the Conservative party, irrespective of whether they had the vote: hence the rationale for establishing

Operative Conservative Societies. These Operative Conservative Societies could be found all over England by the late 1830s. They were designed to educate the working class about the dangers of radicalism. It would, however, be condescending to assume that the workers who frequented these Operative Societies were either unthinking or overly deferential. Evidence from Lancashire suggests that the majority of Operatives appear to have been literate and politically articulate.[34] In the organizational realm, the Conservative party revealed itself to be far more advanced and imaginative than their Whig-Liberal opponents. While the content of this popular Conservatism did not extend much beyond the stuff of conventional toryism (loyalty to traditional institutions), the form in which much of this rhetoric was expressed was novel. The Conservatives used sociability to build up a popular party by holding dinners, festivals and balls.

The Conservative party came close to meeting the criteria of being a party of social integration in the late 1830s and early 1840s: the party was permanently organized (branches met as often as once a week in Lancashire) and attempted to permeate all aspects of their members' lives by providing educational and recreational activities, as well as a range of other services such as sick and burial clubs. Similarly, the Tories were also more socially inclusive than the Liberals, achieved by incorporating women and children into their organizations. This meant that the Tories were equipped with an army of supporters who could canvass at election times and help with the process of registering voters. This was an activity at which the Tories were far more adept than their political opponents long before the arrival of the Primrose League.[35] This was a semi-independent and hugely successful populist organization established in 1883 to convert the masses – men, women and children; those with the vote and those without – to Conservatism by crafting an entertaining and sociable politics that blended political propaganda with leisure. The popularity of the Primrose League, however, was unprecedented: from small beginnings in 1883, by 1910 the League had 2,053,019 enrolled members. In his study of this organization, Martin Pugh noted that in 1900 the total membership of the Independent Labour party was equivalent to the paid membership of the Primrose League in Bolton![36] The League undoubtedly performed a crucial role in mobilizing popular support for the late-Victorian Conservative party, notwithstanding the occasional demarcation dispute between it and other, more formal Tory bodies.[37]

Thus did the Tories prove themselves masters in the art of expanding participation in the political process without conferring the vote, and in rooting politics in the experiences of everyday life. While many of these societies and associations went into decline after 1846 and became dormant in the 1850s, this should not obscure the organiza-tional vibrancy of the 1830s and 1840s.[38] Ultimately, whether one is looking at Conservative party organization in the early, mid or late Victorian period the overall conclusion is the same: far from being a passive beneficiary of social change, the inert recipient of their oppo-nent's weaknesses, or manipulating anti-democratic stratagems, the Conservative party was present at its own transformation by virtue of 'defining and mobilizing its audience and in cultivating cross-class support'.[39]

The Ideology of Popular Conservatism

Conservatives have traditionally presented themselves as a non-ideological and pragmatic party opposed to abstract political theories. As Alex Windscheffel has argued, historians of the Conservative party have, on the whole, reinforced this reading of Conservatism.[40] So, too, have historians of popular politics, many of whom – even in more recent times – have been more interested in organization than in ideas and ideology. The advent of Thatcherism, a deeply ideological politics, called into question the idea that Conservatism was non-ideological. The redefinition of ideology as a more expansive and inclusive term by political scientists and historians over the last 20 years or so has also led to a rediscovery of a distinctive Conservative value and belief sys-tem. Further, as Ewen Green has argued, if ideology is defined as a shared and distinctive body of ideas, and if politics is seen as an arena for defining and solving problems, then Conservatism must surely be ideological since Conservative politicians 'have to find a way of explor-ing and solving problems in a way that is *recognisably* Conservative', to themselves, to their supporters and to their opponents.[41]

A related argument concerns the role of issues in generating electoral support for the Conservative party. As with ideology, so with issues: his-torians have often minimized the importance of them in determining the outcome of elections. For example, James Cornford argued that specific issues at elections did little to influence voting behaviour in the late nineteenth century, which, according to his sociological model, was largely expressive of underlying social cleavages.[42] The working class were thought to be particularly ignorant of issues: only those that related to the immediate material concerns of everyday life attracted their interest. Abstract concepts such as patriotism and imperialism, it was argued, were remote from the quotidian concerns of the electorate. With the attack on electoral sociology and the renewed attention that is being paid to the ideology and rhetoric of popular politics, historians have been rediscovering issues. Paul Readman has shown in his study of the 1900 general election that 'contemporaries were far less circumspect [than historians have been] in ascribing importance to issues on the performance of parties and candidates at the polls'.[43] Contrary to the assertions of Richard Price,[44] Readman demonstrates how important patriotism and imperialism were in generating working-class Conservatism. As he observes of the celebrations that were held throughout Britain in response to the relief of Mafeking by the British Army during the Boer War: 'It is difficult to see how the lifting of a siege in an unknown town in faraway South Africa... had much to do with the down-to-earth realities' of the urban working class.'[45] As for the role of issues more generally, the most cursory examination of the general election campaigns reveals how important issues were, whether it was protection (1841, 1906 and 1910), the position of the Established Church (1837, 1868 and 1885), foreign and imperial policy (1857, 1880, 1886 and 1900), licensing laws (1874 and 1895), parliamentary reform (1832 and 1865), the House of Lords (1892, 1895 and 1910), or the perennial issues of property rights, taxation and social reform. Conservative election addresses were littered with these issues, as were those of their political opponents.

An associated problem with both Conservative ideology and issues is that when historians have paid attention to the party's ideas and policies, this has often been to emphasize how *un*-Conservative they have been. As Bruce Coleman has rightly pointed out, studies of Conservatism have far too often emphasized its progressiveness to the point that one is left wondering what is conservative about Conservatism.[46] Historians of popular politics have rather surprisingly compounded this problem. When not stressing the party's anti-democratic stratagems to stave off mass politics, they have, somewhat paradoxically, presented the party as a progressive, liberal and positive force. The moderate, reforming and integrative creed of Peelite Conservatism; the welfarism that pervaded the tory-radicalism of the 1830s; the party's ongoing interest in, and promotion of, social reform; and the advent of tariff reform: all have been cited as evidence for the party's modernizing, even liberal, pragmatism.[47] To present these policies in such a light is either to misread the objectives of their promoters or to exaggerate the impact of these policies. It is now clear that the growth of popular Conservatism in the 1830s and 1840s owed little to the moderate reformism of Peel[48] who, in any case, showed little interest in popular politics.[49] Neither would such interest have been welcomed: populist tories in and out of parliament distrusted his compromising new Conservatism.[50] The Conservative party's electoral success in the late 1830s and 1840s was the 'result of a Tory revival, not of any "new conservatism'" espoused by Peel.[51] It was the Conservative party's defence of the Church and its pledge to maintain the protective duties on corn that underpinned its electoral success in the later 1830s and early 1840s. Similarly, tory-radicalism was animated by impeccably tory principles – at least for the tories, if not for their fleeting radical allies.[52] If both tories and radicals of this period looked back to a lost golden age of harmony and stability they did so for different reasons. The tory, idealized incarnation of the past was one of hierarchy; for radicals, it was one of popular equality.[53]

As for the party's interest in social reform in the later Victorian and Edwardian period, this was genuine for those Conservatives who kept alive the tory-radical and paternalist traditions, which enabled them to conceive of an interventionist role for the state.[54] The Liverpool Tory boss Arthur Forwood was in doubt that late-Victorian class tensions could be assuaged through a reassertion of paternalism. Under the direction of Forwood, and subsequently Archibald Salvidge, the solution of the Liverpool Tories was to implement a municipal programme of social reform, the centrepiece being cheap housing for the working class.[55] On the other hand, there was a powerful libertarian strain in tory ideology that was opposed to state intervention, and this could also generate popular support for the party by tapping into the long-standing tradition of working-class suspicion of state intervention (fuelled by experiences of the New Poor Law, compulsory elementary education and vaccination of schoolchildren) – especially when that intervention was unwelcome, as were some of the centralized and intrusive welfare reforms introduced by the Edwardian Liberal government.[56]

What stands out in recent work is the extent to which popular Conservatism was shaped by tory ideas on tradition, hierarchy, inequality and the imperfectability of human nature (the pessimistic view that humans are fallible, selfish and emotional). The language of constitutionalism, which has figured much in revisionist work on popular radicalism and liberalism, was no less evident in popular Conservatism. As James Lowther, Tory MP for York, instructed the York Working Men's Conservative Association in 1868, the English constitution had been 'inherited from a wise and provident ancestry' and it was the duty of those in the present to hand it 'down uninjured and unimpaired to a grateful posterity'.[57] Duty was the operative word in tory discourse. As the *Bassetlaw Constitutional Magazine* reminded its readers, 'to no man are rights given without corresponding duties'.[58] This constitution identified by Lowther had to be protected from various forces that were identified as subversive, 'be they Jews, Infidels, Catholic French or Irish, and all those other busy-bodies bent on destroying "Old England" like moral reformers, dissenters and *laissez-faire* industrialists'.[59] Thus, Conservative ideology intersected with the politics of everyday life. The Tories posed as the defenders of pleasures (such as the working man's pint of beer) and popular privileges (such as the freeman franchise) that, it was alleged, were being threatened by Liberal tyranny. The belief in the moral and intellectual imperfection of mankind was also evident in popular Conservatism. As the early Victorian tory-radical Richard Oastler succinctly put it: 'Every Christian believes that man has fallen from perfection, that he is selfish, covetous, and that he needs the unerring teaching of the Almighty.'[60] To the tory-radicals, the tyrannical factory owners who were exploiting women and children had fallen a long way from perfection and, worse still, they were undermining the organic basis of society by forgetting the Burkean dictum that social status and social responsibility were indivisible. For example, Parson Bull, the curate of Bierley, near Bradford, charged the Dissenting manufacturers in the 1830s with replacing the gospel's message of 'love thy neighbour' with the worship of their own wealth.[61]

Far from being ideological aberrations or mere opportunistic pragmatism, Conservative support for factory reform and opposition to the New Poor Law stemmed from an ideological commitment to an organic, interdependent and paternalistic social order. The romantic rhetoric of tory-radicalism contrasted the organic unity of 'The Altar, the Throne and the Cottage' with the divisive effects of capitalist industrialization that was so catastrophically widening the gap and dissolving the bonds between rich and poor. The New Poor Law itself represented an attack on the most personal organic bonds of all: that of the family. The New Poor Law was heavily coloured by the Malthusian belief that overpopulation – the result, it was argued, of excessive breeding amongst the working class – was one of the major causes of unemployment and poverty. To correct this, the new workhouse regime was designed to prevent the poor from marrying and procreating by enforcing a strict separation of husbands from wives, while the new bastardy clauses of the Act overturned the old system whereby Poor Law officials had encouraged unmarried fathers to marry the mother of their children or, at the very least, make financial contributions. To tories, radicals and their working-class followers, this regime was contrary to conventional morality, which held that it was the 'God-given' right of husbands and wives to cohabit and reproduce; it was also believed that sexual activity was an essential and healthy activity. Any ideas, practices (notably divorce and birth control) and institutions that denied these rights were tantamount to denying the humanity of those affected and were 'at variance with the laws of God and man'.[62] Small wonder that the South Lancashire Anti-Poor Law followers of Joseph Rayner Stephens declared their intention 'For child and for wife/ We will war to the Knife.'[63] The romantic idiom of suffering humanity and gothic horror were deployed with gusto on the platform and in the press. The radical newspaper the *Northern Liberator* published a melodramatic account of a starving family who had been forced to enter a workhouse in which the husband had been prevented from seeing his dying wife, and it was also alleged that one of the workhouse keepers had tried to violate his son.[64] The tyrannical factory regime was similarly presented as an attack on conventional domestic family life as it forced women and children out of the home and into the factory. For Oastler and Co., only a restoration of traditional hierarchies would rescue the victimized working class from the oppression of Liberal political economy; the idea that the working class could rescue itself through radical political reform made them anxious.[65]

Sound tory principles also underpinned the Conservative party's advocacy of protectionism. As Anna Gambles has made clear in her reassessment of the politics of protection in the 1840s, protectionism was based on an integrated, coherent and inclusive vision of society that went beyond the polemical focus on the Corn Laws, by embracing a harmonious view of the nation's economy. Protectionists argued that a healthy economy was one in which different economic interests were balanced. Protectionism would supply the means to restore economic and social equilibrium by harmonizing manufacturing and agricultural interests, which had been pitted against one another in consequence of the Whigs making too many concessions to the manufacturing interest. Thus, protectionism, in both its 1840s and Edwardian tariff reform guises, offered an alternative, integrative political economy: tariffs would protect all domestic producers against cheap and inferior foreign goods.[66] Protectionism was also conceived as a means to re-energize the organic bonds of society. The Edwardian tariff reformers articulated their critique of free trade in a gendered language of emasculation, bemoaning the inability of working men to provide for their families. Cheap foreign imports were held responsible for pricing British products – and eventually British firms – out of the market, thus leading to rising unemployment. Sixty years of free trade, it was claimed by the tariff reformers, had brought nothing more than 'poverty, hunger and dirt'.[67]

Moving on to the pessimistic and fatalistic world-view that permeated Conservatism: this could manifest itself in more positive terms. Acceptance of human frailties translated into tolerance of human weaknesses and vices, such as the sinful pleasures of drinking and gambling. Tory aversion to prescription and interference in the private realm also made the party appear less inflexible in their gender politics than their opponents. This explains why Conservatives proved more inclusive towards women, and also why some became supporters of women's suffrage.[68] As for intellectual imperfection: when on the public platform, Tories lost no opportunity to ridicule opponents for their erroneous attachment to abstract ideas and naïve faith in the perfectibility of human nature. To take an example from the 1892 general election, the Leeds Tory W. L. Jackson distinguished himself from what he regarded as the dogmatic beliefs of his Liberal opponent by reminding the voters of Leeds North that elections were to be fought 'upon facts, and not upon theories'.[69] Conservatives preferred to put their faith in experience and tradition. The institutions that Tories valued so highly – the monarchy, the Church, the aristocracy and the United Kingdom itself – were thought to embody a tacit wisdom accumulated over hundreds of years. These were institutional repositories of values and principles such as hierarchy and inequality. For example, the integrity of the United Kingdom was to be preserved by patriotism, which Tories defined as 'a deep devotion…to our fatherland, combined with a proper pride in the deeds of our ancestors, the traditions of their policy, and the heritage of glory they bequeathed to us'.[70] Here, we see the United Kingdom presented in the same way that Lowther presented the English constitution to the electors of York: it was to be preserved and passed on to remote posterity. Conservatives, however, were not opposed to change per se. Drawing on a well-established horticultural idiom, Jackson's colleague Gerald Balfour, Tory MP for neighbouring Leeds Central, told his electors that while Tories 'would dig about the tree, manure it…lop off dead branches and excrescences', the Liberals 'would uproot it, and would have us believe that a new tree would grow up in the morning as fair and bearing as good fruit as the old'.[71]

Inequality and hierarchy were also to the fore in Conservative rhetoric. The tory paternalists of the 1830s and 1840s made no attempt to disguise this. After all, it was 'the security of an ordered, if hierarchical social order' in contrast to the cold, atomizing doctrine of *laissez-faire* political economy that appealed to many members of the working class who were struggling to adjust to the new urban-industrial social order.[72] Hierarchy, though, was not to be confused with polarity. The problem with society in the 1830s and 1840s, as the tory-radical W. B. Ferrand told one Manchester audience, was that it had become divided into extremes: between 'the very rich and the very poor'. This state of affairs could not continue:

> Search history, and you will learn that no country can long exist in which society is broken into such widely distant divisions. We must

have the intermediate links, amalgamating into each other, descending with a regular and even gradation, in order that the monarch on the throne and the peasant in the cottage may alike enjoy the privileges and blessing of our free and glorious constitution.[73]

Similarly, late Victorian Conservatives did not apologize about class; rather, they celebrated class differences and, as Martin Pugh has noted, they attempted to cast hierarchy and inequality 'in a bold, appealing light', not least through the mock medieval hierarchy and pageantry adopted by the Primrose League. The League reached 'deeply into each level of society for its recruits' and enthused 'each part of the hierarchy with a sense of its value as a necessary and equal part of the political community'.[74] Thus, one of the principal ways in which Tories sought to alleviate middle-class anxieties about property and deflect 'sectional' working-class interests was by emphasizing cross-class common interests. When it came to popular audiences, property was presented 'not as the "enemy" but as the "ally" of labour'. British economic prosperity – and, by extension, employment and working-class wages – was dependent on the confidence of commercial men, and that confidence was dependent on the security of property (in the form of capital investment). 'Liberal attacks on property...were presented as destructive of that confidence.'[75] The interests of property and labour were conceptualized in tory thinking as interdependent and indivisible components of an organic commercial community. As one 'Conservative Working Man' from Preston phrased it in the 1890s:

> the success of trade depends primarily on the enterprise of our capitalists, the inventive ability and great commercial acumen of our great trade managers, and last but by no means least the faithful honest labour...of the millions who make up our working class.[76]

One of the major distinguishing characteristics of Conservatism was its blatant appeal to distinctive interests, an avenue that was largely closed to their Liberal opponents who found the idea of 'interests' deeply uncomfortable as they regarded it as divisive. The existence of separate Conservative organizations for the middle and the working classes in the 1830s, and again in the 1870s, was part cause and consequence of this. However, segregating Conservative supporters along class lines was a growing concern for some Tories. This explains why separate class-based associations were rare by the 1880s.[77] The challenge for the Tory party was to weld diverse and often conflicting interests together, a task that proved to be very difficult, if not impossible, as was the case with tariff reform. Although more comfortable with the idea of distinct

interests, class divisions, as opposed to differences, were deeply worry-
ing for Conservatives. This was evident during the debates surrounding
the redistribution of seats in 1884 when many Conservatives voiced concern about the proposed sub-division of boroughs into single-member
constituencies along class lines on the grounds that 'it distanced the
masses from the civilizing influences of property and education'.[78]

The recent focus on ideas, beliefs and values has revealed working-
class Conservatism to be a diverse, multi-faceted and, at times, contradictory and incoherent political culture. Notwithstanding the new
attention to the positive aspects of working-class Conservatism, such
as the party's support for social reform, in many respects this *was* a
defensive, resistant, insular and xenophobic political culture characterized by the beer barrel, downright economic self-interest, and hostility to various 'others', especially puritanical Liberal Nonconformists
and the growing number of alien immigrants allegedly flooding the
late-Victorian labour market. Aspects of this negative political culture
featured in the Edwardian tariff reform campaign. 'Free trade under-
mines the nation's racial strength' was the accompanying caption to
one protectionist cartoon. It was asserted that growing unemployment, due to unfair foreign competition, was driving capital out of
the country and forcing many a good labourer to emigrate, a gap
that was being filled by inferior immigrants.[79] On the other hand,
alien immigrants were not universally blamed for the plight of the
displaced English workman. As one Primrose League article can-
didly put it, the employment of foreign labourers is 'to a certain
extent... caused by the conduct of Englishmen themselves'. The article
went on:

> And there can be little doubt that much of the preference for foreign-
> ers, in many cases, arises from their undeniable readiness for work
> and from their versatility; while the average Englishman, unfortu-
> nately, is unable, or says he is, to do more than a certain specified
> kind and amount of work, and generally grumbles before doing
> that.[80]

On the other hand, working-class toryism could be 'respectable', as
demonstrated by its emphasis on self-improvement, self-education and
self-reliance. These values appealed to the upwardly mobile and socially
aspirant working-class and clerkly voters, and were propagated most
notably by the Primrose League. Even the Conservative party's identification with popular pleasures could be respectable and responsible: the
idealized tory working man was an honest, respectable labourer who
had earned the right to a quiet pint of beer free from the interference

of coercive moral reformers. More importantly, he should be possessed of sufficient 'manliness' to regulate his own consumption of alcohol. It was the responsibility of the individual, not the state to exercise restraint.

Moving on to the Edwardian period, although tariff reform represented a bold attempt to construct a multi-faceted, positive and socially integrative policy, it was hardly the first time that the Conservative party had presented itself in such light. We have already seen how the party promoted protectionism along broadly similar lines in the 1840s.[81] Since tariff reform occupied such a prominent position in the Conservative platform, one has to conclude that it played an important role in revitalizing popular Conservatism, hence the decision by the party to persist with the policy. That tariff reform struck a chord with many working-class electors is hardly surprising, since the Tory party was perceived as offering a dynamic solution to the escalating problem of unemployment in the Edwardian years. Similarly, if Tory candidates were attacked for wanting to tax the people's food (despite official and explicit assurances to the contrary), the Liberal candidates were charged with taxing the people's pleasures. Slogans such as 'Vote Tory' for 'cheaper beer and bacca' abounded at the 1910 general elections. Since the 1909 Liberal budget had proposed further taxes on alcohol and tobacco, the Tory party was able to gain some popular support by playing on their historic defence of the people's pleasures. By deploying shrewd electoral propaganda, the Tories blended their defence of the people's pleasures with tariff reform, an ingenious example being the production of 'Tariff Reform Cigarettes', with each packet containing a leaflet outlining the essentials of the policy.[82]

By 1910, tariff reform had played an important part in revitalizing the Conservatives as the party of property. As John Belchem argues, 'Conservatives upheld tariff reform as the best defence against "socialist" redistribution, a means of financing necessary social reforms and rearmaments without recourse to confiscatory taxation and punitive land duties', as represented by the 1909 Liberal budget.[83] Combating the threat of 'socialism' gave Conservatism a renewed clarity of purpose. This enabled the party to win back some of the middle-class support, especially in the south-east, that had been lost in 1906 due to the then Tory government's education policy of giving state grants to Anglican schools (thus offending Nonconformist sensibilities), its failure to bring the South African War to a speedy conclusion, and due to the confusion surrounding tariff reform. For all the constructive and positive aspects of tariff reform, by 1910 it had been made to serve conservative ends, and arguably subordinated to traditional organic style toryism.[84] Tariff reform would renew and strengthen the organic bonds of the local, national and imperial communities by promoting class harmony, defending national interests and identity, and binding the colonies to the mother country through imperial federation. While the Tories were kept from forming a government after 1906, there can be little doubt that tariff reform won the party unprecedented levels of cross-class support, so much so that the Tories had their political opponents on the run.

Chapter 8: The Decline of Liberalism and the Rise of Labour I: A Narrative

Of all the historical debates surrounding popular politics, none has been more contentious than the one that has raged on the realignment of progressive politics in the late nineteenth and early twentieth centuries. This was the period when the Labour party established itself, and soon replaced the Liberals, as the main party of the British left. The facts appear straightforward: after their landslide victory of 400 seats at the 1906 general election, by 1924 the Liberal party had been reduced to a rump of 40 MPs. Labour, on the other hand, enjoyed a meteoric rise: from humble beginnings in 1900 as the Labour Representation Committee, which only managed to elect two MPs at the general election held in that year, the Labour party (as it was renamed after the 1906 election) had 191 MPs by 1923. Less than one year later, Labour formed its first government. The rapidity and scale of this realignment has been forensically analysed by generations of historians; there has, however, been little agreement about why and precisely when this happened. Put simply, the debate has been divided between 'inevitablists' and 'accidentalists': the former have emphasized longer-term structural changes, pre-eminently the rise of class-based politics; the latter have stressed short-term, contingent factors, such as the far-reaching changes associated with the First World War.[1]

Before launching into this historiographical minefield in Chapter 9, this chapter will provide a narrative overview of the political changes of the late-Victorian and Edwardian period. It will be argued that, far from being the inevitable outcome of the transition to class-based politics, the rise of Labour and the continuing success of the Edwardian Liberal party were due to changes in the political sphere. While the electoral map was characterized by pockets of growing Labour strength before

1914, on the whole the Liberal party, despite some serious difficulties, was able to contain Labour.[2]

The Challenge of Independent Labour Politics, c.1880–1906

The so-called 'Age of Equipoise' – with its relative prosperity, social harmony and political quiescence – reached its apogee in the late 1860s. Thereafter it began to disintegrate: slowly and unevenly in the 1870s, and then rapidly in the 1880s. The onset of economic depression in the late 1870s, the associated rise in unemployment in the early 1880s, and the growth of militant trades unionism in the late 1880s (facilitated by the return of more secure employment) all fuelled the growth of popular unrest. The foremost manifestation of this unrest was the rising number of trades union strikes. What was remarkable about the wave of strike activity in the late 1880s (initially concentrated in East London) was not only the success achieved by the strikers, but also the fact that many of them were drawn from the hitherto largely non-unionized semi-skilled and unskilled workers. This was dramatically underlined by the strikes of the matchgirls at Bryant & May in June 1888, and in the following year by the Beckton gas workers in March and the dockers in August. Their success stimulated the growth of trades unionism throughout the country between 1889 and 1893, a development that used to be characterized as the 'new unionism'. This was distinguished from the 'old' unionism by its broader social basis (not only being confined to skilled artisans in the craft trades) and by its socialist sympathies and growing desire for independent political representation.[3] This wave of unionism no longer seems as new as was once thought. Not only could some of the older generation of trades unionists (such as Robert Knight of the Boilermakers' Society) be just as militant, progressive and class conscious as any of their 'new' successors; it has also come to light that it was the older, more established craft unions (and those new ones that aped the ethos and practices of the old) that survived the frenetic wave of industrial unrest once it dissipated in the early 1890s.[4] Either way, this wave of strike activity played an important role in creating the conditions for the rise of Labour.

Yet, we might ask why the discontented sought a political solution to their grievances. Three factors combined to produce that outcome. First, it was not the initial success of Metropolitan trades unionism but, as E. P. Thompson argued, the subsequent failure of some unions in the industrial districts of the North of England and Scotland to achieve their objectives (notably preventing wage cuts and improving working conditions) 'which turned... workers into channels of independent political action'. Having exhausted the strike weapon, 'political action was seen as the only effective remedy for industrial grievances'.[5] This failure made the more militant and younger trades unionists receptive to the socialist ideas that were being disseminated by those activists who had played a leading role in organizing the new unions and strikes (Annie Besant at Bryant & May's, Will Thorne at Beckton and Ben Tillett at the docks). Thus, as in the Age of the Chartists, what we are seeing is the politicization of discontent. Second, that politicization was due to the realization that the tyrannical and unjust employers with whom the strikers were in conflict (notably over attempts to cut wages as a means to maintain profit margins) were often the very same men who dominated the local parties, especially the Liberal party with its dictatorial 'caucuses'. These oligarchic organizations were perceived to be increasingly hostile to the interests of organized labour due to their frequent refusal to nominate labour representatives as candidates, by their failure to support legislation designed to protect labour interests, and by their often tacit approval of the state's repression of strike activity. Indeed, the clash between the strikers and the local authorities resolved itself into the age-old dispute over rights of popular access and freedom of assembly. To take one local example: in Bradford, the local Labour Union was formed in 1891 as a direct result of the attempt by the Council's Watch Committee to prevent the strikers from holding public meetings and by their reliance on the military to enforce the ban.[6] Third, enter the committed band of socialist activists who began to tap into the growing popular discontent with the established two-party system and fuse the desire for independent labour representation with socialist ideas and ideals.

What, precisely, was the nature of these socialist ideas, and why was there a 'socialist' revival in the 1880s? These socialist ideas were shaped more by currents of indigenous radicalism than by continental ideas of Marxist socialism, ideas that in any case only began to appear in English from the later 1880s. This socialist revival was due to the coalescing of three radical currents. The first of these had been simmering away throughout the mid-Victorian years. This was the independent-style radicalism associated with the campaigns for manhood suffrage in the 1860s and 1870s, the popular struggle on behalf of Charles Bradlaugh (ironically, an anti-socialist), and the allied secularist and republican movements of the 1870s and 1880s. Many of the activists involved in organizing these campaigns were subsequently converted to socialism in the 1880s.[7] Much of this independent radicalism was animated by opposition to the idle rich and to dictatorial and exploitative party elites, such as Alfred Illingworth in Bradford. As Ben Tillett told a Bradford audience at the time of his parliamentary candidature in 1892: 'We will have proper representation without the patronage of the rich, and we will not give in to the cadjoling [sic] and lying of the wirepullers'.[8]

The second current emerged from the radical fringes of the land reform movements that were particularly strong in Ireland and Scotland. This current had been charged by the immensely popular ideas of the American land reformer Henry George and his book *Progress and Poverty*, published in 1879, of which 400,000 copies a year were being sold by 1884. George advocated the replacement of the various taxes on labour and capital with a punitive 'single tax' on land values. Many of the Labour party's first MPs claimed to have been heavily influenced by Henry George who, in Keir Hardie's words, 'unlocked many of the industrial and economic difficulties which then beset the mind of the worker trying to take an intelligent interest in his own affairs'.[9] Although this radical agrarianism was disseminated throughout Britain by the radical press and by George's itinerant lecture tours,[10] it was most powerful in Scotland due to the Highland crofters' land agitation against exploitative landlords, which had raged throughout the late 1870s and 1880s. This agrarian radicalism was carried to the lowlands by crofters' migration to Glasgow, where it was fused with lowlands trades unionism. The product of this fusion was the establishment of the Scottish Labour party in 1888, the precipitating factor being the refusal of the Mid-Lanark Liberal party to endorse the candidature of Keir Hardie who, at this stage, was still a radical Liberal.

The third current was supplied by an indigenous English socialism that was heavily indebted to the socialistic Chartism of Bronterre O'Brien, kept alive and nurtured in the mid-Victorian years by Metropolitan radical club-land.[11] This indigenous socialism had been given a substantial fillip by John Ruskin's impassioned attacks on political economy and his ideas on the value and dignity of labour, which were taken forward and further popularized by Edward Carpenter, William Morris and Robert Blatchford. Carpenter, Ruskin, Morris and Blatchford – with their eclectic mix of tory, utopian and Marxist socialism, and, above all, their celebration of a pre-capitalist age of joyful, creative and fraternal labour – were the most influential socialist thinkers in the pioneering generation of Labour activists. When the periodical *Review of Reviews* asked those Labour MPs elected in 1906 to list the books that had most influenced their thinking, one of the most frequently mentioned was Ruskin's *Unto This Last*, a devastating attack on *laissez-faire* political economy, published in 1862. Almost as frequently mentioned was the Bible.[12] This eclectic mix of ideas and values coalesced into ethical socialism that, as David James has argued, was more often 'a matter of feeling and emotion rather than precisely defined beliefs'.[13] The mantras of ethical socialism were justice, morality, freedom, fraternity and equality; a socialism that reached its literary apogee in William Morris' hugely inspirational utopian novel *News From Nowhere*, published in 1890.

By the 1880s, the influence of a more recognizably Marxist socialism was, nevertheless, beginning to take hold of some of the advanced radical elements, and nowhere more so than in the Social Democratic Federation (SDF), founded by the maverick H. M. Hyndman in 1884. A fine specimen of the bourgeoisie, complete with tall hat and frock coat, Hyndman did more than most to popularize the ideas and works of Marx and Engels before they were made available in English, albeit in a caricatured, selective and dogmatic fashion. Yet, Hyndman's dogmatic Marxism should not be allowed to obscure the SDF's impeccably radical origins. The SDF was actually a successor to an earlier radical organization – the Democratic Federation (DF), established in 1881 by metropolitan radical clubs in reaction to the dictation of 'Caucus' politics, and to the Gladstone government's coercionist Irish policy.[14] The DF had restricted itself to what were largely Chartist objectives for parliamentary reform, although it did anticipate the socialism of the SDF with its demand for land nationalization. Compared with the DF, the SDF certainly appeared more socialistic, as illustrated by Hyndman's assertion that only 'the collective ownership of the means of production, distribution and exchange, managed by a democratic state in the interests of the whole commonwealth' would bring about 'a complete emancipation of labour from the domination of capital and landlord'.[15] However, as Jon Lawrence notes, this aspect of the SDF's programme was usually subordinated to what were largely traditional 'ideas of radical democracy': adult suffrage, annual parliaments, proportional representation, payment of members and abolition of the House of Lords.[16] Further evidence of its radical origins, and continuing affinity with such groups, is furnished by the co-operation that existed between many local SDF activists, radicals and trades unionists, and by the SDF's willingness to use the existing political framework and promote active participation in electoral politics as a means to bring about the transition to socialism.[17]

Some of the more ethical and utopian socialists came to reject the SDF's strategy of working within the existing political system – and, in some cases, political channels altogether. The result was a split and the secessionists – prominent amongst whom were William Morris and Marx's daughter, Eleanor – left to form a rival organization, the Socialist League, in 1885. They were motivated, in part, by growing personal animosity towards Hyndman's dictatorial leadership, his xenophobic nationalism, and by his dogmatic adherence to a scientific understanding of socialism to the exclusion of ethical, moral and even religious concerns.

In contrast to the perceived bureaucratic and politically focused SDF, the members of the Socialist League sought what Noel Thompson has termed a 'decentralized socialism' that concentrated more on 'making socialists' and preparing for the new socialist life, which would be based on co-operative communes.[18] This was to be brought about by fomenting industrial conflict; hence the League's willingness to work with the trades unions. Some of the more extreme members of the League subsequently rejected co-operation and communal ideas, and became anarchists. The anarchists had gained control of the League by the early 1890s and it would remain under their control until it was disbanded in 1901. Although the League did not survive long, the ethical socialism that it had originally espoused was taken forward by the Labour Church movement. As the religious embodiment of organized labour, the Labour Churches were also concerned with making socialists and were especially influential in the 1890s.[19]

And yet, powerful countervailing currents were also at work. Some socialists, such as those who had started out in the 'Fellowship of the New Life' – founded in 1883 to work for 'the perfecting of individual character' based on simple living[20] – were becoming frustrated with their apparent lack of progress and wanted to use political institutions and organizations to bring about *social* transformation. The result was the establishment of a new society in 1883 whose aim was 'the re-organisation of Society by the emancipation of Land and Industrial Capital from individual and class-ownership, and the vesting of them in the community for the general benefit'. This was the Fabian Society, which sought to 'promote these ends by the general dissemination of knowledge' and by 'permeating' state institutions with its ideas.[21]

In contrast to what it regarded as the narrow precepts of the SDF's radicalism, the Fabian Society expanded that radicalism to provide a new political diagnosis of the nation's socio-economic ills. For the Fabians, the pinnacle of 'Old Corruption' was no longer the monarch and the aristocrat (their unjust privileges were merely the symptoms rather than the cause) but the idle, unproductive capitalist who lived off unearned income (in contrast to the productive and socially useful capitalist) – a state of affairs politically legitimized by the state.[22] The solution was to break this capitalist monopoly by democratizing the state through franchise extension and by taxing unearned income as a means of emancipating land and industrial capital from individual and class ownership. This was a form of socialism that looked back to the radicalism espoused by Thomas Hodgskin and William Thompson in the 1820s and 1830s, which had similarly attacked idle, exploitative capitalists.

The significance of the Fabians to the rise of Labour is to be found in their attempts to broaden the ideological parameters of radicalism and in appreciating the need to forge an alliance between trades union-ism and popular radicalism.[23] Despite these achievements, Fabianism – while serving an important long-term educational strategy – did not provide the kind of activism that was being sought by many frustrated labour and trades union activists. This is not to suggest that Fabianism, as is traditionally argued, was perceived as being bureaucratic, elitist and far removed from the world of popular politics. As recent work has made clear, Fabian societies sprang up all over the country and, in their pragmatic attempts to forge local alliances with organized labour, they were forerunners of the Independent Labour Party (ILP). What is also becoming clear is that the rigid boundaries that existed between organizations at a national level were seldom replicated in the localities: activists were often members of several organizations.[24] Nevertheless, the objective of the younger, more radical and impatient socialists was the immediate mass mobilization of organized labour. The aim was sim-ple: to convert the trades unions to socialism by means of promoting the idea of independent political representation for labour. This led to conflict and divisions within local trades councils between 'Lib-Labs' (those representatives of organized labour, some of whom were elected as Liberal MPs, who formed themselves into a pressure group *within* the Liberal party to further labour interests) and advocates of independent labour politics. In some cases, this led to the formation of rival trades councils, as happened in Sheffield.

No doubt some of the trades unionists that agreed to work with the socialists did so largely out of pragmatic, self-interested motives and with the expectation of anticipated gain for their members, rather than through any genuine, deep attachment to socialism. On the other hand, as Keith Laybourn and Jack Reynolds have rightly argued in relation to West Yorkshire, the activities of the ethical organizations such as the Labour Church, the Clarion movement (which promoted the cul-tural aspects of the labour movement through a whole range of leisure activities) and the Socialist Sunday Schools 'were not so much counter-vailing as complementary' to the trades union alliance.[25] It is unduly simplistic, therefore, to caricature the nascent Labour party as the political mouthpiece of a conservative and defensive 'labourist' trades union consciousness. Even if one accepts that the majority of Labour activists were trades unionists, the majority of trades unionists were not Labour supporters – at least, not until the wave of industrial unrest of 1911–13. The most cursory examination of Labour's electioneering rhetoric reveals that the party had wider concerns than trades union issues. We might also note that not all Labour activists were enthusiastic supporters of the trades unions, especially when the wider ethical vision of the former conflicted with the perceived narrow economistic goals of the latter.[26]

To return to the growing discontent in the 1890s, in the first instance, this led to the rise of a plethora of local organizations in the late 1880s and early 1890s that were dedicated to securing representation of labour interests separate from the established political parties. Representatives of the new independent local bodies (along with the Fabians, the SDF and the Scottish Labour party) came together at a conference held at Bradford in January 1893, out of which the ILP was formed. Although the ILP committed itself to the socialist objective of securing 'the collective ownership of all means of production, distribution and exchange', this was part of a broader set of objectives encompassing social, political and fiscal reform. This represented a new, dynamic recomposition of the popular radical tradition and socialism. Many of these reforms had their origins in the radical ideas of Tom Paine, the factory movement and Chartism, and had been developed and supplemented by the SDF and the Fabians, who fused these aspects of popular radicalism with socialist ideas, notably collective ownership.

The rise of these various organizations, especially the ILP, was evidence that radicalism was beginning to fragment. The outcome was a fracturing of the Liberal coalition due to its ultimate failure to contain the representatives of organized labour and their radical allies. Initially, in the 1880s, the older and more traditional radical elements were pushed back into the Liberal party, albeit uneasily on the margins, due to their opposition to socialism and the declining salience of traditional causes such as secularism and republicanism. Bradlaugh, the Newcastle radical Joseph Cowan and the 'old' trades unionist George Howell were notable, if rather different, examples of this latter-day traditional radicalism. It would, however, be wrong to write off these radical Liberals as outdated and conservative. As John Shepherd has shown in his study of the 20 'Lib-Labs' who sat as Liberal MPs in the House of Commons for varying periods between 1874 and 1906, and as Alistair Reid illustrates in his rehabilitation of 'Old Unionist' labour activists, the moderate ideas along with the gradual and practical policies of these working-class Liberal radicals continued to resonate with popular audiences.[27] For example, as Reid shows with the 'old' trades unionist Robert Knight, it was not that he was opposed to the socialist policy of nationalization per se; rather, it made little sense to transfer control to the state without making it more democratically accountable, the lack of accountability being one of the reasons why many radical Liberals remained sceptical about state sponsored social reform. Similarly, if Knight and the Lib-Lab MPs were opposed to a statutory uniform working day, it was because 'national legislation was likely to be too rigid in its application to local conditions'.[28] These Liberal radicals continued to put their faith in the independent, collective agencies of working-class self-help and looked to the state to protect, promote and extend these forms of self-government. Beyond their role as political representatives of organized labour, Liberal radicals, many of whom were either Nonconformists or secularists – were stalwarts of 'old' Gladstonian Liberalism and they campaigned for temperance reform, Home Rule, disestablishment, unsectarian education and free trade. Their presence and popularity in the late-Victorian and Edwardian Liberal party not only helps to explain the continuing electoral success of popular Liberalism, but also why the emerging Labour party went to great lengths to incorporate this Liberal radicalism into its programme.

In establishing independent labour politics as an alternative to the existing political parties, one cannot help being impressed with the tenacity and millenarian anticipation shown by the pioneering socialist activists who did so much to disseminate their ideas among the trades unionists and the working classes in the 1880s and early 1890s. One can appreciate why subsequent generations of activists and historians looked back on this period as a golden age, one filled with optimism, idealism and great expectations that were captured so eloquently by Morris, Blatchford and Carpenter. In addition to the formal political organizations of the SDF and ILP, these years saw the rise of Labour Churches, Socialist Sunday schools, Ethical Societies, Clarion cycling and ramblers corps and a whole range of other organizations, activities and experimental communities that blended recreation, camaraderie, education and politicization. All of this was part of an attempt to create an alternative socialist culture.

By the late 1890s, those members in these organizations who looked for political solutions to social problems, and who were the majority, increasingly threw in their lot with the ILP, bringing their ethical brand of socialism with them. While the SDF and Socialist League had laid much of the groundwork, the ILP soon eclipsed these rival organizations. One of the main reasons for this was that the SDF and the League were divided amongst themselves and sceptical about either working within the existing political system (the League) or about the efficacy of trades unions (the SDF). By contrast, the ILP – and, subsequently, the Labour party – while not rejecting socialism, was more pragmatic and desirous of immediate action. During the 1890s, and to a lesser extent in the 1900s, there were moves to bring about 'Socialist Unity' by drawing the various socialist organizations together. Advocates of Socialist Unity could be found in all the labour and socialist organizations, especially at a local level. Historians have been divided over when Socialist Unity ceased to be a viable option: for some, the point of no return was reached in the mid-1890s; for others, 1900 – or even 1914.[29] As Keith Laybourn has convincingly argued, Socialist Unity was unlikely after the mid-1890s given the opposition of the ILP which, having quickly established itself as the dominant expression of organized labour and socialism, was never going to consent to Hyndman's plan of making the SDF the dominant force in any future united socialist party.[30] Thus, while it would be wrong to argue that there was no alternative to the ILP's parliamentarism and pragmatic strategy of pursuing trades union support after the mid-1890s, for all the alleged benefits that would come from joining forces, Socialist Unity was not practical politics.

And yet, despite this pragmatism, for the remainder of the 1890s the ILP had a chequered history, as did the Labour party after 1906. In the 1895 general election, the first to be held after the founding of the party, the ILP failed to win any of the 28 seats that it contested. The newly formed Labour Representation Committee (LRC) faired little better at the 1900 'Khaki' general election, when only two of its 15 candidates were elected. The LRC, as had the Liberal party, suffered at the 'Khaki election' due to its 'pro-Boer' sympathies.[31] Similarly, ILP membership also plummeted: from just over 10,000 members in 1895, this figure had been halved by 1901.[32] The road to 1906, let alone 1914, was far from straight. It would take several more bouts of industrial unrest, employer counter-attacks, adverse legal decisions, government intransigence and Liberal opposition in the late 1890s and early 1900s to convince more trades union leaders of the necessity of independent political representation. The adverse legal decisions affecting trades unions were the most important, principally making picketing to encourage strike action illegal in 1899 and the Taff Vale Judgement of 1901 making unions financially liable for damages incurred during strikes. A crucial breakthrough with the unions occurred in 1899, when a resolution to hold a conference with labour and socialist organizations to further the cause of independent political representation was passed by a narrow majority at the Trades Union Congress. The leaders of these trades unionists met with representatives from the ILP,

Fabian Society and the SDF in London in February 1900 for talks. The outcome was the formation of the LRC.

Under the impact of Taff Vale, the affiliated membership of the LRC increased from 350,000 in 1901 to 861,000 by 1903. Recognition of the LRC's growing power, and affinities with the Liberal party, came in 1903 when Herbert Gladstone, the Liberal Chief Whip, entered into secret negotiations with Ramsay MacDonald, Secretary of the LRC. The result was an electoral pact designed to maximize the anti-Conservative vote in which the Liberals agreed to give the LRC a free run in a number of constituencies at the next general election provided that they did not intervene in Liberal strongholds. Largely as a result of this pact, 29 LRC candidates were returned at the 1906 general election, at which point they formed themselves into the Labour party.

This informal electoral pact mediated the relationship between the Liberal and Labour parties until the First World War and, in the hands of its most enthusiastic supporters, it was both cause and consequence of a mutual commitment to the tenets of progressivism, an ideological synthesis of moderate socialism and 'New Liberalism'. The New Liberalism envisaged a more positive and interventionist role for the state in which collectivist social reform, financed through graduated taxation of unearned income, would remove the structural obstacles (notably poverty) that were stifling individual development. The result would be the elimination of class antagonism and the creation of an ethical and efficient political economy that would maximize liberty and reward the productive classes at the expense of the idle, while guaranteeing a minimum standard of living for all.[33]

The Dynamics of Progressive Politics, c.1890–1914

The establishment of an independent political party was a remarkable achievement for the combined forces of organized labour and their radical-socialist allies. The Labour party had already come a long way by 1906, such a distance and so rapidly that Labour's advance between 1906 and 1914 appeared much less impressive. Although the number of Labour MPs rose to 40 after the general election of January 1910, and to 42 after the December election of 1910, on the eve of the First World War there were only 37 Labour MPs, the losses being due to by-election defeats. In municipal elections, Labour's fortunes were similarly mixed, although it is undeniable that Labour had made advances, and some were substantial. This section explores the dynamics of Liberal–Labour relations and how that dynamic shaped the electoral map of late-Victorian and Edwardian Britain. The precise

electoral balance between the Liberal and Labour parties in the localities was shaped by a combination of factors: the responsiveness of local
Liberal establishments (itself conditioned by the strength of popular
Conservatism), and the extent to which Labour was able and willing to
build cross-class constituencies of electoral support. In those parts of
the north-west and London where the Liberal party had been historically weak in the face of popular Conservatism, from the 1890s Liberal
radicals were able to exert a powerful influence over the local Liberal
agenda to shape a progressive politics, often by forming alliances with
the Labour party. In these hitherto Liberal deserts, the Liberal party
had everything to gain by forming electoral pacts with the Labour party.
In those constituencies where the Liberals knew they stood little chance
of success, Labour, they calculated, might fair better. In return for giving Labour a free run in a handful of these constituencies, Labour (as
stipulated in the Gladstone–Macdonald Pact of 1903) would not contest
seats where Liberals were standing, who – in the absence of Labour –
were able to maximize their support by emphasizing their progressive
credentials.

The Labour party, when it tried, was unable to make much headway
as an independent force in these localities. Indeed, in parts of London
and Lancashire the torch of independent labour, such as it existed, was
carried by the SDF, the secular ethos of which was more congenial to
many of the ex-Conservatives who objected to the Nonconformist and
moral tone of the Labour party and its Liberal allies. It was no coincidence either that the SDF did well in these places, as the forces of trades
unionism – the mainstay of Labour – were often relatively weak and
divided in their political loyalties. For all its radical antecedents, the SDF
was becoming a more class-conscious organization by the early 1900s,
particularly after it metamorphosed into the Social Democratic Party in
1907 and, subsequently, into the British Socialist Party in 1911. Despite
this refashioning, independent socialism ultimately made few dents in
the progressive alliance, not least because it often proved willing at the
local level to co-operate with Labour.[34]

This progressive politics synthesized aspects of traditional radicalism (targeting 'Old Corruption'), New Liberalism and socialism. This
synthesis underpinned the experiments in municipal socialism, the
national welfare reforms of the Liberal Government, and the commitment to extending democratic accountability as part of the traditional
radical attack on privilege. Liberals of this hue appealed to the common
humanity of the many against the selfish propertied few. In a number
of places, this progressive spirit dated back to the 1890s. If the national
Liberal party was finding it difficult in the 1890s to repackage its messages in ways that resonated most effectively with popular audiences,[35]

evidence from Leicester and Manchester suggests that local Liberals had no such difficulty and were evolving municipal versions of 'New Liberalism' a decade before it made its appearance on the national scene.[36]

By contrast, in those places with a longstanding successful Liberal presence, such as existed in Scotland and in the textile districts of the West Riding, local Liberal elites saw little reason to make common cause with the infant, upstart Labour party, especially when organized labour was either weak and divided or willing to work within the Liberal party. Hostile Liberal elites lost no opportunity to argue that the Liberal and Labour parties were ideologically incompatible, and thus it made little sense to enter into an alliance, tactical or otherwise as, sooner or later, the two parties would be locked in conflict.[37] One such vocal opponent was the Sheffield Liberal Imperialist W. E. Clegg, who attacked the progressive sympathies of those in his own local party. In 1909, Clegg circulated a 'Memorandum on Socialism' in which he pleaded the absolute necessity for the local and national Liberal party to 'disassociate itself publicly and by its actions from the "red-tie" brigade'. Failure to do so would 'alienate a large number of supporters who make themselves felt at the ballot box and by their financial support of the party'. To continue aiding Labour was an act of electoral suicide that Clegg dismissed as nothing more than assisting 'the robber ... to enjoy the fruits of his robbery'. But opposition to socialism did not necessarily entail opposition to working-class 'interests' more generally. Clegg emphasized that he was 'not opposed to Labour in the moderate sense', as he had 'hearty sympathy with all the reasonable and moderate movements to improve the conditions, hours of work, and wages of the workmen'. Rather, he was against Labour in the extreme sense, which advocated transferring capital to the state; communal ownership; the state as sole employer to control all manufactories, distribution and exchange; and abolition of private property, profits or rents.[38] This was the stance taken by many moderate Liberals who were on the right of their party, particularly those who had embraced Liberal Imperialism in the later 1890s and early 1900s.

Originally conceived as a reaction to the outdated individualism of Gladstonian Liberalism, obsessed as it was with destructive causes such as Irish Home Rule, the Liberal Imperialists advocated a more vigorous pursuit of imperial interests and linked this imperial expansion with domestic social reform: such expansion, it was alleged, was conditional on bringing about a more efficient state and healthy society at home. Although much of the Liberal Imperialist critique was drowned out by the revival of traditional Liberalism in the Edwardian years, some of its vigour survived and animated moderate Liberalism's hostility

towards socialism. Such hostility was not, however, the exclusive preserve of latter-day Liberal Imperialism. Old-fashioned, individualist
Liberal Nonconformity could be equally as hostile towards socialism
and even the Labour party. In Bradford, it was the Nonconformist wool
manufacturer Alfred Illingworth who spearheaded Liberal opposition
to the rise of Labour and the more general drift towards collectivist
social reform, a role that was similarly played by Sir James Kitson, a
Unitarian manufacturer, in neighbouring Leeds.

If the 'old' style traditional Liberalism continued to reap electoral dividends (as was the case in Scotland, parts of Wales and the north-east)
Labour, although able to establish itself as an alternative to the Liberal
party, found it difficult to dislodge the 'Lib-Lab' politics of the organized working class and thus experienced limited electoral success.[39]
For example, in those constituencies dominated by the coalfields the
miners were so great in number and the single most important group of
electors that their representatives were the de facto local Liberal establishment. In these Lib-Lab oases, upstart Labour candidates could find
themselves the object of intense hostility, as Pete Curran found when he
contested the Barnsley by-election for the ILP in 1897.[40]

The continuing electoral success of the Liberal party could result
in frustration within Labour circles at the party's limited electoral
progress, which was attributed to its moderation and co-operation with
the Liberal party. In Sheffield, this led to the local ILP withdrawing
from the LRC.[41] Elsewhere, this frustration could translate into support for rival socialist individuals, the most famous example being the
election of the 'independent socialist' Victor Grayson at Colne Valley in
1907. It could also translate into support for rival organizations, such as
the SDF, which had seceded from the LRC in 1901 because of the latter's diluted socialism, but few were able to mount a serious challenge
to mainstream Labour and the progressive alliance. [42]

Where old Liberalism reigned supreme, and appeared sectional and
selfish, as in Bradford and Leeds, the Labour party could experience a
spectacular rise.[43] But even when the Liberal and Labour parties were
locked in electoral conflict, more often than not this resolved itself into
a contest over which party was the rightful heir of the radical tradition
and the authentic voice of progressivism. In its most consensual form,
Labour was presented as merely completing the work begun by Liberalism; when conflict predominated, Labour was fulfilling that which
the Liberals refused to acknowledge as the next logical step.[44] As Jon
Lawrence has argued, 'despite apparent disagreement over electoral
matters, the two parties nonetheless spoke a common political language
(even if that language was used to argue that the other side were less
worthy champions of the "cause")'.[45]

One has to conclude that the fragmented electoral map of Edwardian Britain provides few clues as to the nature and extent of the political realignment that took place after the First World War. As Pat Thane has argued in relation to municipal politics, 'before 1914 it was still not clear whether Labour or the Liberals or some realignment of the two would be the long-term beneficiaries of the appeal of reforming politics'.[46] Whether or not one attaches much significance to municipal election results is somewhat of a moot point. The fact remains that Labour often failed to maintain or consolidate its municipal victories – an uneven performance that tells against narratives of the inevitable triumph of Labour. What is clear, as Chris Cook pointed out many years ago, is that Labour was struggling in many places to establish itself as a popular alternative to the established parties: 'outside a very few heavily industrialized wards of major cities, Labour's municipal advance prior to 1914 was either negligible or non-existent'.[47] Thus, whether judged from the national or local perspective, Labour was still the junior party of the Left. Certainly, Labour was becoming too big for its boots in places, buoyed up by the tidal wave of industrial unrest that swept the country between 1911 and 1913. But, on the whole, the Liberal party was able to contain the threat in the immediate years before the war. Even in West Yorkshire, an area identified as a pre-1914 Labour heartland, Labour's advances at municipal level were largely limited to Bradford and Leeds, and the fact remains that the Liberal party still controlled 20 of the 23 parliamentary seats in the region. Clearly, the West Riding had its fair share of Liberals, such as Alfred Illingworth, who were hostile to Labour; however, the region also had some of the most radical reformers and advanced Liberals as MPs, such as Charles Trevelyan.[48] And what was true of the West Riding was generally true elsewhere.

Further, the trades unions were far from being united in support of Labour. Granted, a crucial breakthrough for Labour came when the leaders of the miners finally decided to affiliate with the Labour party in 1908. However, many of the rank-and-file were opposed to this and continued to support Liberal candidates at the 1910 general elections. For all that trades union membership mushroomed in the years before the war, this was not a self-sufficient reservoir of innate Labour support. Only one in three workers was unionized by 1914; when the unions held ballots on whether to affiliate with the Labour party, of the 420,000 members that voted 298,702 were in favour, with 125,310 against. Clearly, a majority favoured Labour – but not overwhelmingly: so ingrained was the Lib-Lab tradition.

Those historians who have emphasized Labour's strength before 1914 have argued that Labour would have achieved unprecedented electoral success at the anticipated general election of 1915, which would have been held had it not been for the suspension of party political conflict due to the outbreak of war in 1914. Yet, it was unlikely that Labour would have achieved many election victories in the 120–150 or so three-cornered contests that it was allegedly planning (latest estimates suggest that the figure was more like 60 candidates).[49] Since electoral conflict had been renewed between the Liberal and Labour parties in 1912, Labour finished last in every single by-election, even in the seats that it was defending. It is, therefore, hardly surprising that Ramsay MacDonald was negotiating with the Liberals for a new electoral pact in the years immediately before the outbreak of war. Throughout, MacDonald had 'wished to expand *within* the Progressive Alliance'.[50] In those constituencies that Labour held, there was a fear that, even though Liberal candidates had no likelihood of success if they stood, their intervention could split the progressive vote and prevent Labour from winning. This would most probably have played into the hands of the Conservative party. Of the three political parties, it was the Tories who stood to benefit the most from the anticipated general election.

On balance, therefore, it seems that the political realignment of the postwar years owed more to the war itself and its consequences than to any pre-1914 developments. The war years were catastrophic for the Liberal party. Wars were corrosive of Liberal values and beliefs such as toleration, pacific internationalism and civil liberty – especially 'total' warfare, which required the mobilization of the nation along collectivist lines. Such was the challenge presented by war that the Liberal party split in 1916 when Lloyd George, who was pressing for a more efficient prosecution of the war effort, ousted the cautious Asquith and replaced him as Prime Minister of the coalition government. The failure to patch up these differences, and the decision of Lloyd George and his supporters to continue the wartime coalition with the Conservative party into peacetime, allied to the ideological battering Liberalism had suffered, gave the Labour party its chance at the 1918 general election. Labour candidates, with some justification, were able to argue that Lloyd George, through his decision to extend the life of the coalition, had shifted the Liberal party to the right, thus betraying the radical Liberal tradition: an argument that clearly resonated with many of the ex-Liberal activists, who defected to Labour at the 1918 general election.

The war years were far from being uniformly beneficial to the Labour party, as the early divisions between the pacifists and those who supported the war illustrate. However, the party's inclusion in the wartime coalition government gave its leaders valuable experience and the creation of a more uniform nationalized political culture organized along collectivist lines undoubtedly benefited Labour. The party's continued rise was by no means inevitable: despite the enfranchisement of all adult males in 1918, the Labour party never polled more than 38 per cent of the popular vote between 1918 and 1935. Further, the Liberal and Labour parties had similar levels of aggregate electoral support up to and including the general election of 1923. Indeed, in suburban and rural parts of the United Kingdom the Liberal party was still a significant – and, in some cases, the dominant – electoral force in the interwar years. But, for all the many twists and turns in the road to 1945 – the year of Labour's first landslide electoral victory – by 1918 the Labour party had nevertheless become a serious contender for political power. The battle to crack the established two-party system had been fought and won: the battle for supremacy had now begun.

Chapter 9: The Decline of Liberalism and the Rise of Labour II: The Debate

One of the leitmotifs of this book has been the way hindsight has often given rise to narratives that have distorted the past. Nowhere is this more evident than in relation to the political change that resulted in Labour replacing the Liberals as the main party of the left. Formulaic and teleological narratives of 'rise' and 'decline' have been the main culprits here. Just as teleological narratives of the 'forward march of Labour' are difficult to reconcile with the uneven and often poor electoral performance of the Labour party, so is the Liberal party's revival after the split over Home Rule in 1886, culminating in the Liberal landslide victory at the 1906 general election, at odds with notions of interminable decline.

There has been an almost habitual historical obsession with constantly assessing the relative strengths of the two parties. As a result of this, an unrealistic set of expectations and assumptions have been projected onto both of the parties. With the exception of a few voices, no Edwardian Liberal in 1914 would have foreseen their future collapse and replacement by the Labour party. It is also unlikely that anyone in the Labour party in 1914 would have predicted the election of a Labour government ten years later. Looking back on Labour's prospects in 1914 from the vantage point of the early 1930s, Philip Snowden recalled how it 'looked as if the Party was destined to remain a mere group, depending for what representation it had upon the goodwill of the Liberals'.[1] Notwithstanding all the debates about the electoral strength and ideological coherence of the Edwardian Labour party, could anyone have realistically expected such a newly established party to have been more successful? Granted, there were discontented, critical voices in the party, but this hardly made the Labour party exceptional. And if those debates were a little more fractious than was the norm, then this was only to be expected from a party that was still finding its political feet. In addition, it should be pointed out that the Labour party was actually more of a coalition than either of the two established political parties. What emerged in 1906 was a federation, an alliance of various organizations and groupings: the Social Democratic Federation (SDF), the Independent Labour party (ILP) and the Fabians. And, for a party in such a position, it is remarkable that they were able to mount a serious challenge to the established parties at all. Labour had achieved that which has eluded so many other would-be political parties: cracking the two-party system. Furthermore, given the constitutional tradition out of which Labour emerged, it seems unfair to criticize the Labour party (and the working class) for its reformism and lack of commitment to revolutionary socialism.[2] The projection of that unrealistic expectation was the work of Marxist historians, who, having failed to find evidence of their idealist view of revolutionary class consciousness, resorted to a range of largely unnecessary sophisticated arguments to explain the gap between theory and practice.[3] In reality, what had emerged by 1914 was a composite Labour party, underpinned by an alliance between the trades unions and pragmatic ethical socialists, although not without its right- and left-wing critics.[4]

The Liberal party also had its difficulties; the problem here, however, is that historians have often been guilty of interpreting the party through a lens tinted with the fading glow of Gladstonian Liberalism. Such were the heights scaled by this Liberalism in the mid-Victorian decades, according to this view, that there was only one way for the Liberal party to go. As argued in Chapters 4 and 5, Liberalism never really commanded such heights. However, there is no reason why the downsizing of Gladstonian Liberalism should necessarily lead one to locate the origins of Liberal decline in Gladstone's time or in the immediate aftermath of his retirement in 1894. In many localities, the Liberal party was a more coherent and positive force in the 1890s than traditionally believed – evidence that the divisions within the party leadership and vying of activists to have their particular 'fad' prioritized made, at best, small dents in popular Liberalism.[5] As for the party's allegedly dismal performance at the 1900 'Khaki' general election, when the Liberals were divided between pro-Boer sympathizers and Liberal Imperialists, the party still polled 44.6 per cent of the popular vote (although it did leave a large number of seats uncontested). Neither is it necessary to resort to grand claims about the party's elaboration of a New Liberalism to explain its revival.

Revisionist work on both Gladstonian and post-Gladstonian Liberalism has brought into sharper focus the continued existence and popularity of what historians of the Edwardian Liberal party term 'old-style' traditional Liberalism.[6] This was underlined by the 1906 general election, when the Liberal party was swept back into power on a traditional ticket of 'free trade'; Nonconformist-led outrage at the Conservative government's tacit approval of the use of indentured Chinese labour in South African Mines; and its Education Act, which had provided state funding for Anglican schools. Most historians are now agreed that there was little evidence of any New Liberalism at the 1906 general election; when social reform was mentioned at all, it appeared way down on the election addresses.[7] The general elections of 1910 were also fought out on the battleground of traditional Liberalism, thanks largely to the House of Lords' refusal to pass Lloyd George's 'People's Budget' in 1909. This enabled the Liberal party to mobilize the people in an epic struggle of Gladstonian proportions against the Peers who, it was argued, had selfishly rejected a budget that had been designed to finance important welfare reforms through the introduction of graduated income tax, death duties and other 'super' taxes on the very wealthy. Free trade versus protection also dominated the two general elections of 1910.

Thus, opposition to new forms of 'Old Corruption', hostility to various exploitative middlemen, the electorate's preoccupation with the moral character of politicians, and the moral basis of politics continued to inform popular Liberalism in the years until the First World War.[8] To take the example of free trade, Frank Trentmann has recently argued that this was ultimately a moral issue, rather than one based on the rational economic self-interest of securing cheap food – although it would be unduly naïve to suggest that this was not a factor. For popular Liberals, free trade was the hallmark of the disinterested state that refused to recognize and reward distinctive interests. Thus, free trade came to symbolize social justice, fairness, prudence and pacific internationalism (the unrestricted flow of goods between nations, it was argued, promoted peace; tariffs incited rivalry and conflict). Protectionism was the moral antithesis of free trade, as it was based on a naked appeal to individual and national economic selfishness. The moral dimension of free trade explains why Liberals of all shades were so vitriolic in the denunciation of tariff reform. Indeed, Liberals had few reservations about appealing to the emotions of the electorate by deploying crude national stereotypes about life in protectionist countries such as Germany, where it was claimed that the workers were forced to live on a diet of black bread (as opposed to the much coveted British white loaf), horsemeat and even dog. This defence of free trade symbolically empowered the citizen-consumer as the ethical custodian of the wider public interest, the bulwark against selfishness and unfair taxation. Popular Liberals were the self-restrained, morally upright and sober antithesis to the over-indulging and hedonistic popular Tory.[9]

As the renewed attacks on feudalism and the Liberal party's prioritizing of land reform in the years before the First World War illustrates, opposition to the idle, parasitical rich was still a central component in popular Liberalism.[10] Only recently have historians begun to rediscover the genuinely radical antecedents of this Liberalism.[11] Prior to this, it was remarkable how often historians of the Edwardian Liberal party not only equated old Liberalism with radicalism, but also presented that radicalism as outdated and increasingly unpopular, a mere fig-leaf for narrow middle-class interests.[12] Once again, it is evident how class-based paradigms have obscured the populist dimensions of Liberal ideology and rhetoric. The fact that the Edwardian Liberal party and the Labour party was shaped by this radical tradition and continued with the crusade against 'Old Corruption' shows just how resonant and popular that tradition still was in the early twentieth century, itself a reflection of the continuing political and social power exercised by the aristocracy.[13]

This is not to suggest that New Liberalism had no impact on Edwardian popular politics. The problem with many studies that have claimed there was no evidence of New Liberalism is that – as the Marxists with class consciousness – they look for a pure, idealist form of the phenomenon, unsurprisingly find it missing and conclude its absence. As the work of Duncan Tanner, Pat Thane and, more recently, James Moore has shown, the influence of New Liberalism was far more subtle than this and often fused with older Liberal concerns to produce a broad spectrum of overlapping, but in some ways competing, progressive positions that Tanner describes as Radical, Centrist and New Liberal. Each of these groupings, to varying degrees and in different ways, represented a challenge to the forces of Liberal conservatism.[14] The extent to which New Liberalism and the progressive alliance were undermined by class-based tensions is the subject of the next section.

The Rise of Class

Conventional interpretations of the rise of Labour and the decline of the Liberal party revolved around the paradigm of class-based politics and, in particular, whether a nationalized political culture organized along class lines had arrived by the Edwardian period.[15] To outline: following the 'remaking' of a relatively coherent and united working class from the 1880s, the rise of independent labour politics was virtually inevitable. This 'remaking' was expressed in the growth of trades unionism, co-operatives and a distinctive working-class lifestyle that was physically and culturally separate from, and increasingly in conflict with, the middle class. Conflict in the workplace over wages, and the erosion of skill and authority (due to foreign competition and further mechanization) previously enjoyed by labour aristocrats transcended the existing divisions between skilled and unskilled workers.[16] Allied to this was the widening gap between employer and employee consequent on the widespread replacement of smaller, family run units of production with large, impersonal factories run by absentee boards of directors. This change in the size of business units was corrosive of the factory paternalism that had been one of the structural props of the mid-Victorian social harmony.[17] For those workers not embroiled in workplace conflict, consciousness of class was felt no less in the wider community. This was due to greater residential segregation along class lines, declining social mobility, more uniform living standards and participation in a range of cultural activities – football, music halls, the eating of fish and chips – that were quickly establishing themselves as 'working class'. The outcome was an insular, defensive and, in many respects, conservative class-based identity.[18] The political manifestation of this was the creation of a Labour party in 1906 rooted in working-class consciousness and dedicated to ameliorating the harsh conditions of working-class life – an outcome that owed more to the tactical considerations of pragmatic trades unionists than to socialist ideology.[19] As a result, parties and the electorate polarized along class lines – transcending previous divisions based on religion, ethnicity and locality – between a middle-class Conservative party that was better equipped to defend propertied interests, and a working-class Labour party. The Liberal party, with its ideological aversion to representing class interests, went into interminable decline due to its inherent inability to reconcile the conflicting class-based interests of its core Nonconformist middle-class activists and wider working-class supporters.

The simplicity and totality of this rather circular argument proved very seductive to a generation of historians. As George Bernstein commented in an account that represented the apotheosis of the conventional wisdom, published in 1986: 'If class politics was coming, so was the decline of the Liberal Party – not imminently perhaps, but eventually and inevitably.'[20] The writing was on the wall by 1914, if not earlier. According to some interpretations, these structural changes had their origins in the 1880s, when the Liberal party began to alienate its propertied supporters, who defected to Conservatism in ever increasing numbers long before the party was faced with the problem of how to prevent the haemorrhaging of working-class support. Some historians have located the seeds of the party's destruction in 1886. Gladstone's policy of Home Rule, perceived as the latest in a long line of attacks on the propertied classes and the whig tradition of disinterested government, split the Liberals in two as the propertied classes took refuge in the arms of the Conservative party, through Liberal Unionism: a split from which the party never recovered.[21] According to this interpretation, on closer inspection the 'Liberal landslide' at the 1906 general election was a 'freak result' – as were the much reduced Liberal victories at the two 1910 general elections. The Liberals won simply by virtue of not being the Conservative party.[22]

Thus, the rise of class-based politics was well under way by 1914; it was only a matter of time before it caught up with the Liberal party. The Liberals were only kept alive artificially in the Edwardian years by an unexpected last flowering of traditional Liberal issues (free trade and 'peers versus people'), and by Labour's inability to remove the various obstacles that stood in its way. There can be little doubt that the Labour party suffered from acute financial hardship and organizational weakness (many of its potential working-class supporters lacked the time and money for political activism), a problem exacerbated by the adverse Osborne Judgment of 1909. This prohibited trades unions from raising money for political purposes (overturned partly in 1913). These financial pressures, however, were further eased in 1911 when pay for MPs was finally introduced. Labour, it seems, was also handicapped by structural constraints, nowhere more so than in the restrictive nature of the franchise, which deprived many of Labour's 'natural' working-class supporters of the vote.[23] While some historians denied that class politics spelt inevitable doom for Liberalism by showing how the elaboration of a New Liberal agenda of social reform and a progressive pact with the infant Labour party enabled the party to maintain its working-class support,[24] few questioned the rise of class politics itself. Some questioned the timing of its arrival, but not its eventual triumph.[25]

The Forward March of Labour Halted

Much of this traditional interpretation has been overturned in the last 20 years. Even if one accepts that the working class was becoming more socially, economically and culturally unified than it had been in the mid-Victorian decades – which is, at least, debatable – it does not follow that this translated into a distinctive working-class consciousness, let alone a relatively uniform class-based political identity. Empirically, the class-based interpretation of the rise of Labour and the decline of the Liberals simply does not square with the evidence. As Duncan Tanner and Jon Lawrence have shown, Labour was often *least* successful in those seats that were the most heavily industrialized and proletarianized; that is, in those very places where theory and assumption would suggest that Labour should have been most successful.[26] Such places were, in any case, few and far between since, contrary to the predictions of Marx and Engels, the economy was still dominated by small specialized workshops in which skilled labour remained important, rather than by factories with a proletarian workforce.

As for the 'franchise factor', this can only be made to explain so much. As Tanner has shown, the registration process did not systematically and overwhelmingly discriminate against the working class who, in any case, dominated the electorate after 1867, and more so after 1884.[27] He concluded that if there was a bias in terms of who was excluded, it was young, single working- *and* middle-class men who lodged (the lodger franchise being notoriously difficult to claim and maintain).[28] To buttress his argument that Labour was not handicapped before the war by low levels of enfranchisement, Tanner – drawing on earlier work by Michael Hart – showed in a later study that '[t]he areas of lowest enfranchisement before 1914 (and therefore the areas where new male voters were most numerous in 1918) were not necessarily the areas where Labour was most successful in post-war parliamentary elections'.[29] Clearly, many younger, single men were disfranchised before 1914, the majority of whom were probably working class. Some of these younger disfranchised men, unencumbered with long-standing attachments to the established parties reinforced by years of voting, might have been more inclined to vote Labour, as argued by Michael Childs.[30] However, this would have been insufficient to bring about a decisive shift in the electoral map of Edwardian Britain had they been enfranchised. For one thing, capturing the votes of a single group – in this case the young, defined as the 21–30 age cohort – was never going to bring about overall electoral victory. In terms of other ways in which the electoral system disadvantaged Labour, Keith Laybourn has argued that the Labour party could not afford anywhere near the number of full-time agents employed by the Liberal and Conservative parties.[31] This may have been so, but the extent to which this actually worked against Labour is not clear. Consider, in areas where some form of the progressive alliance was in existence, it was just as much in the interests of the Liberal party to ensure that Labour supporters were entered onto the electoral register. Thus, it is quite probable that Liberal registration agents acted as a surrogate for the Labour party in many constituencies.

As the continuing electoral success of the Liberal and Conservative parties suggests, one of the reasons for the Labour party's frequently poor electoral performance was precisely because the working class continued to be divided in its political loyalties. For those who were unionized, many were still loyal to the Liberal party – a reflection of the long-standing tradition of 'Lib-Lab' politics. The great reforming tradition of 'Liberty, retrenchment and reform', supplemented in some places by the New Liberalism, retained the loyalty of the working class. The New Liberalism and the progressive alliance supplied the means with which to prevent the rise of class-based politics and, while that alliance was prone to fracture, it is overly simplistic to reduce this to evidence of class tension.

John Belchem has argued that the Liberal-Radical formula of uniting the productive classes against the idle was outdated by this stage, as it ignored the 'increasing unity of propertied interests in late-Victorian and Edwardian Britain' under the protective banner of Conservatism.[32] As Chapters 6 and 7 illustrated, the Liberal party still retained a sizeable middle-class support base. Middle-class villa Liberalism was a significant electoral force until 1910, and beyond. Certainly, the Liberals seem to have suffered from a pronounced swing towards the Tories in middle-class seats in 1910. However, the first time the Liberals had won most of these seats was in 1906, so the loss of them hardly represented a seismic shift in middle-class political loyalties. In any case, it seems that this swing was mainly confined to the south; there were few dents in northern and eastern business Liberalism, which remained a significant electoral force into the interwar years, especially in the medium-sized and smaller towns of Lancashire and the West Riding and in such places as Norwich, Leicester and Sunderland.[33] It would also be wrong to dismiss this middle-class Liberalism as a fig leaf for a penny-pinching and selfish municipal ratepayer politics. As James Moore has shown in a study of the Manchester middle class, the suburban middle class often looked to a progressive collectivist Liberalism to provide the urban community with the necessary amenities, financed out of the rates and the profits of municipal enterprises. What stands out, once again, was the blend of old and new Liberalism:

> Suburban Liberal programmes tended to combine traditional denominational and Nonconformist concerns with campaigns for improvements to local municipal services...Denominational loyalties and demands for the 'development' of suburbia meant that a large portion of the middle class remained loyal to the Liberal party and reinforced its moves towards a more Radical and collectivist municipal agenda.[34]

Middle-class Liberal businessmen were not always conservative opponents of Labour, as the progressive sympathies of the Cadbury and Rowntree families testify.[35] Some members of the middle class were active supporters of the ILP and the Labour party. Members of the professions, shopkeepers, shop assistants, clerks, commercial travellers and even employers of labour were, collectively, a significant element in the party's memberships.[36]

When it came to the Labour party, it was most electorally successful not when it espoused the politics of class hatred but, rather, when it was closest to the radical tradition of uniting the productive classes against the idle rich, a tradition that lived on in ethical socialism. In an early declaration of the ILP's aims, the trades unionist Tom Mann (who would become a communist in later life) defined them as 'the establishment of a state of Society where living upon unearned incomes shall be impossible for any but the physically enfeebled'.[37] In contrast to its political opponents – who, Labour claimed, governed in the interests of land and property – Labour represented the interests of the people as a whole. Socialism had something to offer everyone. As Keir Hardie was at pains to emphasize: 'To the poor it offers release from the bondage of thankless toil and harassing poverty; to the middle class it promises freedom from tyranny of the market, and to the rich it holds out the hope of joy in life in exchange for the burden of property.'[38] In this respect, the Labour party's attitude towards class, especially the middle class, was remarkably similar to that of the Chartists. It was the exploitative, tyrannical and unproductive members of the middle class (grasping capitalists and lawyers) and aristocracy against which Labour defined itself. As Fred Jowett, Labour MP for Bradford West, told one of his audiences, the three evils were 'Rent, Interest, and Profits...three suckers' which have 'vampire-like fastened on this land of ours'.[39]

Even the socialism that was espoused by those on the left of the party, such as Keir Hardie and Philip Snowden, was rooted in and fused with this radical tradition. Their socialism was more ethical than economic, with its emphasis on morality, purity, justice, freedom, humanity and fraternal Christianity. As with many Labour activists, they took this from the Nonconformist culture in which they were steeped. Men like these carried over the politics of the moral passion that Gladstone had once so ably roused, and no one more so than Keir Hardie. In his autobiography, Snowden recalled Hardie as the seer and prophet of the movement:

> His speeches were not those of the politician, but of the man with a mission and a message. His fine, rugged appearance, his powerful

and resonant voice, the character of his popular addresses, brought
to one's imagination the old Hebrew prophets thundering forth
denunciation of the evils of their day and prophesying the coming
of a better time.[40]

It was no coincidence that Hardie, Snowden and Ramsay MacDonald
were opposed to industrial unrest and class warfare as a means
of resolving problems. In the words of the trades union and ILP
activist Ben Tillett, this was a politics for those who shouted ' "Glory,
Hallelujah" for the democracy', which he defined as 'the men and
women who love their children, love their country, love justice, and
love the God of humanity and the religion of humanity and purity and
truth'.[41] Similarly, Tom Mann, who came from an Anglican background
but was subsequently influenced by the teachings of the Quakers, boldly
stated that 'according to the standard of sound religion . . . no man shall
exploit another man'. This 'ethical or moral law' called 'for right relationships between all citizens, none taking advantage of another'.[42] For
Keir Hardie, socialism was underpinned by 'the great basic truth of
human equality; not that all are alike, but that all are to be equal, which
is a very different thing'.[43] For socialists, no less than for Conservatives,
society was conceived of as an organic whole.

   As this brief survey of ideology and rhetoric suggests, religion did
more to shape the emerging Labour movement than any Marxist or
even indigenous conception of class. For the many Labour activists
with religious backgrounds, socialism was merely applied Christianity.
Thus, in the 1880s and 1890s socialism and Christianity were seldom regarded as being incompatible, although the resulting blend
was invariably the outcome of a crisis of faith experienced by the
individual.[44] For some, socialism was an outgrowth of their Christianity
and, although a minority came to jettison religion for scientific socialism, most retained their faith. The antithesis between socialism and
Christianity was, for the most part, an invention of anxious, paranoid
and narrow middle-class minds.

   This blend of Christianity and socialism was institutionalized in the
Labour Church movement. This flourished briefly in the 1890s until
it was undermined by conflict between religious purists (who, like the
Socialist League before them, wanted to focus on making socialists) and
political activists (who wished to subordinate such lofty goals of making
socialists to electioneering and winning political power for the Labour
movement). The *raison d'être* of the Labour Church was broadly similar to that of the ILP: just as the established political parties had failed
to represent the interests of organized labour so, too, it was argued,
had the established churches. In an appropriately titled article in the

opening issue of *The Labour Prophet* – the organ of the Labour Church –
Philip Wickstead asked: 'Is the Labour Church a Class Church?'[45]
Wickstead's answer was a resounding 'no'. On the contrary, its purpose
was to bring about a fraternal union of all classes in which everyone
did 'work enough to provide the *means* for his own living', 'living a full
life, in fellowship with his fellow workers'. This was not only about providing the necessities of life, but also living life to the full through the
exercise of 'human faculties, knowledge, enjoyment, fellowship, love,
active interchange of thought and feeling with man, joyful communion
with nature and with God'. The members of the Labour Church movement were inspired to live by the example of Christ's life as a means to
spread joy and happiness in this life, and to focus on God's Kingdom
on earth rather than the other-worldliness of life beyond the grave,
as was the case with the established churches. As Keir Hardie contro-
versially announced, 'the reason why the Labour party to-day turns its
back upon the Church is because the Church has turned its back upon
Christ'.[46] The established churches had become the slaves of rich men.
In this respect, the Labour Church movement represented an attempt
to revert to the fundamental teachings of Christ; these, it was argued,
had been subordinated to the selfish pursuit of profit. To quote Hardie
again:

> Clearly, the modern system of wealth accumulation, which is rooted
> and grounded in land monopoly, usury, and the fleecing of the poor,
> finds no support in such teachings as are contained in the Old Tes-
> tament Scriptures... the Socialist who denounces rent and interest
> as robbery, and who seeks the abolition of the system which legalizes
> such, is in the true line of apostolic succession with the pre-Christian
> era prophets, with the Divine Founder of Christianity, and with those
> who for the first seven hundred years of the Christian faith main-
> tained even to the death the unsullied right of their religious faith to
> be regarded as the Gospel of the poor.[47]

The Labour Church movement was actually little concerned with
doctrinal controversy or sectarian rivalries, the absence of which –
allied to its fundamentalist Christianity – explains why Nonconformists,
Anglicans and even secularists could all be counted amongst the Labour
Church's membership.[48]

Perhaps the greatest single piece of evidence against the class interpretation of the rise of Labour is the party's inability or unwillingness
to appeal to all sections of the working class. Labour found it difficult
to attract the poorest sections of the working class. Appeals based on
the promise of a bountiful socialist future offered little to those who

were struggling in the present. Of course, it did not take long for the more practical Labour activists to realize that they would have to remedy the most pressing immediate social grievances before establishing socialism. For activists such as John Wheatley and Fred Jowett, the local architects of municipal socialism in their respective cities of Glasgow and Bradford, the 'passage to the Socialist City' was to be brought about 'by means of municipal trading, housing reform, municipal coal, municipal milk supply, and – education'.[49] But what the eventual 'Socialist City' was to look like, or how it was to be brought about, was far from clear. However, the infant Labour party did not only run aground on the rocks of strategy and tactics. In many localities Labour was still faced with the challenge of legitimizing its claim to speak for the people, a claim that was not helped by the frequent condescending bewilderment that its activists often displayed towards the poor. An early example of this attitude was voiced by the Bradford *Labour Echo*, the organ of the ILP, in 1895 and is worth quoting at length:

> The South Ward is a Liberal anti-Labour ward. What we have to think about the position is very little. It is not from people such as those who are to be found in this locality that our emancipation will ever come. Socialism is a science of government. It requires intelligent men and women to grapple with its tenets and to look for such among the mass of unfortunate wretches who make the sum total of wretchedness in the South Ward is to look in vain. The very people for whom we are working and toiling are our worst opponents – bitter and intolerant, unsympathetic and insolent, prone rather to live on charity than upon the rights of manhood and womanhood and if ever such places are captured at all, they must be captured from outside, for not until the death rate, the insanitation and the horrible mode of life are changed shall we ever see the South Ward of Bradford taking an intelligent interest in the affairs mostly concerning it. This is no skit but a sorrowful admission of the plain facts as I see them.[50]

As the work of Jon Lawrence has shown, these attitudes and assumptions were an enduring feature of the Labour party's early years, and their persistence was one of the reasons why Labour's electoral performance was so poor before 1914. As Lawrence shows in relation to Wolverhampton, not only did a significant proportion of Labour activists live apart from those they sought to represent, this gap was also widened by their constant desire to 'improve' working men, in marked contrast to the Tories whose appeal was based on their celebration of the people's pleasures and an acceptance of the people for who they were.[51]

In towns with sizeable Irish populations, Labour's failure to appeal to the poorest sections of the working class could assume an ethnic dimension. Evidence suggests that most Irish electors remained loyal to the Liberal party on the grounds that a Liberal government was far more likely to confer Home Rule on Ireland. But this was not the only reason. As Steven Fielding has shown, some of the political representatives of Irish Nationalists in Britain subscribed to the wider radical Liberal agenda and supported the progressive alliance with organized labour.[52] While a small, but growing number of Irish working-class Catholics became more sympathetic to the Labour party, few were willing to abandon Liberalism outright and transfer their loyalties; hence the periodic frustration of Labour leaders towards the Irish. Keir Hardie, for one, could never understand why Irish workers in Britain put Home Rule before their economic emancipation.

Labour's ability to construct broad-based coalitions of support was also limited by its equivocal attitude towards women. Although women could not vote in parliamentary elections, they could vote in municipal elections, be elected as Poor Law Guardians and to the School Board and, from 1907, women could stand as local councillors. On the one hand, Labour had much to offer women: its democratic and egalitarian rhetoric of freedom and justice for all could be gender-inclusive, encompassing the rights of downtrodden women. Women were often to the fore in the early years of the socialist movement, as it was widely believed that socialism had the potential to bring about their own emancipation. The Women's Social and Political Union (WSPU) – which soon achieved notoriety for its militant deeds, undertaken as a means to bring about women's suffrage by enlisting the support of working-class women – started out in 1903 as a 'ginger group' within the ILP. As with the ILP before it, the WSPU originated as both a reaction to attempts by the authorities to restrict freedom of assembly and free speech in public areas, a right that the WSPU had to continually fight for throughout the Edwardian years. In this respect, both movements bore the stamp of the popular radical tradition of the mass platform and the popular access campaigns of the nineteenth century. As Krista Cowman has shown, even after the WSPU became officially independent of any party-political affiliation in 1906, many of the WSPU's socialist members continued in their 'dual work for socialism and suffrage' and there continued to be strong links between the WSPU and the ILP.[53] For women such as Isabella O. Ford – a socialist and suffragist of national repute – who saw women's oppression as a product of capitalist exploitation, it made little sense to jettison their socialist loyalties. Both the Labour and women's movements 'sprang from the common evil of economic dependence'.[54]

For all these overlaps and parallels, there was also a good deal of gender prejudice running through Labour, especially amongst many of its trades union supporters who, as tenacious supporters of the 'male breadwinner wage', wanted women out of the workplace: as a source of cheap labour, they threatened the privileged status of better paid male labourers. Although women were incorporated into Labour's organizational infrastructure, in practice this did little to challenge the subordinate role of women in either the workplace or the home. The types of activities that ILP women performed also tended to reinforce the prevailing 'separate spheres' model, with women undertaking tasks that were seen as an extension of their domestic roles, such as organizing teas. And yet, as June Hannam has shown, such responsibilities accorded women a prominent role in the construction of a socialist culture through their organization of Sunday schools, trips and concerts, so crucial in the early years of the movement.[55] This ambivalent attitude towards women was also revealed in the Labour party's stance on women's suffrage. The logic of their own ideology and rhetoric pointed towards the need to support women's suffrage but, in practice, many Labour activists subordinated this to the wider need to enfranchise all adults – a stance that placed them at odds with the WSPU's strategy of enfranchising women on the same restrictive basis as it had been given to men in 1867 and 1884. There were few who shared Hardie, George Lansbury and Victor Grayson's support for what was, in effect, a female householder's franchise. In fact, mainstream Labour's lukewarm support for women's suffrage and its deferment towards the Liberal government's own less than enthusiastic stance was the occasion for a wider left-wing revolt against the Labour party's centralizing dictation and its subservience to the Liberal government. The highpoint of this revolt occurred when George Lansbury, Labour MP for Bow and Bromley, resigned his seats in 1912 and fought a by-election on a pro-suffragette platform.

Labour was most successful when it was closely identified, and in sympathy with, those it sought to represent. Take the example of Joseph Pointer, Labour MP for Sheffield Attercliffe between 1909 and 1914. Pointer, a local unemployed patternmaker, trades unionist and Labour Councillor, was able to fashion a community-based politics that united the people against the 'noble idlers', as he termed his opponents. It was no coincidence that Pointer emphasized the need for land reform: Lords Norfolk and Fitzwilliam owned large parts of Sheffield. His success, in the first instance, was due to the pressure that the local ILP placed on the National Executive to drop their choice of a carpetbagger and endorse Pointer. The National Executive surrendered to local pressure and, tellingly, Pointer was nominated in the open air by a show of hands at a meeting of some 250 local workers outside Attercliffe baths. Interestingly, Pointer also received official support from the SDF. This politics, grounded in the community, was underpinned by a highly developed organizational infrastructure (based on an ILP branch, a Labour Club and Institute) and a rich associational culture. When Pointer won the seat at a by-election in 1909, a crowd of 30,000 people celebrated his victory outside Sheffield Town Hall, singing the Red Flag and Edward Carpenter's *England Arise*. However, even Pointer's victory was the product of fortuitous circumstances: there were two rival Conservative candidates and the Liberals, who by this stage had a reputation for hostility towards organized labour, nominated an ineffectual carpetbagger. By way of comparison, it is instructive to note that, in the neighbouring Brightside constituency, Labour made little headway before 1914 due to the popularity of the progressive Liberal MP Tudor Walters.[56]

In some crucial respects, the left-wing critics of mainstream Labour were more in tune with the working class. In contrast to the moralizing disapproval of the likes of MacDonald and Snowden, left-wing critics such as Lansbury, Jowett and Grayson were far less critical of working-class culture and far more optimistic about its potential for bringing about socialism. A complementary current, identified by Martin Pugh, that fed into this tolerance for working-class vice and tapped into popular hostility to the moralistic preaching of the state came from a Conservative political tradition: this was fused by some into a 'Tory-socialist' politics.[57] Although this politics did not really take off until the interwar years, it had roots stretching back to the 1880s and 1890s. This could be seen in Blatchford's newspaper *The Clarion*, which blended politics and entertainment. A tory streak was also evident amongst those trades unionists sympathetic to tariff reform and who exhibited xenophobic attitudes, while a more diffuse conservatism could be seen in the popular patriotism and in enthusiasm for the monarchy and empire exhibited by many Labour supporters. An early example of Labour's ability to tap this Conservative political tradition occurred in parts of Lancashire, which was hardly surprising given that many Labour supporters were originally Tories, although, as we have seen, Labour did not always escape from the charge of moral earnestness, especially when it co-operated with like-minded Liberals. While the Liberals and the Labour activists who emerged from Liberal backgrounds were often shaped by a Nonconformist religious culture, many of these tory-socialists had Anglican and Catholic backgrounds, no doubt explaining their tolerance for popular vice. For the moment, this tory-socialism was confined to a few pockets, and it would take the experiences of two world wars before Labour succeeded in fully adapting to this Conservative political culture.

Ultimately, the continuing success of the Liberal party and Labour's limited electoral success was largely dependent on their respective abilities to relate their ideas and policies to the needs and interests of the electorate, and how effectively they built broad-based coalitions of electoral support. As Duncan Tanner has argued:

> The connection between economic conditions, the causes of those conditions and the political remedies which they [Labour] advocated was less clear to the majority of workers. There was no 'objective' social experience which was inevitably translated into a Labour allegiance by an increasingly class-minded electorate. The connection between social experience and political behaviour was something which had to be manufactured and maintained. Labour had not succeeded in making that connection before 1914 in such a way that it was a major threat to the older parties.[58]

If Labour had succeeded in finding the right marching tune before 1914, they were not yet marching to it in time.

Chapter 10: The Modernization of Popular Politics

By way of conclusion, this chapter will assess how far the framework and political culture outlined in Chapter 1 was subverted, revised and overturned between the 1832 Reform Act and the First World War. One school of historians has argued that this period witnessed the birth of a modern system of party politics in which 'political principle defined in national terms by the parties at Westminster took the place of the local, factional, and idiosyncratic concerns' that had hitherto characterized the system.[1] While this school of historians might disagree over the timing of this development, broad agreement exists about the factors responsible for this ultimately inevitable development: the Reform Acts of 1832, 1867 and 1884, the associated growth of centralized party machines and a burgeoning cheap daily press.[2] As more and more men had the vote, so the parties went to greater lengths to integrate them into their organizations.

In contrast to these conventional narratives, which interpreted such developments as progressive and empowering, revisionists have argued that they were little more than cynical attempts by the state to stifle what had been a genuinely participatory popular politics. This chapter subjects this debate to critical analysis. While this period witnessed the rise of a more homogenized political culture, little overall evidence exists to suggest that popular politics was either disciplined or disabled; and, although a more nationalized political framework was established, this framework was still sensitive to local issues and interests.

Standardizing the Franchise

Franchise reform, and its modernizing impact on party politics, was a crucial factor in bringing about a more uniform political system. The

161

ignition for this process was supplied by the 1832 Reform Act, which gave a substantial boost to partisanship. Partisanship, defined as consistent electoral support or involvement in the organizational apparatus of a political party, was clearly not *established* in 1832. As Frank O'Gorman has argued, 'before 1832 party attachments may have been less formal and more intermittent than they later became, but they were not noticeably less assertive nor less popular'.[3] What is clear, as John Phillips and Charles Wetherell have demonstrated through their statistical analyses of poll books, is that only the post-1832 electorate displayed long-term trends of partisan consistency over time (that is, voting for the same party), which contrasted with the randomness of the unreformed system.[4] It was this degree of consistency that was the hallmark of modern partisanship. One statistical measure Phillips and Wetherell used to illustrate this trend was the overall reduction in 'split' voting. Before and after 1832, many urban electors had two votes by virtue of their constituency returning two MPs to the House of Commons. This often meant that both political parties would each nominate two candidates. Thus, electors had two votes that they could use in one of four ways: by casting their two votes for the two candidates of one party (a 'straight'); by giving a single vote if a party fielded only one candidate (a partisan 'plump'), thus wasting the second vote; by casting one vote for one candidate of each party (a 'split'); or they could cast only one vote (a non-partisan 'plump') despite there being two candidates for a particular party. Phillips and Wetherell note the overall trend toward 'straight' voting and partisan 'plumping' after 1832. This leads them to conclude that the 1832 Reform Act, rather unintentionally, destroyed the old political world and replaced it with a modern electoral system based on rigid partisanship and clearly articulated political principle.

As has been shown by Philip Salmon, the registration clauses of the 1832 Reform Act were one of the main reasons for this rise in partisanship. Prior to 1832, voters had been relatively few, and the eligibility of those electors claiming the right to vote was checked when they actually voted. With the expansion of the electorate in 1832, it was felt that this already laborious process would no longer be practical, so a system of prior electoral registration was introduced. As we saw in Chapter 1, stringent criteria were to be met by those claiming the vote: those who qualified as owners or occupiers of property worth £10 had to be in possession of that property for at least one year, have paid all relevant taxes and not have been in receipt of poor relief. In addition, and this was the real struggle in terms of time and money, those on the electoral register had to renew their claim annually: failure to do so resulted in being struck off the register. Further, the voting lists were publicly displayed and any claimant had the right to challenge names on the list without having to state the nature of their objection. Anyone whose claim was challenged had to defend their qualification in the annual registration court before the revising barristers. These stringent criteria account for the slack take-up of the franchise in the immediate aftermath of 1832, and are the reasons why the political parties subsequently assumed control over registration procedure. As we saw in the chapters on popular Liberalism and Conservatism, attending to the contentious business of registering votes necessitated the establishment of local Conservative and Liberal associations, and this explains why so many were established, or re-established, on a semi-permanent basis in the wake of 1832. Thus, the complexities and cost of registering a vote fostered partisanship by encouraging voters to ally themselves with one of the two political parties who very quickly began to permeate all levels of urban politics after 1832. With the establishment of many elected Town Councils under the terms and conditions of the 1835 Municipal Corporations Act, partisan politics increased in the council chamber due, in part, to the overlap between the parliamentary and municipal franchise: the electoral registers for both were compiled simultaneously. Many of those who qualified for the parliamentary franchise also qualified for the municipal franchise (although the latter was often more restrictive than the former), and partisan voting could be just as evident in choosing town councillors as it could be for MPs.[5]

The 1832 Reform Act therefore 'profoundly altered the legal and constitutional framework of political activity on the ground' and the 'franchise became a more permanent and personal possession, which was defined on a national basis by law'.[6] Thus, under the combined impact of the polarizing effects of national political issues (notably parliamentary reform) – the popular resonance of which was stimulated by the frequency of general elections in the 1830s and the local organizational drive unleashed by the registration clauses of the Reform Act – the electorate became unprecedentedly partisan after 1832. Perhaps more significant was that the popular experience of electoral politics began to change. As Salmon argues, these legal and constitutional changes 'encouraged voters to think of themselves as individuals, critical agents, stimulating their sense of self-importance and the notion of inviolate electoral rights'.[7] These changes were of a permanent nature and withstood the relatively apathetic mid-Victorian years, during which time general elections were less frequent. As new studies have made clear, less frequent general elections did not necessarily weaken partisanship. The annual registering of voters, canvassing, participation in local political organizations, municipal elections and the growth of the press all encouraged people to regard themselves as partisans, irrespective of whether a general election took place.[8]

In creating a more recognizably 'modern' political system, 1832 was far more significant than the Second Reform Act of 1867. Conventionally, historians used to interpret 1867 as the moment when modern political parties emerged: mass parties that attempted to permeate all aspects of their members' lives.[9] Yet, as the chapters on popular Conservatism – and, to a lesser extent, on popular Liberalism – revealed, such 'parties of social integration' were hardly novel features by 1867. Unlike 1832, 1867 did not create a new political structure; rather, it was the scale of popular participation and the attempts to organize it that increased. Hundreds of associations and clubs were established, but the type of organization had been pioneered in the aftermath of 1832. As for the franchise, notwithstanding its dramatic expansion, it could be argued that the 1867 Reform Act actually represented a significant step backwards from a uniform national electoral structure, due to the ways it introduced or compounded the complexities and local idiosyncrasies surrounding electoral law, which were only partially corrected by subsequent legislation.[10]

The Third Reform Act proved to be as 'modernizing' as its 1832 predecessor. Gladstone certainly took this view, and his Chancellor of the Exchequer, Hugh Childers, went even further – perhaps too far – when he remarked that it was 'the largest Constitutional Change since the Revolution of 1688'.[11] The Third Reform Act created a constitutional framework based on the notion of equal voting rights for the four nations of the UK. For the first time, there was to be a uniform franchise across boroughs and counties, and across the United Kingdom; previously Scotland and Ireland had been dealt with in separate legislation and had distinct franchises, as did the English counties and boroughs. The widespread introduction of single-member constituencies also represented a constitutional departure. It was argued that the creation of single-member constituencies in the past had been unavoidable and largely ad hoc. Those that had been created in 1832 were 'by reason of one Member being taken away from double-Member constituencies ... and by reason of a single Member being given to such new constituencies as were not entitled to a greater share in representation'.[12] Now, it was proposed to introduce them virtually wholesale by carving up hitherto unified boroughs and counties. Single-member constituencies substantially reduced the scope for parties to compromise by sharing the representation, as had often been the practice in many constituencies. As result, the Redistribution Act acted as a booster to partisanship, by making contested elections more common.[13]

Perhaps the most far-reaching and modernizing change associated with the Third Reform Act was the shift away from 'interests' to 'population' as the basis for participation in the national political process. As the *Manchester Courier* tellingly observed, 'For the first time in our history it has been openly proposed to base the Constitution upon numbers.'[14] No longer would 'interests' be entitled to representation that was grossly disproportionate to their numerical size. This shift was registered in the stipulation that population was to be proximately equalized across the constituent divisions within boroughs, thereby reducing significantly the disparity that had hitherto existed in the ratio between MPs and their constituents. Consequently, this represented a serious challenge to the legitimacy of 'virtual representation'.

Political Communication and the Rise of Party

Democratization and modernization used to be interpreted as different sides of the same coin; the former was evidence of the latter, and vice versa. The standard textbook narrative of nineteenth-century British politics was the whiggish celebration of the rise of democracy. Yet, as we saw in Chapter 1 in relation to the franchise, some revisionist historians have inverted this narrative. The most assertive and controversial statement of this position is James Vernon's *Politics and the People*.[15] Vernon argues that rigidly controlled party caucuses, the secret ballot, indoor 'ticketed' meetings (the assumption being that tickets were only distributed to known supporters) and the proliferation of cheap partisan newspapers were part of an insidious attempt to undermine the open, libertarian crowd politics of the street. In short, we are told that the nineteenth century witnessed 'the closure of democratic political forms', both in terms of the nature of political practice and the sorts of people who were permitted to participate in it. Vernon has made an important contribution to the historiography – although he has undoubtedly exaggerated the disabling and disciplining functions of these processes, as more recent work has shown.

Take Vernon's argument about the undermining of crowd politics and how this disempowered the unenfranchised masses. He argues that the first major curtailment came with the 1832 Reform Act. This stipulated that constituencies had to provide at least one polling booth for every 600 electors; previously, many had only one central polling place on the hustings. Vernon claims that the latter state of affairs allowed those without the vote to exert maximum influence on the electors by virtue of their concentrated intimidating presence. The proliferation of polling places throughout constituencies 'represented a considerable set-back, for by dispersing the crowd at the central hustings it significantly reduced their collective power to regulate and intimidate their enfranchised neighbours'.[16] Possibly so, but one needs to weigh these 'popular' losses with participatory gains. The geographical dispersal of polling places facilitated participation by reducing the distance electors had to travel to cast their vote. Previously, this had often been a costly affair, both in time and money, especially in county constituencies. It is probable that one of the knock-on effects of providing more polling booths was increased voter turnout at elections, by making it easier to vote.

What of the spread of cheap partisan newspapers and the introduction of the secret ballot in 1872? Vernon argues that these innovations took politics off the street and into the privacy of the home (by means of the press) and the polling booth. Further, these developments paralleled a shift that was taking place in the realms of political communication in which print was replacing oral and visual media, thereby disadvantaging the illiterate. To take the first of these, the spread of cheap newspapers: if print was such a restricting medium, then it is difficult to explain why working-class radicals campaigned for the abolition of the 'taxes on knowledge' (the legal and financial restrictions that had been imposed on the press by the government) without resorting to tired accusations of 'false consciousness'. These restrictions were designed to suppress radical newspapers by increasing the stamp duty on newspapers to fourpence in 1815 (the intention being to make them too expensive for the working class) and by reinforcing the laws against blasphemous and seditions publications in 1819 (thus rendering publishers more liable to prosecution and imprisonment). The radicals fought a long and bitter campaign to defy these restrictions through the 'war of the unstamped' in the 1830s (the illegal publishing of cheap newspapers; cheap by virtue of not adding the statutory government tax to the price of the newspaper). They also campaigned to end these restrictions through the Society for the Diffusion of Useful Knowledge in the 1830s, the Newspaper Stamp Abolition Committee (1849), and the Association for the Promotion of the Repeal of the Taxes on Knowledge (1851). Stamp duty was lowered to one penny in 1836, but the duty was not completely repealed until 1855; the last of the restrictions was only finally removed in 1869. The removal of these restrictions, allied to technological changes that speeded up production and dissemination, made the newspaper the dominant medium of political communication by the end of the nineteenth century.

It is difficult to measure how far the ascendancy of print eroded the public and collective character of oral and visual politics, as argued by Vernon. The spread of cheap newspapers undoubtedly enabled an increasing number of the literate working class to purchase their own newspaper, giving them the potential to read them in their own homes. But the extent to which cheap newspapers served the intentions of placing 'as much distance as possible between the oral and the literate, and between one politically conscious working man and another' is far from clear. The implied intention is that it was to undermine the long-established tradition of working men clubbing together to buy a newspaper and for it to be read aloud, discussed and debated in the pub or coffee house.[17] Even if this had been so, it is virtually impossible to quantify the effect. What is clear is that an oral and communal culture persisted down to at least the end of the nineteenth century, partly because the pub remained an important venue for working men, despite the moralizing efforts of Liberal reformers. For example, trades union branches and friendly societies were often based at pubs. Similarly, Marc Brodie's study of politics in the East End of London has shown how this oral culture thrived in the lodging houses and among the street-sellers in the late-Victorian and Edwardian period.[18] Vernon himself concedes that there was no linear and dramatic shift from an oral–visual culture to one based on the printed written word. On the contrary, as James Thompson has demonstrated through his work on political posters, there was an increase in the volume of visual material at the turn of the last century, as political organizations began to produce an unprecedented amount of visual propaganda.[19] What stands out throughout this period is the interdependencies of oral, visual and printed culture: visual material often incorporated text (such as banners and handbills), and vice versa. Indeed, some of the political street literature from the early nineteenth century demanded a relatively high level of literacy.

Vernon also contrasts what he sees as the elasticity, inclusiveness and empowering nature of oral and visual culture with the restricting, exclusive and disempowering nature of print. In this reading, the widespread existence of outdoor meetings and processions, and the local and communal production of banners, placards, effigies and other iconography was inclusive and empowering, much of it being made by the community. This 'popular, flexible, and formulaic oral and visual' culture contrasted with printed material, as this was usually the product of a single author, centrally produced and 'imposed fixed, verbatim meanings'.[20] This juxtaposition exaggerates the empowering potential of oral and visual culture, and underestimates the empowering effect of print. Not wishing to trivialize what was clearly an important part of popular culture: how empowering was it to make a banner or display cockades and ribbons at elections (the display of which was, in theory, restricted by legislation)?[21] Further, it could be argued that oral and visual culture was so open-ended and polyphonic that it collapsed under the weight of the multiplicity of meanings, thus rendering it powerless.

As for print, the act of reading and writing promotes political participation by providing those with these skills access to the information upon which the exercise of power is based. As literacy was on the rise during the nineteenth century, this information was being made accessible to a wider audience. The press, by reporting speeches and voting divisions in the House of Commons, supplied the means for constituents to monitor the activities of their political representatives – and potentially to censure them, either through the letters columns or, subsequently, at the ballot box. The changing nature of newspapers also facilitated this. At mid-century, the main function of the press was to educate. This meant that 'views' rather than news dominated. From the 1880s, the competitive pressures of commercialization undermined the educative role of the press. The emphasis shifted away from views to news, at least in the popular press: information sold newspapers, not lengthy moralizing editorials. Similarly, this now meant that newspapers spent more time trying to reflect, rather than create, public opinion, and incorporating the views of the masses. This might well have come at the price of 'dumbing down' (by appealing to the emotions rather than to reason) and less discussion of political issues, but at least it reduced the power of the press to act as an instrument of social control, such as that had ever existed. Politicians came to view the press as the voice of the electorate, and were doubtful that it could be used to mould public opinion.[22] As for the reception of the messages contained in the press, the reading masses were far from being the passive and uncritical bearers of dominant discourse. Given that Vernon has been so heavily influenced by poststructuralism, with its emphasis on the instability of meanings, it is ironic that he plays down the potential for readers to subvert the meaning of texts. Finally, although a *single* text might be the result of one author,[23] some print forms brought a range of texts together written by different people, such as newspapers and periodicals, and, in the case of newspapers, provided an opportunity for readers to contribute through letters columns. In short, print was, and is, a more dialectic and inclusive medium than Vernon argues.

Turning to the secret ballot: even if one accepts that these developments represented losses for the largely male non-electors of the hustings and nomination crowds, not only did it allow voters to exercise their independence with relative impunity, the very act of domesticating and privatizing popular politics also represented gains for another significant group of popular political actors: women. Although the illiterate (who were declining in number anyway) were disadvantaged by print replacing oral forms of political expression and protest, access to print was not as gender-exclusive as the male dominated election crowd. The partisan press went to great lengths to court and cater for a female readership, especially from the 1880s, and there is no reason to assume that women were any less politically aware than men.[24] It was not only middle-class women who gained from these developments. Rooting politics more firmly in the home had the effect of augmenting the importance of door-to-door electoral canvassing. As Matthew Cragoe has recently shown, canvassing provided women from all classes with many opportunities to become involved in elections. Candidates and their supporters deliberately targeted women for the assumed influence they exerted over their husbands – an influence that might well have increased due to the secret ballot breaking the coercive power of male non-electors. Many women came to regard the vote 'as a piece of family property'.[25] Nevertheless, as Cragoe observes, the secret ballot not only shielded a man's vote 'from the gaze of his landlord, employer, or co-religionist, but also from his wife'.[26] More generally, though, the canvass afforded an opportunity for popular, albeit informal, participation in the electoral process. By the late nineteenth century, women were not only those being canvassed; many of the canvassers were themselves women. The Corrupt Practices Act of 1883 had left the parties with little choice but to rely on unpaid volunteers to undertake canvassing, registration and leafleting – routine work that was increasingly undertaken by women.

For all the participatory gains afforded by these developments, it would be wrong to exaggerate the shift towards a privatized, domesticated and disciplined politics. Parties continued to employ a range of traditional electoral practices that legitimized their claims to represent the people: holding meetings outdoors (rather than indoors), acceptance of what Jon Lawrence describes as the 'politics of disruption' (such as heckling and disorderly behaviour by the crowd), and by demonstrating physical bravery.[27] Platform politics was a test of manliness; to avoid the platform was, in the eyes of the crowd, to forfeit legitimacy.[28] Frank Trentmann has shown how the Edwardian free traders resorted to traditional methods of political mobilization such as outdoor meetings.[29] As with the radical hostility to formalized party-politics, this open political culture was more pervasive and enduring than the 'rise of party' narrative suggests. Further, the secret ballot might well have represented attempts to regulate and sanitize the conduct of elections, but intention did not always translate into effect. Although instances of drunken and disorderly behaviour at elections were declining by the late nineteenth century, election contests could still be rowdy affairs, and not just in the provincial backwaters.[30] For example, there were riots between free traders and protectionists at the 1910 general elections.[31] Thus, one should not exaggerate either the rapidity or extent of the changes brought about by the secret ballot: the pre-election canvass still took place, candidates continued to address public meetings, and some still demanded a show of hands at nomination-style meetings.[32]

It would, however, be wrong to assume that, where popular politics did move indoors, it was either inherently rational and respectable or de-politicized. To take the example of working men's clubs, it used to be assumed that their rise in the mid-Victorian years symbolized the parallel emergence of an aspirational, improving and initially politically moderate – and subsequently de-politicized – working class.[33] But, as Tony Taylor has demonstrated in a reassessment of metropolitan club life, this does not square with the small, but influential, number of radical political clubs that kept alive an underworld of 'conspiracy, discontent and subversive excess',[34] originally associated with a period from the early nineteenth century until at least the late nineteenth century.

Despite growing partisanship amongst the electorate, little evidence can be found to suggest that parties succeeded in disciplining and controlling voters. There was a powerful undercurrent of anti-party sentiment in the late Victorian and Edwardian years, and, although it did little to stem the growth of partisanship, it made parties far more inclusive and responsive to popular interests. Electoral success went to those candidates who made serious attempts to construct broad-based coalitions of support that represented the interests of as many electors as possible. In conventional historiography, it was urban political elites – through economic, social and political power – that instilled partisanship in the masses.[35] However, revisionist work has made it clear that the power of local urban elites and 'modernized' political parties to control the electorate was heavily circumscribed.[36]

The limits to partisanship were also evident in the survival of the eighteenth-century culture of electoral independence. The powerful anti-party sentiment that pervaded Victorian popular politics represented a reworking and updating of the eighteenth-century 'country-party' ideology and the associated culture of electoral independence outlined in Chapter 1. Although the mid- to late Victorian years saw the re-emergence of parliamentary reform and other momentous political issues, there remained considerable electoral value in appealing to civic ideologies of electoral independence, protecting local rights and privileges, and in proclaiming one's manly independence from the dictates of party politics. Various attempts were made by disaffected political groupings to use this ideology as a stick to beat political opponents, usually dictatorial liberal elites and the tyrannical and unrepresentative organizations that they headed. Many places in the late Victorian period still had their own localized incarnations of 'Old Corruption', and the way in which it manifested itself was dependent on the political dynamics of the locality in question. In places where either the Tory party was weak or the position of the liberal elite less secure, this discontent could take the form of independent radical politics, as was the case in London, Newcastle and Nottingham. By contrast, in places such as the Black Country, Lancashire and Yorkshire the power of the local liberal elites was so entrenched that popular hostility towards them fuelled the rise of popular Conservatism. Somewhat paradoxically, the Conservative party was well placed to tap into this anti-party spirit due to the emphasis it placed on local and national patriotism, and by presenting itself as the custodian of national (as opposed to party) interests along with its defence of a traditional way of life. Thus, we begin to see how the Conservative party's reworking of the traditional language of electoral independence was made to serve partisan ends. The Tories were also well placed to exploit this tradition, due to the large number of independent-style gentlemen on their back-benches, most of whom sat for old boroughs such as Exeter, Ipswich, Plymouth and York.[37] The Liberals, on the other hand, were saved (to some extent) by the widespread popularity of Liberalism as a national movement, which many radicals 'felt a profound loyalty towards . . . without overcoming their deep suspicion of its local representatives'.[38]

Given the boisterous and fractious nature of party politics, it is not surprising that there remained a powerful undercurrent of opinion that regarded party as a disruptive and divisive force. Patricia Lynch has shown that in many rural constituencies political organizations were thought to be disruptive of village life, and that party divisions upset an otherwise relatively harmonious social order.[39] There was a similar attitude towards party in urban municipal politics and, to a lesser extent, in parliamentary politics. At the municipal level, there was a widely held belief that party divisions should not be allowed to interfere with council affairs and that it was important to elect the best men, irrespective of party identity. What mattered in municipal politics, certainly in the 1870s and 1880s, was the 'character' and personality of politicians.[40] When party rivalry increased in council chambers in the 1870s and 1880s, it was much lamented and resisted.[41]

In terms of parliamentary politics, again, what stands out is the electorate's preoccupation with 'character' and personality, which could just as easily weaken partisanship as cement it.[42] The most popular and successful politicians were those who drew not only cross-class but also cross-party support. Civic politicians – such as Joseph Chamberlain in Birmingham, W. L. Jackson in Leeds and Archibald Salvidge in Liverpool – were often best placed to transcend party divisions, followed by other paragons of patriotic and civic virtue such as country gentlemen, military men, self-made men, and paternalistic and benevolent elites – provided, of course, that they were not associated with dictatorial actions.[43] More generally, it was surely no coincidence that it was during the late Victorian years that the patriotic cry of placing 'country before party' was deployed on an unprecedented scale. This was also a reflection of the growing popular frustration with established party politics by the 1890s, and of party politics more generally among some groups such as the Socialists. Neither is it a coincidence that the trope of independence was to the fore in the establishment of Labour politics, hence the name of the *Independent* Labour party. While the Labour party itself eventually fell victim to the dictatorial trappings of party, it grew out of, and developed, the culture of electoral independence: it represented the most sustained challenge to the power of liberal elites, and to tory elites for that matter.[44]

But it was not only working-class radicals who were disillusioned with the political system. Arguably, the legion of radical-right wing leagues that sprang up in the Edwardian period was evidence of middle-class frustration with conventional party politics. In some respects, the radical-right critique of conventional party politics also represented a reworking of the rhetoric of 'Old Corruption'. Those who shared the criticisms of public figures such as Hilaire Belloc, Cecil Chesterton and Leo Maxse were convinced that the corrupting effects of the concentration of political power in the hands of small wealthy cliques was undermining parliamentary government.[45] While it is possible to dismiss these figures as cranks, their views did resonate, however briefly, with popular disillusionment with conventional party politics in the years leading up to the First World War.[46]

Ultimately, political traditions and rituals placed a significant limit on the power and influence of party, so much so that the open, libertarian and boisterous politics of the street, and the language of electoral independence all survived down to 1914. This is not to postpone the triumph of party and the disciplining of popular politics to a future unspecified date. To do so would be to conclude, inadvertently, that parties can effectively control those that they claim to represent: in liberal democracies, this will always remain an unachievable desideratum. Representing the people is a difficult business, especially when the representativeness of the system is called into question.[47] By the early years of the twentieth century, few were more vociferous in questioning the representativeness of the system than women. Yet, if the intensity of that questioning was novel, the questioning was not. This dated back to at least the early nineteenth century.

Women and the Quest for Citizenship

The conservative backlash against the French Revolution in the spheres of politics and religion, allied to changes in the organization of economic life (the growing separation between home and work, consequent on the rise of the factory) had, by the early years of the nineteenth century, circumscribed the public role of women.[48] Part cause, and part consequence, of these changes was the rise of the prescriptive ideology of 'separate spheres', based on the assumption that the private, domestic sphere was the 'natural' female domain, while the public world of work and politics was the preserve of men: hence the formal exclusion of women from the parliamentary franchise in 1832.

In practice, these boundaries were seldom drawn so rigidly, as evidenced by the various ways middle- and working-class women participated in politics: as canvassers, petitioners, marchers, members of the electoral crowd, boycotters of businesses that did not support their political agenda, as organizers of political social events like teas and dinners, and, eventually, as voters and candidates in local government.[49] These forms of participation were, for so long, obscured by the historical obsession with the vote. Notwithstanding the various ways in which the state redefined the public citizen as male and the growing cultural constraints that policed the boundaries of the 'masculine' public sphere, many women (and not merely those who were members of the elite) skilfully negotiated their entry into the public political sphere – and long before the emergence of an organized women's suffrage movement in the later nineteenth century.

In the first half of the nineteenth century, one strategy employed by radical women to legitimize their public presence was to position themselves as part of a wider radical 'counter-public' political sphere; one that challenged the exclusivity, elitism and, occasionally, the masculinism of the 'official' public sphere. As Helen Rogers has shown, in the early to mid-nineteenth century, women 'did not always, or only, identify themselves as "women"'; they also conceived of themselves as a distinct part, or in some cases as leaders, of the 'people' in their battles against monopoly, injustice and self-interest.[50] Radical women drew on a range of arguments to legitimize their putative transgression of the feminine private and masculine public divide. A frequent claim was that their male kinsmen were unable (or unwilling) to mount an effective challenge to the forces of political exclusion that were held responsible for social, and especially domestic, misery. Thus, it was the breakdown of 'virtual representation' that induced women to enter the public political sphere as a means to bring about its restoration.[51] This argument was frequently used to justify women's involvement in the Factory and Anti-Poor Law movements, and by Chartist women to justify their active support for universal manhood suffrage by the setting up of female Chartist associations.[52] Only by the grant of the vote to their male kinsmen, Chartist women argued, would their social miseries be alleviated. Few Chartists were in favour of enfranchising women. While male Chartists clearly objected to the prevailing assumption that working men were virtually represented, most of them had no problem in yoking that very same theory to patriarchal assumptions as an argument against enfranchising women.[53] Even in the supposedly sexually egalitarian Owenite communities, it was the women who usually performed the domestic chores.[54]

Another argument that was used to legitimize (particularly middle-class) women's direct political participation was the claim that their domestic role and experiences, along with their assumed heightened sense of morality and religiosity, gave them unique and valuable insights into humanitarian, moral and religious issues. This gave rise to the language of 'Women's Mission', which became so prominent in arguments justifying the enfranchisement of women. The involvement of women in political campaigns that centred on 'moral imperatives' – or, subsequently, on social and welfare issues, especially at the local level – was regarded as acceptable, not least because it was regarded as a logical extension of their domestic and caring role.[55] This had the effect of blurring the boundary between the public and private spheres, although again it would be wrong to assume that women were perfectly contented to act as auxiliaries, or in ways that did not challenge their subordination.[56] A number of political movements began, albeit in carefully orchestrated ways, to incorporate women into their organizations, claiming that 'female influence' raised the moral tone of debate and had a civilizing impact on the conduct of politics. Movements such as the Anti-Corn Law League and, later, the Conservative Primrose League, harnessed what were seen as 'peculiarly feminine techniques of agitation':[57] collecting signatures for petitions, door-to-door canvassing (an extension of the tradition of district visiting performed by women), holding tea parties and organizing bazaars – all regarded as 'women's work' for the simple reason that much of it was indirect and occurred 'behind the scenes'.[58]

But it was not only middle-class women that were involved in these great moral campaigns in the first half of the nineteenth century. Working-class women campaigned against the New Poor Law, 'factory slavery' and the Corn Laws, not only on grounds of moral outrage but also on account of the direct impact these had on their lives.[59] The participation of working-class women in these popular movements was evidence of the extent to which domestic family life was being politicized in the early nineteenth century. Thus, the 'failure' of women to reorient radical politics towards genuinely universal suffrage should not be allowed to obscure some of the other ways in which women made aspects of political culture more gender-inclusive and more sensitive to their interests. For example, Kathryn Gleadle has argued that the emphasis placed by Chartist women on tea parties, outings and family events represented a shrewd attempt by Chartist women 'to encourage their males kinsmen to eschew the public house', as drink was 'held to be responsible for widespread domestic violence and for exacerbating the financial problems of the poor'.[60]

With the ending of these great campaigns, and the parallel rise of a more prescriptive 'separate spheres' model of gender relations between the 1830s and 1850s, it is argued that popular politics thereafter became increasingly 'masculinized', thereby further excluding women in the process. Popular radicalism became suffused with the rhetoric of domesticity as working men sought to demonstrate their fitness for citizenship by emphasizing their independence and respectability.[61] This independence was based on the ideal of the male breadwinner wage – a wage that was sufficient to support a domesticated wife and family. The logic of the male breadwinner wage entailed the removal of women from the masculine workplace.[62] The reality could, in fact, be much different. Many working-class men could not afford for their wives and daughters to cease employment. Further, it would be wrong to assume that this process of masculinization went uncontested. With the emergence of a more polarized gendered order, various currents – feminism, liberalism and radicalism – began to coalesce into an organized women's movement from the 1850s. Many of these 'pioneers' had backgrounds in radical politics, especially in the Anti-Slavery and Anti-Corn Law campaigns.[63] The final catalyst, one that placed suffrage at the centre of gender politics, was supplied by the re-emergence of parliamentary reform in the 1860s, culminating in John Stuart Mill's amendment to the 1867 Reform Bill to exchange the word 'man' for the word 'person'. The women's movement was hampered by the failure of this first attempt to secure votes for women, and the subsequent divisions over the desirability of prioritizing the campaign for the repeal of the intrusive Contagious Diseases Acts of 1864–69. The Contagious Diseases Acts sanctioned the compulsory detention, and intrusive medical examination and treatment, of women suspected of prostitution and carrying venereal disease in garrison towns.[64] However, growing frustration over their failure to secure a quick repeal of these Acts, allied to the further 'masculinization' of politics in the 1870s and 1880s, restored women's suffrage to the centre of gender politics. Consequently, feminist women began to jettison their former identification as part of the people and emphasize the separate claims of 'womanhood'.

By the 1890s, a growing number of women were becoming frustrated by the lack of recognition and support they received from the political parties, especially when it came to the vexed issue of women's suffrage. This led to a series of splits among political women continuing into the Edwardian years over the competing claims of party loyalty and commitment to votes for women.

Throughout this period, the supporters of women's suffrage drew on a range of arguments – some new and some old – to justify the extension of the vote to women. As radicals before them had demanded the vote for working men, some advocates of women's suffrage looked to the past and historic precedent to show how the exclusion of women from political power was a recent and novel invention.[65] Some harnessed the constitutional argument that taxing people without giving them political representation was tyranny,[66] and linked this to a wider critique of arbitrary government that drew on an older radical notion that citizens had the right to resist tyrannical power.[67] Others drew on Lockean notions of individual rights and Enlightenment faith in human capacity for reason and rationality.[68] These ideological positions became enmeshed with strategic and tactical considerations. A long-standing division that came to a head in the Edwardian years was the question of whether property should form the basis of citizenship. Some took the pragmatic (or elitist) view that it would be more desirable to enfranchise women on the same basis as men (as householders), and that this proposal would be more likely to command wider support if it were limited to unmarried women, who could legitimately claim to be independent. Others, drawing on more radical definitions of citizenship, were committed to all women (and also, in some cases, all men) being enfranchised.

Overlapping with these arguments were debates about the purpose of giving women the vote. This, in turn, led to disagreements and divisions over how the vote was to be won. Some women saw the vote as both a means (to challenge sexual inequalities and promote women's rights) and an end (as an ennobling and obliging badge of citizenship); others tended to place more emphasis on the vote as either a means or an end in itself. These different emphases were, in part, a reflection of a more fundamental gender debate about the ways, and degrees to which, women were equal to, or different from, men.[69] Those who maintained that women were equal to men in the public sphere drew on a model of citizenship that was grounded in the notion of equal rights, thereby minimizing sexual difference. The more radical and militant Women's Social and Political Union (WSPU), established in 1903, tended to adopt this stance, which underpinned their commitment to gender solidarity and willingness to employ militant tactics. The problem with this argument was that public opinion was, for the most part, against gender equality. Equality-based arguments played into the hands of the anti-suffragists who interpreted this as evidence that women – particularly those who engaged in violent (and, therefore, masculine) antics – were 'unsexing' themselves.

By contrast, arguments based on gender 'difference', although no less contentious, circumvented the 'unsexing' argument by justifying votes for women on the grounds that they were distinct from, but complementary to, men. According to this argument, which became closely identified with the National Union of Women's Suffrage Societies (NUWSS) – the moderate and constitutional wing of the Edwardian suffragette movement – moral superiority, purity and feminine authority over the domestic sphere entitled and fitted women for electoral citizenship. Unfortunately, opponents of women's suffrage could also turn arguments based on difference on their head.[70] In the prevailing gender hierarchy of Victorian and Edwardian Britain, difference implied inequality and, worse still, an inequality that was religiously and biologically 'naturalized'.

Continuing divisions over objectives and tactics within the women's suffrage movement, the ambiguous position of the political parties, the cool response of the Liberal government, and public opposition collectively account for the failure to grant women the vote before 1914. And yet, despite all this opposition and internal wrangling, women were beginning to secure more political and legal rights from the 1860s. If masculinity was the fundamental basis of citizenship after 1832, then this was only the case in relation to the parliamentary franchise. In the sphere of local government, women found an increasing number of opportunities to participate as citizens, 'and at a time when the local state was playing a larger role in the daily lives of most Britons, and an infinitely larger role than the central state did'.[71] As early as 1834, single or widowed women ratepayers (that is, women of property) could vote in elections for Poor Law Guardians and, from 1875, they could stand as candidates, although the stiff property qualification prevented many women from voting and standing as candidates until it was relaxed in 1894. The same class of women were able to vote in municipal elections from 1869. The Education Act of 1870 stipulated that women who were municipal and parish electors were eligible to vote and stand as candidates in the school board elections, the important new local bodies responsible for educational provision. In 1888, women ratepayers were allowed to vote for the new county councils established under the Local Government Act of that year. From 1894, women were also eligible to vote and stand as candidates for election to parish and district councils and, in 1907, this was finally extended to county and borough councils.

Thus, against the background of the enactment of the Third Reform Act – which, it will be recalled, marked a shift away from interests to population – the rise of a women's suffrage movement marked the beginnings of what would become a powerful challenge to the legitimacy of virtual representation by the early years of the twentieth century. In 1918, the Fourth Reform Act finally introduced the most important and coveted point of the People's Charter: universal manhood suffrage. In addition, 8 million women who were over 30 years of age and already local government electors (or married to a municipal elector) were also enfranchised; this constituted approximately 40 per cent of the overall electorate. The lingua franca of representative politics was no longer 'interests' but 'numbers'. Britain had finally become a democracy, albeit a peculiar kind. In describing Britain's journey towards democracy between 1832 and 1918, most historians would probably agree with the following characterization by Hoppen that: 'The roads to democracy were never motorways, and rarely highroads; more often a set of meandering byways.'[72]

Conclusion

By 1914, a more standardized electoral system had replaced much of the heterogeneity and local idiosyncrasies that had existed in the early nineteenth century. Some anomalies remained. Although a more uniform franchise existed across the United Kingdom after 1884, the ancient voting rights, such as the freeman franchise, were still in existence in the pre-1832 boroughs. Although single-member constituencies were the norm, the Third Reform Act had left 22 pre-existing double-member boroughs intact in England and Wales, largely as a sop to Gladstone's insistence that the integrity of historic boroughs should not be completely obliterated by the new system. Further, we have already noted that, despite the clamping down on electoral malpractice, elections could still be riotous affairs. A more nationalized and integrated political culture was, no doubt, brought into existence by a cheap daily press, but the basis of the electoral system remained the local constituency. If the system itself had become more standardized across the nation, little evidence exists of any linear shift towards the dominance of national issues in popular politics during this period.

What stands out throughout this period is the continual interplay of local, regional, national and imperial identities; again, there was no linear shift from the local to the national. As the work of John Brewer, Frank O'Gorman, Nicholas Rogers and Kathleen Wilson has made clear, even in the eighteenth century urban voters were aware of national and international issues.[73] If there was an overall shift towards national and imperial issues during the nineteenth century, then it was change in terms of degrees, not of dramatic proportions. By the end of this period, local issues could still determine the outcome of a general election in a constituency. Electors did not always take kindly to national pressure groups 'invading' their local constituency, a charge that the Suffragettes often found levelled against them.[74] Conversely, there can be no doubting the importance of national issues in the early nineteenth century: one thinks of the various protest movements, notably Chartism and the Anti-Corn Law League, and of the ways in which itinerant activists, newspapers such as the *Northern Star* and tactics such as petitioning focused attention on national issues and created national political movements. The press was crucial in bridging the gap between the local, the regional and the national.

Perhaps one of the most evident and significant changes over this period was the shift away from traditional forms of protest, pre-eminently petitioning and the mass platform, towards the vote and the electoral system.[75] This was part cause and part consequence of the rise of modern party politics. From mid-century, party became the dominant, though by no means exclusive, means by which the masses participated in the political process. Again, one should not exaggerate the extent of this shift, as the example of the Suffragettes illustrates. They employed a range of tactics, many of which had been pioneered by earlier reformers: petitioning parliament; holding demonstrations, large public meetings and, symbolically, occupying public space; setting up newspapers; employing, or threatening to employ, physical force; exclusive dealing; and working through the parties (as well as against them). And as those before them, they were all too often divided over the efficacy of these various tactics. Further, they drew on a familiar range of arguments to legitimize their tactics and claims: that which they demanded, and the way in which they were demanding it, was sanctioned by the imaginary English constitution.[76] The parallels with Chartism, the greatest popular movement of the nineteenth century, are striking.

This is not to suggest that the Suffragettes were deploying 'outdated' arguments and employing old-fashioned tactics. The Suffragettes, as the radicals before them, were shrewdly legitimizing their objectives and methods by recourse to precedent. But appealing to what was 'old' should not blind us to what was 'new' in Suffragette politics, and in the type of political culture heralded by the Suffragettes. Their campaigns represented an attempt – unprecedented in its scale – to feminize public politics by curbing what they regarded as the violent and unthinking aspects of the male polity, such as existed in the visceral traditions of street politics. The irony, as Jon Lawrence has pointed out, was that the Suffragettes themselves mimicked 'men's volatile forms of political protest' in their own quest for the vote (at least, until this contradiction became apparent in the years immediately before the First World War), thus illustrating the tensions that often existed between the 'old' and the 'new' in popular politics.[77] As Lawrence goes on to show elsewhere, although the Suffragette campaign played a part in bringing about the feminization of the polity, this was a development that owed far more to the changes wrought by the First World War. The War had raised fears about violence and of the need to expunge it from civilian (and political) life, thought to be all the more imperative against the background of strained wartime class relations and, subsequently, as a means to distance Britain from the hyper-masculinity of continental fascist politics. Of further significance was the Fourth Reform Act of 1918: the partial enfranchisement of women presented the parties with a new and relatively unknown constituency, which was widely believed to have rendered traditional manly 'hurly-burly' street politics unsuitable to the new 'feminized' electorate. Such practices, it was argued, would have alienated women. Similarly, the sheer size of the new electorate overwhelmed old electioneering practices. The role of politics in these altered conditions was to create and maintain a sober, rational and domesticated public opinion, which left little space for outbreaks of the old crowd politics.[78] The extent to which the 'old' ways declined and the impact these broader changes in political culture had on the form and content of politics in twentieth-century Britain is another story.

Notes

Introduction

1. Marc Brodie (2003).
2. Maurice Cowling (1971); A. B. Cooke and J. Vincent (1974).
3. Jon Lawrence (1998: 61–9).
4. Kevin Jefferys (2007: 6–19).
5. Kelly Boyd and Rohan McWilliam (2007: 37).
6. For a critical review of this perspective, see David Mayfield and Susan Thorne (1992: 170–3).
7. An interpretation stated most forcefully in James Vernon (1993).
8. James Vernon (1994: 85).
9. Henry Pelling (1967); John Vincent (1967); Peter Clarke (1972).
10. Norman Gash (1953); H. J. Hanham (1959); John Vincent (1972) [1966].
11. For a critical introduction to postmodernism and its application to nineteenth-century popular politics, albeit from a rather hostile perspective, see Neville Kirk (1994a).
12. Geoffrey Crossick (1987: 30).
13. Patrick Joyce (1991).
14. Catherine Hall, Keith McClelland and Jane Rendall (2000).
15. Patrick Joyce (1991); Frank O'Gorman (1992); James Vernon (1993); James Thompson (2007: 177–97). Work on symbolic practices, however, has not universally 'attacked class'. See Paul Pickering (1986); James Epstein (1994).
16. Gareth Stedman Jones (1982: 3–58), an expanded version of which appears in Gareth Stedman Jones (1983).
17. Rohan McWilliam (1998: 33).
18. James Epstein (1994; 2003); Jon Lawrence (1998: 61–9).
19. Michael Bentley (1999: 899).
20. Jon Lawrence (2003: 195).

21. Patrick Joyce (1991; 1994); James Vernon (1993).
22. Patrick Joyce (1993); cf. Patrick Joyce (1991: 27–8); James Vernon (1994: 84–5 and 89).
23. David Mayfield and Susan Thorne (1992: 175).
24. Jon Lawrence and Miles Taylor (1993: 11).
25. Neville Kirk (2000: 89).
26. Patrick Joyce (1991: 27–9).

1   Citizenship, the Franchise and Electoral Culture

1. Anna Clark (2003: 263).
2. Catherine Hall (2000: 111).
3. *The Times* (1884) 28 March.
4. Catherine Hall, Keith McClelland and Jane Rendall (2000); Matthew McCormack (2005).
5. James Vernon (1996).
6. J. G. A. Pocock (1975).
7. Matthew McCormack (2007: 27).
8. Ben Griffin (2003).
9. Matthew McCormack (2005: 2).
10. Leonore Davidoff and Catherine Hall (1987: 416–49).
11. Quoted in Catherine Hall, Keith McClelland and Jane Rendall (2000: 98).
12. *Hansard*, House of Commons, vol. 175, cols 324–5.
13. Matthew McCormack (2004: 27).
14. Matthew McCormack and Matthew Roberts (2007: 192).
15. James Vernon (1993: 164, 172–7); Jon Lawrence (2006); Matthew Roberts (2006b). See also Alex Windscheffel (2005).
16. D. A. Hamer (1977: 14).
17. Kathryn Gleadle and Sarah Richardson (2000: 11).
18. Frank O'Gorman (1992: 79).
19. The division of opinion amongst the assembled crowd was the basis for demanding an official poll.
20. John Vincent (1972 [1966]: 138).
21. Bruce L. Kinzer (1978).
22. Catherine Hall, Keith McClelland and Jane Rendall (2000); Matthew McCormack (2005).
23. James Vernon (1993).
24. John Davis and Duncan Tanner (1996); Miles Taylor (1997: 57).
25. Chris Cook and John Stevenson (1988: 68).
26. Asa Briggs (1956: 69–70).
27. Norman Gash (1953); D. C. Moore (1966).

28. Frank O'Gorman (1989: 393; 1992); James Vernon (1993); Richard Price (1999: 264–79).
29. Frank O'Gorman (1989: 182).
30. James Vernon (1993: 33).
31. T. J. Nossiter (1975); Frank O' Gorman (1992); Miles Taylor (1995: 10); Edwin Jaggard (1999: 112–32).
32. Philip Salmon (2002); John A. Phillips and Charles Wetherell (1995).
33. K. Theodore Hoppen (1994: 605); K. Theodore Hoppen (1996: 558); cf. Justin Wasserman and Edwin Jaggard (2007).
34. Frank O'Gorman (1989: 179). On the other hand, if the number of enfranchised males is taken as a proportion of all adult males, the growth rate between 1833 and 1866 appears extremely low: from 17.2 per cent to 18.4 per cent. See K. Theodore Hoppen (1998: 238–9).
35. Frank O'Gorman (1993: 177–8).
36. Eric J. Evans (2000: 27–8).
37. Miles Taylor (1997: 56–8).
38. Mark Pack (1995: 75).
39. See Chapter 10.
40. Philip Salmon (2002: 27).
41. Charles Seymour (1970 [1915]: 27–8); Philip Salmon (2002: 200–6).
42. Philip Salmon (2002: 200–1).
43. Miles Taylor (1997: 58–9); Matthew Roberts (2006b: 221).
44. Matthew McCormack (2004: 27).
45. James Vernon (1993: 39).
46. Boyd Hilton (2006: 354); Jane Rendall (1999: 484).
47. Catherine Hall (2000: 125).
48. Philip Salmon (2002: 219); Derek Fraser (1976). The Act, however, did not do away with all existing closed corporations: 68 were omitted on the grounds that they were either too big (as was the case with London) or too small to warrant reform.
49. Miles Taylor (1997: 61).
50. Only those towns that had borough status were permitted to establish corporations to manage the affairs of the town.
51. Derek Fraser (1976: 27).
52. Neville Kirk (1994b: 75).
53. Philip Salmon (2005: 94).
54. Boyd Hilton (2006: 498).
55. The residency requirement for the municipal franchise was reduced to one year in 1869. Harling (2004: 221).
56. K. Theodore Hoppen (1985: 210, 215).

57. John Davis and Duncan Tanner (1996).
58. For this interpretation of 1832, see Dror Wahrman (1995).
59. James Vernon (1993: 100); Richard Price (1999: 278).
60. Eric J. Evans (2000: 61–2).
61. John Davis and Duncan Tanner (1996).
62. Marc Brodie (2004: 54–69); Michael Childs (1995).
63. Catherine Hall, Keith McClelland and Jane Rendall (2000: 182).
64. Quoted in Catherine Hall, Keith McClelland and Jane Rendall (2000: 166).
65. *Birmingham Daily Post* (1865) 19 January, quoted in Catherine Hall, keith McClelland and Jane Rendall (2000: 222).
66. Peter Mandler (2001); Andrew Thompson (2005: 132).
67. Catherine Hall, Keith McClelland and Jane Rendall (2000: 139–51).
68. Eric J. Evans (2000: 134); G. R. Searle (2004: 132–3).
69. Figures taken from F. W. S. Craig (1981: 159).
70. Quoted in Anna Clark (1996: 230).
71. *Hansard*, House of Commons, vol. 284, col. 103.
72. John Garrard (2002: 13).
73. *Hansard*, House of Commons, vol. 284, col. 111.

2   Radicalism in the Age of the Chartists

1. Raymond Williams (1988: 251).
2. *Northern Star* (1841) 2 January.
3. There were groups of radicals, especially those connected with skilled trades, that based their claims to citizenship on property, but it was a form of property that they claimed was inherent in all persons: labour.
4. Matthew McCormack (2005: 27).
5. Gareth Stedman Jones (1983: 102).
6. Paul Pickering (2001: 378).
7. Paul Pickering (1991).
8. Betty Fladeland (1982: 99); Robert Gray (1996: 37–47).
9. Quoted in Cecil Driver (1946: 42–3).
10. David Brion Davis (1966) [1988].
11. Seymour Drescher (1981).
12. Antony Taylor (2002).
13. Timothy Randall (1999: 173–4).
14. Francis Burdett, *Reform of Parliament: To the Electors of Westminster* (London: W. Robson & Co., 1820: 7).
15. Patrick Joyce (1996: 186).

16. Joanna Innes (2003: 87).

17. Joanna Innes (2003: 90).

18. *Bradford Observer* (1838) 15 October.

19. *Leeds Times* (1835) 26 December; *Northern Star* (1848) 1 July.

20. Robert G. Hall (2007: 59); Malcolm Chase (2007: 41).

21. Occassionally, the Chartists went even further back in time to celebrate the 'Kyfr-y-then', the imagined democratic republic of the Ancient Britons that was actually suppressed by the Saxons in the middle of the fifth century. See *McDouall's Chartist and Republic Journal* 1841 8 and 15 May.

22. *Northern Star* (1839) 4 May.

23. Robert G. Hall (1999b).

24. *Northern Star* (1839) 3 August.

25. Antony Taylor (1999a: 58).

26. Paul A. Pickering and Alex Tyrrell (2000: 42).

27. Robert G. Hall (2007: 40).

28. Thomas Paine (1987b [1795]: 464).

29. Thomas Paine (1987a [1792]: 279).

30. James Epstein (1994: 124).

31. Richard Carlile, *An Address to that Portion of the People of Great Britain and Ireland Calling Themselves Reformers, on the Political Excitement of the Present Time*, reprinted in Gregory Claeys (2001 [1839]: vol. 2, 129).

32. Joanna Innes (2003: 93, n.77).

33. James Epstein (1990: 556).

34. See, for example, the article on universal manhood suffrage in *The Chartist* (1830) 3 March.

35. James Epstein (1989).

36. James Epstein (1996: 32).

37. Mark Hovell (1918: 306).

38. Mark Hovell (1918: 305).

39. Edward Royle (2000: 4).

40. Andrew Messner (1999).

41. John Belchem (1996: 1).

42. For a succinct discussion of these tactical positions, see Martin Hewitt (1996: 232–48).

43. G. D. H. Cole (1948: 94); Asa Briggs (1959a: 26).

44. Gareth Stedman Jones (1983: 94–104); Robert G. Hall (2007: 3).

45. Mark Hovell (1918: 303).

46. Malcolm Chase (2000a: 156).

47. *Northern Star* (1842) 16 July.

48. Stewart Angas Weaver (1987).

49. *Fleet Papers* 1841 20 March.

50. *The Charter* (1839) 10 and 17 February.
51. *Northern Star* (1838) 24 March.
52. Michael J. Turner (2001).
53. London Working Men's Association, *An Address from the Working Men's Association to the People of England, in Reply to the Objections of the Press*, reprinted in Gregory Claeys (2001 [1838]: vol. 1, 148).
54. Phillip Harling (1995).
55. 'The Chartist Petition, 1848', in S. MacCoby (1952: 140).
56. See, for example, 'An Address From the Universal Suffrage Association of Manchester to the Unrepresented of Great Britain and Ireland', *Northern Star* (1838) 19 May.
57. William Lovett, *Manifesto of The General Convention of the Industrious Classes*, reprinted in Gregory Claeys (2001 [1839]: vol. 2, 139).
58. Gareth Stedman Jones (1983: 118).
59. Joanna Innes (2003).
60. Derek Beales (1999: 161).
61. Miles Taylor (1999: 1).
62. Miles Taylor (1999: 6–7).
63. Antony Taylor (1999a: ch. 2).

3   The Culture and 'Failure' of Radicalism

1. Cited in David Jones (1975: 33).
2. Patrick Joyce (1991: 31).
3. Speech at Manchester, 19 October 1843, quoted in John Morley (1906: 141).
4. *Northern Star* (1838) 29 September.
5. *The Communist International* (1919) no. 1, May, col. 34.
6. E. P. Thompson (1966 [1963]: 9).
7. John Belchem (1996: 1–2).
8. Edouard Dolléans (1949: 319).
9. See Chapter 1.
10. F. C. Mather (1972: 8).
11. Patrick Joyce (1991, Part III).
12. Stewart Angas Weaver (1987: 14); Robert Gray (1996: 56–7).
13. Paul A. Pickering and Alex Tyrrell (2000: ch. 7).
14. Gareth Stedman Jones (1983: 104).
15. S. MacCoby (1952: 130).
16. *Hansard*, House of Commons, vol. 49, col. 227.
17. Gareth Stedman Jones (1983: 170).
18. James Vernon (1993: 309).
19. Neville Kirk (1985: 20–1); cf John Foster (1974).

20. Miles Taylor (2003).
21. Theodore Koditschek (1990: 488).
22. Neville Kirk (1987).
23. P. F. Taylor (1995); Michael Winstanley (1993).
24. Robert G. Hall (2007: 55).
25. Malcolm Chase (2007: 30).
26. This was an attempt to unite middle-class reformers with members of the more working class National Charter Association.
27. On the affinity between these 'opposing' interpretations, see Miles Taylor (1996).
28. Dorothy Thompson (1984).
29. Iain McCalman (1993: 205–6).
30. Iain McCalman (1993: 234).
31. Matthew McCormack (2005: 209).
32. Anna Clark (1992).
33. David Jones (1975: 46); Hugh McLeod (1984: 29).
34. John Belchem (2005: 4).
35. J. E. King (1982).
36. Edward Royle (1971: 9).
37. Eileen Yeo (1981).
38. For a summary of this debate, see Hugh Macleod (1984).
39. E. P. Thompson (1966 [1963]: 41–2).
40. Hugh Macleod (1984: 48).
41. Paul A. Pickering and Alex Tyrrell (2000: 88).
42. A claim made by 'Radical Jack' of Stockton, quoted in Eileen Janes Yeo (1981: 109).
43. Patrick Joyce (1991: 33).
44. Miles Taylor (2003: 85).
45. Asa Briggs (1959c).
46. Detlev Mares (2005: 121–43).
47. Hugh Cunningham (1981).
48. Robert G. Hall (2007: 34, 40).
49. John Belchem (2005: 2–8).
50. *Northern Star* 1842 2 April.
51. Robert G. Hall (2007: 51).
52. James Epstein (1989).
53. Antony Taylor (1995); James Vernon (1993: 48–79); James Epstein (1994); James Epstein (2003).
54. Paul Pickering (1986: 162).
55. James Epstein (1989: 78).
56. Dorothy Thompson (1996).
57. John Belchem (2005: 2).

58. Cf. John Belchem and James Epstein (1997) in James Epstein (2003: 132).
59. Patrick Joyce (1991: 34).
60. Miles Taylor (2003: 80).
61. Patrick Joyce (1991: 36–55); Miles Taylor (2003); John Belchem and James Epstein (1997) in James Epstein (2003).
62. John Knott (1986: ch. 10); James R. Simmons, Jr (2007).
63. James Gregory (2007: ch. 4).
64. G. R. Wythen Baxter, *The Book of the Bastilles* (London, 1841: iv).
65. D. J. Rowe (1967: 75–6).
66. Edward Royle (1996: 16).
67. James Epstein (1982: 221).
68. Paul Pickering (1991).
69. Timothy Randall (1999: 173); Paul Pickering (2001: 380).
70. Malcolm Chase (2000a: 173).
71. Stewart Angas Weaver (1987: 267).
72. John Saville (1987).
73. Henry Weisser (1981).
74. John Belchem (1982: 277).
75. James Vernon (1993: 222); Martin Hewitt (1996: 193–229, 262–93).
76. *Northern Star* (1840) 16 May.
77. Paul A. Pickering (2003: 246).
78. Antony Taylor (1999a: 53–4).
79. John Foster (1974); Trygve R. Tholfsen (1976); Gareth Stedman Jones (1983: 177–8).

4 The Making of Mid-Victorian Popular Liberalism

1. W. L. Burn (1964).
2. Dona Torr (1936: 469).
3. Dona Torr (1936: 356).
4. Asa Briggs (1959b: 402–12); Eric J. Hobsbawm (1968a: ch. 6).
5. Eric J. Hobsbawm (1968b [1964]); John Foster (1974).
6. Robert Gray (1981).
7. R. Q. Gray (1976); Geoffrey Crossick (1978); Patrick Joyce (1982) [1980].
8. John Foster (1974).
9. Patrick Joyce (1982) [1980].
10. Neville Kirk (1985: xi, 25). A similar interpretation, albeit one that is more explicitly Marxist, is advanced in Theodore Koditschek (1990).

11. Neville Kirk (1998: 24, 60–70).
12. Theodore Koditschek (1990: 429).
13. Neville Kirk (1985: 17–24); V. C. Barbary (2008).
14. Neville Kirk (1985: 22–3, ch. 7); Janet Toole (1998); Robert G. Hall (2007: 109, 133).
15. Peter Bailey (1979).
16. Malcolm Chase (2000b: 47).
17. Neville Kirk (1998: 115–37); Malcolm Chase (1991: 325, 342).
18. Joan Allen (2007: 58–78).
19. Martin Hewitt (1996: 201).
20. Andrew August (2001); Antony Taylor (2005a).
21. D. A. Hamer (1972: ch. 1).
22. Eugenio F. Biagini (1992); Jonathan Parry (1993).
23. Eugenio F. Biagini (1992: 11).
24. Jonathan Parry (1993: 4).
25. John Vincent (1972 [1966]: 29–30).
26. T. M. Webb, 'The Liberal's Creed', *Bee-Hive* (1868) 5 September.
27. *Weekly Times* (1867) 20 October.
28. D. A. Hamer (1977: 4).
29. Patrick Joyce (1996: 179–203).
30. Derek Fraser (1976).
31. *Labourers' Union Chronicle* (1873) 7 June.
32. Philip Harling (2001: 78–88).
33. Peter Mandler (1990); Jonathan Parry (1993); Philip Harling (1996). For an overview of the complex historiography on mid-Victorian disinterested governance, see Philip Harling (2003).
34. Frank Trentmann (2008: 48–9).
35. Quoted in Eugenio F. Biagini (1992: 93).
36. *National Reformer* (1865) 30 July.
37. Quoted in Eugenio F. Biagini (1992: 167–8).
38. Eugenio F. Biagini (1992: 253).
39. Matthew McCormack (2005: 198); D. A. Hamer (1972: 14).
40. Malcolm Chase (1991).
41. Peter J. Cain (1995: vii).
42. See Chapter 1.
43. Peter J. Cain (2006: 178).
44. Catherine Hall, Keith McClelland and Jane Rendall (2000: ch. 2).
45. Miles Taylor (1995); Derek Fraser (1976: 252).
46. J. P. Parry (2006: 73).
47. Harry Browne (1979: 46).
48. Jon Lawrence (1992: 168ff); Rohan McWilliam (1991); Nadja Durbach (2005).
49. Eugenio F. Biagini (1992: 161).
50. J. P. Parry (2006: 93).

51. Eugenio F. Biagini (1992: 257).
52. Jon Lawrence (1998: 73–98, 169–77).
53. Council Meeting of the Reform League, 21 April 1865, George Howell Collection, Reform League Papers, 95922/4.
54. Eugenio F. Biagini (1992: 268).
55. For a critical overview of the debate on the background and passage of the Second Reform Bill, see Catherine Hall, Keith McClelland and Jane Rendall (2000: 1–20).
56. Adullamite was the name given by John Bright to those renegade parliamentary Liberals who voted against their own government's Reform Bill. This was an allusion to the Biblical story of the Cave of Adullam where those in distress took refuge.
57. Derek Fraser (1976: 264).
58. Hypatia Bradlaugh Bonner (1908 [1894]: I, 222).
59. Margot C. Finn (1993: 249).
60. *Hansard*, House of Commons, vol. 185 col. 324–5.
61. John Davis and Duncan Tanner (1996: 312).
62. Cf. Eugenio F. Biagini (1992: 310).
63. Eugenio F. Biagini (1992: 297).

5 Post-Chartist Radicalism and the (Un)making of Popular Liberalism

1. Eugenio F. Biagini and Alistair J. Reid (1991: introduction).
2. John Vincent (1972 [1966]: 19).
3. Jonathan Parry (1993); Joseph Coohill (2005); Philip Salmon (2002: ch. 2).
4. Angus Hawkins (1998: 311).
5. Jonathan Parry (1993: 1–2).
6. Philip Salmon (2002: 58–73).
7. Eugenio F. Biagini and Alistair J. Reid (1991: 5).
8. Eugenio F. Biagini and Alistair J. Reid (1991: 1).
9. Patrick Joyce (1991: 36–40, 45–55).
10. Patrick Joyce (1994: 192–213).
11. John Belchem and James Epstein (1997).
12. Cf. Neville Kirk (1998: 9).
13. Gareth Stedman Jones (1983: 174–8).
14. Miles Taylor (1995).
15. Miles Taylor (1995: 103).
16. Miles Taylor (1991); Rohan McWilliam (1991); Jon Lawrence (1991).
17. An argument put forward most explicitly by Miles Taylor (1995: 99). See also Michael Winstanley (1993).

18. Michael J. Turner (2001).
19. For the classic statement of this interpretation, see Brian Harrison and Patricia Hollis (1967). For a recent rehabilitation of this interpretation, see Colin Skelly (2005).
20. Paul Adelman (1984: 15).
21. David Nicholls (1997: 129).
22. Robert G. Hall (2007: 45).
23. Theodore Koditschek (1990: 336).
24. Theodore Koditschek (1990: 332).
25. Stewart Angas Weaver (1987).
26. Patrick Joyce (1994: 132).
27. See Chapter 2.
28. Quoted in Margot C. Finn (1993: 95).
29. R. E. Swift (2007: 688).
30. Simon Szreter (1997: 705–10).
31. Margot C. Finn (1993); Eugenio F. Biagini (1992: 159–62).
32. Quoted in Theodore Koditschek (1990: 521).
33. D. G. Wright (1966: 244–5).
34. For a local case study, see V. C. Barbary (2008: 132–43).
35. Robert Cooper to Joseph Cowen, 28 July 1862, from the Cowen Collection, reprinted in Edward Royle (1976).
36. Neville Kirk (1998: 26).
37. Martin Hewitt (1996: 229).
38. Richard Price (1996: 231).
39. Antony Taylor (2004b: 117).
40. Antony Taylor (1997: 190); Robert G. Hall (1999a).
41. Antony Taylor (1997: 185).
42. Margot C. Finn (1993: 61, 103, 143, 158–9).
43. Margot C. Finn (1993: 187).
44. David Nicholls (1996: 342).
45. John Vincent (1972 [1966]: 159).
46. Catherine Hall, Keith McClelland and Jane Rendall (2000: 94–5).
47. Antony Taylor (2005b: 75–96, 96–120).
48. Antony Taylor (2005a: 78).
49. Stan Shipley (1971).
50. Joan Allen (2007: 94, 113–14).
51. Jon Lawrence (1992: 169–75).
52. *Reynolds's Newspaper* (1868) 13 September.
53. Malcolm Chase (2000b: 49–50).
54. *Yorkshire Post* (1874) 3 February; (1880) 17 March.
55. Moisei Ostrogorski (1970 [1902]: 195–203, 228–40); Jon Lawrence (1998: 173–6).

56. For Bradlaugh see Hypatia Bradlaugh Bonner (1908) [1894]; Edward Royle (1980); W. L. Arnstein (1965).
57. Antony Taylor (1995).
58. Gertrude Himmelfarb (1966: 104).
59. Edward Royle (1980: ch. 8).
60. W. L. Arnstein (1965: 34).
61. Edward Royle (1980: 29–31, 268–71).
62. Rohan McWilliam (1991; 2007). Ironically, Bradlaugh regarded the Tichborne Case as a farce and waste of time, as did Joseph Cowen. See Joan Allen (2007: 98–9).
63. Cf. John Belchem and James Epstein (1997).

6 Rethinking the 'Transformation' of Popular Conservatism

1. R. McKenzie and A. Silver (1968); E. A. Nordlinger (1967).
2. Henry Pelling (1967); Paul Thompson (1967); Gareth Stedman Jones (1976) [1971]; Ross McKibbin (1984).
3. Gareth Stedman Jones (1974).
4. Martin Pugh (1985: 2).
5. James Cornford (1963).
6. Figures compiled from Nicholas Crowson (2001).
7. Derek Fraser (1980: 273–6).
8. Theodore Koditschek (1990: 153).
9. Patrick Joyce (1982 [1980]: ch. 1).
10. Christopher Stevens (1997: 32).
11. John Ward (2002: 47).
12. David Walsh (1991).
13. Richard Oastler, *A Letter to the Shareholders of the Bradford Observer* (Bradford, 1836: 13).
14. Robert Stewart (1978: 165).
15. Stewart Angas Weaver (1987); Felix Driver (1991).
16. David Gadian (1996: 267).
17. Janet Toole (1998).
18. Matthew Roberts (2003: 116–25).
19. Neville Kirk (1998: 103).
20. John Ramsden (1999: 87).
21. Catriona Burness (2002: 16–35).
22. Matthew Cragoe (2004: 23, 27).
23. K. Theodore Hoppen (1985: 202–3).
24. Matthew Roberts (2006b).
25. E. H. H. Green (1995: ch. 2).
26. Paul Readman (2001a).

27. Two examples being the late 1870s – when Disraeli's government was embroiled in the Eastern Question as well as colonial conflict in the Transvaal and in Afghanistan – and in the early 1900s, due to the failure of the Unionist government to bring the South African War to speedy and favourable close. See Alex Windscheffel (2007: 171).
28. Quoted in Andrew Roberts (1999: 262).
29. Martin Pugh (1988: 256).
30. Matthew Roberts (2006c); Alex Windscheffel (2007: 6–9).
31. James R. Moore (2006).
32. P. J. Cain and A. G. Hopkins (1987: 6).
33. Hugh McLeod (1996: 22).
34. For one local instance of these insecurities, see T. A. Jenkins (2004).
35. J. P. D. Dunbabin (1994: 241–67).
36. Richard Shannon (1996: 109).
37. Peter Clarke (1971: 32).
38. E. H. H. Green (1995: 137).
39. E. H. H. Green (1995: 1).
40. Martin Pugh (1988: 255).
41. Peter Clarke (1971: 32).
42. James R. Moore (2001: 994).
43. Jon Lawrence (1998: 126, 249).
44. Martin Pugh (2002a). See Chapter 9.
45. Chris Cook (1976: 63).
46. Tony Adams (1990: 26).

7   Defining and Debating Popular Conservatism

1. For the classic statement of this view, see James Cornford (1963).
2. E. H. H. Green (1995: 125).
3. For a discussion of the critique of electoral sociology as applied to popular Conservatism, see Matthew Roberts (2006c: 217–19).
4. Martin Francis and Ina Zweiniger-Bargielowska (1996: 4).
5. Patrick Joyce (1982) [1980].
6. V. C. Barbary (2008: 124).
7. Jon Lawrence (1998: 166).
8. Alex Windscheffel (2007: 6–8).
9. James Cornford (1963).
10. For examples of socially heterogeneous suburban constituencies post-1885, see *Birmingham Daily Gazette* (1885) 19 January; *Yorkshire Post* (1885) 17 January; Timothy Cooper (2005); Alex Windscheffel (2007: 6). Even Henry Pelling's *Social Geography of British Elections,*

1885–1910 (Pelling, 1967) – electoral sociology *par excellence* – made numerous references to the social heterogeneity of suburban constituencies (pp. 36–7, 65–7, 250, 293–4, 299).

11. See, for example, the chorus of opposition – mostly culled from provincial tory newspapers – in the *Pall Mall Gazette* (1884) 4 December.
12. Richard Shannon (1996: 109).
13. Patrick Joyce (1982 [1980]: 324).
14. R. F. Foster (1983: 147).
15. Jeremy Smith (1997: 27).
16. Patrick Joyce (1982 [1980]: 324).
17. Sandra O'Leary (2004: 160).
18. Modest estimates put the proportion of working-class voters at under 60 per cent: H. C. G. Matthew, R. I. McKibbin and John Kay (1976). Revisionist estimates suggest that it could have been as much as 76 per cent: Duncan Tanner (1990: 119).
19. Jon Lawrence (1993: 641–2).
20. James Cornford (1963: 54–6).
21. Marc Brodie (2004: 99, 113, 200–1).
22. For the argument that Liberal weaknesses and divisions have been exaggerated, see Paul Readman (1999: 470–3).
23. Jon Lawrence (1993); Paul Readman (1999); Matthew Roberts (2006a); Matthew Roberts (2006c); Alex Windscheffel (2007).
24. C. S. Ford (2002: 125).
25. Janet Toole (1998: 175).
26. Patrick Joyce (1982 [1980]: 250–62); P. J. Waller (1981).
27. Sandra O'Leary (2004: 159, 166).
28. Sandra O'Leary (2004); Marc Brodie (2004: 185–98); Michael Savage (1987: 136); Joan Allen (2007: ch. 4).
29. Patrick Joyce (1982 [1980]: 190).
30. *Pall Mall Gazette* (1895) 23 July, cited in Paul Readman (1999: 479).
31. James R. Moore (2006: 17).
32. Jon Lawrence (1993); Paul Readman (1999: 477–8); Alex Windscheffel (2007).
33. Jon Lawrence and Jane Elliot (1997); Paul Readman (1999: 487–90); Alex Windscheffel (2007: 216–23).
34. David Walsh (1991: 198–221).
35. Philip Salmon (2002: 58–69).
36. Martin Pugh (1985: 2, 27).
37. Alex Windscheffel (2007: 99–100).
38. Patrick Joyce (1982 [1980]: 251); David Walsh (1991: 410).
39. Alex Windscheffel (2000: 15).
40. Alex Windscheffel (2007: 85).

41. E. H. H. Green (2002: 3–4).
42. James Cornford (1963: 36–7).
43. Paul Readman (2001b: 127).
44. Richard Price (1972).
45. Paul Readman (2001b: 136).
46. Bruce Coleman (1988: 3).
47. For these perspectives see R. L. Hill (1929); Norman Gash (1972); Matthew Fforde (1990).
48. Ian Newbold (1983).
49. Philip Salmon (2002: 51).
50. John Ward (2002: ch. 4).
51. David Eastwood (1992: 31).
52. Felix Driver (1991).
53. Stewart Angas Weaver (1987: viii, 293–9).
54. Paul Readman (1999).
55. Sandra O'Leary (2004: 162).
56. Pat Thane (1984: 894–5); Martin Pugh (2002b: 776).
57. Matthew Roberts (2006b: 233).
58. *Bassetlaw Constitutional Magazine* (1887) May, Retford Local Studies Library.
59. James Vernon (1993: 301).
60. Quoted in Cecil Driver (1946: 468).
61. G. S. Bull, *Public Meeting in Bradford on the Ten Hours Bill* (Bradford, 1833).
62. Robert Blakey, *Cottage Politics; Or Letters on the New Poor Law* (London, 1837: 170).
63. Quoted in Patrick Joyce (1991: 347).
64. *Northern Liberator* (1838) 1 December.
65. Anna Clark (1995: 187–95).
66. Anna Gambles (1999).
67. Frank Trentmann (2008: 52).
68. Matthew McCormack and Matthew Roberts (2007: 193).
69. *Yorkshire Post* (1892) 12 May.
70. *Bassetlaw Constitutional Magazine* (1887) May.
71. *Yorkshire Post* (1885) 11 September.
72. David Walsh (1991: 269).
73. Quoted in John Ward (2002: 54).
74. Martin Pugh (1985: 141).
75. Paul Readman (1999: 476).
76. *Preston Herald* (1895) 3 August, cited in Michael Savage (1987: 143).
77. Martin Pugh (1985: 9); Alex Windscheffel (2007: 92).
78. Alex Windscheffel (2000: 30).

79. Frank Trentmann (2008: 54).
80. *Bassetlaw Constitutional Magazine* (1887) July.
81. Anna Gambles (1999).
82. Burngreave (Sheffield) Conservative Association, Minute Book, Meeting of the Executive Committee, 20 October 1910, Sheffield City Archives.
83. John Belchem (1990: 30–1).
84. Philip Williamson (2002: 9).

8   The Decline of Liberalism and the Rise of Labour I: A Narrative

1. J. A. Thompson (1990).
2. While this chapter, and Chapter 9, are concerned with the relationship between the Liberal and Labour parties, more attention has been paid to the rise of independent Labour politics, partly because it constituted the most novel development in popular politics during this period, but also because this has been the focus of much of the 'new political history'. For a critical overview, see Lawrence Black (2003).
3. Paul Adelman (1986: 10–18).
4. Eugenio F. Biagini and Alistair J. Reid (1991:13).
5. E. P. Thompson (1960: 285–6).
6. Jack Reynolds and Keith Laybourn (1978: 326–7).
7. Stan Shipley (1971); Eugenio F. Biagini and Alistair J. Reid (1991); Jon Lawrence (1992); Antony Taylor (1999b).
8. *Bradford Daily Argus* (1892) 16 June.
9. 'The Labour Party and the Books that Helped to Make It', *Review of Reviews* (1906: 571).
10. Antony Taylor (2004a: ch. 2).
11. Stan Shipley (1971).
12. 'The Labour Party and the Books that Helped to Make it'.
13. David James (1995: 163).
14. Joan Allen (2007: 129).
15. Noel Thompson (1996: 5).
16. Jon Lawrence (1992: 177).
17. Martin Crick (1994); Keith Laybourn (1997: xxii).
18. Noel Thompson (1996: 5).
19. Mark Bevir (1999).
20. A. M. McBriar (1962: 2).
21. Sidney Webb, 'Socialism in England', *Publications of the American Economic Association*, 4 (1889: 13–14).

22. Antony Taylor (2004a: 51).
23. Jon Lawrence (1992: 179–85).
24. Martin Crick (1994).
25. Keith Laybourn and Jack Reynolds (1984: 95).
26. Keith Laybourn (1997: 36).
27. John Shepherd (1991); Alastair J. Reid (1991).
28. Alastair J. Reid (1991: 238).
29. Stephen Yeo (1977); David Howell (1983: 389–97); Martin Crick (1994: 83–92, 238–60); Keith Laybourn (1994).
30. Keith Laybourn (1997: xxii).
31. 'Pro-Boer' was the somewhat overly simplified, derisive term applied to those who opposed the Conservative Government's policy of fighting the Boers in South Africa.
32. Gordon Phillips (1992: 6).
33. Michael Freeden (1978).
34. Peter Clarke (1971); Duncan Tanner (1990: 130–3, 162–4).
35. Jon Lawrence (1998: 208–9).
36. James R. Moore (2001).
37. Keith Laybourn and Jack Reynolds (1984: 205).
38. W. E. Clegg, 'Memorandum on Socialism' (1909) 17 December, H. J. Wilson Papers, Sheffield City Archives MD5906.
39. Kenneth Morgan (1973); A. W. Purdue (1981).
40. David Rubinstein (1978).
41. *Sheffield Guardian* (1906) 31 March.
42. David Clark (1981); Keith Laybourn (1997: 47).
43. George L. Bernstein (1983: 640).
44. *Keighley News* (1895) 6 July.
45. Jon Lawrence (1999: 148).
46. Pat Thane (1991: 261).
47. Chris Cook (1976: 58).
48. Duncan Tanner (1990: 253).
49. Cf. Ross McKibbin (1974: 76); Duncan Tanner (1990: 329).
50. Duncan Tanner (1990: 74).

9   *The Decline of Liberalism and the Rise of Labour II: The Debate*

1. Snowden (1934: vol. 1, 319).
2. Cf. Gareth Stedman Jones (1974).
3. Ross McKibbin (1984).
4. For a forensic analysis of these dynamics, see Duncan Tanner (1990: chs 2 and 3).

5. James R. Moore (2006).
6. Patricia Lynch (2003);Michael Dawson (1995).
7. Michael Bentley (1987: 110).
8. Marc Brodie (2004: ch. 4).
9. Frank Trentmann (2008).
10. Ian Packer (2001).
11. Eugenio F. Biagini and Alistair J. Reid (1991).
12. Keith Laybourn and Jack Reynolds (1984).
13. Antony Taylor (2004a: 8-16).
14. Duncan Tanner (1990: ch. 1); Pat Thane (1991); James R. Moore (2006).
15. Peter Clarke (1971); Ross McKibbin (1974); George L. Bernstein (1986); Keith Laybourn and Jack Reynolds (1984).
16. Eric J. Hobsbawm (1984: 194–213); Mike Savage and Andrew Miles (1994).
17. Patrick Joyce (1982 [1980]: 331–42).
18. Stedman Jones (1974); Ross McKibbin (1984).
19. Ross McKibbin (1974).
20. George L. Bernstein (1986: 201).
21. Jonathan Parry (1993).
22. For this characterization, see Bentley (1987: 110).
23. H. C. G. Matthew, R. McKibbin and J. A. Kay (1976).
24. Peter Clarke (1971).
25. David W. Bebbington (1984); Kenneth D. Wald (1983). For further elaboration of this characterization, see Jon Lawrence (1997: 81).
26. Jon Lawrence (1998: 122–33); Duncan Tanner (1997).
27. See Chapter 7, footnote 18.
28. Duncan Tanner (1990: 99–129).
29. Duncan Tanner (1997: 115); Michael Hart (1982).
30. Michael Childs (1995: 131).
31. Keith Laybourn (1995: 212).
32. John Belchem (1990: 4).
33. G. R. Searle (1983); George L. Bernstein (1986: 1–5, 135–65, 197–201); Barry Doyle (1995); James R. Moore (2003).
34. James R. Moore (2006: 270–1).
35. Duncan Tanner (1990: 88).
36. Carl Levy (1987); Jon Lawrence (1998: 143).
37. Tom Mann, 'What is the ILP Driving at?'(Labour Press Society, 1895: 2), Philip Snowden Collection, Keighley Library.
38. Keir Hardie, 'The ILP. And all about it' (ILP Publications, n.d.: 7).
39. *Keighley Labour Journal* (1894) 21 January.
40. Snowden (1934: vol. 1, 315).
41. *Bradford Daily Argus* (1892) 5 July.

42. Tom Mann (1895: 4).
43. Keir Hardie (n.d.: 9).
44. Stephen Yeo (1977).
45. *Labour Prophet* (1892) January.
46. *Labour Prophet* (1892) November.
47. Keir Hardie, *From Serfdom to Socialism* (London: George Allen, 1907: 38 and 44).
48. Mark Bevir (1999).
49. Fred Jowett, *The Socialist and the City* (London: George Allen, 1907: 8); Joan Smith (1984: 36).
50. Quoted in Jack Reynolds and Keith Laybourn (1978: 319).
51. Jon Lawrence (1998: 122–7, chs 6 and 9).
52. Steven Fielding (1993: 88–92, 95–100).
53. Krista Cowman (2002: 134).
54. Isabella O. Ford, *Women and Socialism* (Keighley: Rydal Press, 1904: 3).
55. June Hannam (1987: 220).
56. *The Attercliffe Elector* (1909) 1 May; *Sheffield Guardian* (1910) 4 February.
57. Martin Pugh (2002a).
58. Duncan Tanner (1997: 112).

10 *The Modernization of Popular Politics*

1. John A. Phillips and Charles Wetherell (1995: 415).
2. Peter Clarke (1972); J. P. D. Dunbabin (1980); Gary Cox (1986); H. J. Hanham (1959); Eric J. Evans (1985); Angus Hawkins (1989); John A. Phillips and Charles Wetherell (1995).
3. Frank O'Gorman (1989: 357).
4. John A. Phillips and Charles Wetherell (1991: 626; 1995).
5. Philip Salmon (2002: chs 1 and 7).
6. Philip Salmon (2002: 7).
7. Philip Salmon (2002: 8).
8. Edwin Jaggard (2004).
9. John Garrard (1977).
10. See Chapter 1.
11. *Bradford Observer* (1884) 2 December.
12. *Hansard*, House of Commons, vol. 294, col. 660–1, 699–700.
13. G. R. Searle (2004: 138).
14. *Manchester Courier* (1884) 15 October.
15. James Vernon (1993: 337).
16. James Vernon (1993: 102).

17. David Vincent (1989: 235). For evidence of Chartist communal reading, see Malcolm Chase (2007: 45).
18. Marc Brodie (2004: 35–43, 159–79).
19. James Thompson (2007: 180).
20. James Vernon (1993: 147).
21. Cf. James Vernon (1993: 112).
22. Mark Hampton (2001: 214–15).
23. James Vernon (1993: 110).
24. Matthew Roberts (2006a: 135); Simon Morgan (2007: 151–2).
25. Matthew Cragoe (2000).
26. Matthew Cragoe (2004: 11).
27. Jon Lawrence (1998: ch. 7).
28. Kit Good (2007); Jon Lawrence (2006: 188).
29. Frank Trentmann (2008).
30. Justin Wasserman and Edwin Jaggard (2007: 132).
31. Frank Trentmann (2008).
32. Jon Lawrence has recently argued that the number of outdoor political meetings actually increased in the later nineteenth century. He further concludes that 'there is little evidence that disruption and disorder were declining as features of British public politics during the Edwardian era'. See Jon Lawrence (2006: 189, 191).
33. Gareth Stedman Jones (1974).
34. Antony Taylor (2005a: 75).
35. John Garrard (1977).
36. Jon Lawrence (1998: 163ff.); V. C. Barbary (2008).
37. Mathew Roberts (2006b: 238).
38. Jon Lawrence (1998: 169).
39. Patricia Lynch (2003: 85).
40. Julie Light (2005).
41. *Sheffield Daily Telegraph* (1878) 2 November.
42. Marc Brodie (2004: 13, 75ff.).
43. Jon Lawrence (1998: 166).
44. Jon Lawrence (1998: 141).
45. Hilaire Belloc and Cecil Chesterton, *The Party System*, 2nd edn (London, Latimer, 1911) [1913].
46. Frans Coetzee (1990).
47. Jon Lawrence (1998).
48. Leonore Davidoff and Catherine Hall (1987).
49. Kathryn Gleadle and Sarah Richardson (2000).
50. Helen Rogers (2000: 2).
51. Jutta Schwarzkopf (1991: 226).
52. Robert Gray (1996: 29); Eileen Janes Yeo (1998: 10).

53. *The Chartist* (1839) 3 March.
54. Barbara Taylor (1983: 248).
55. Patricia Hollis (1987: 471–2).
56. See, for example, Clare Midgley (1992: 116).
57. Simon Morgan (2007: 136).
58. Linda Walker (1987: 172–3).
59. Clare Midgley (1992); Anna Clark (1995: Part 3).
60. Kathryn Gleadle (2001: 35).
61. Anna Clark (1992).
62. Anna Clark (1995); Catherine Hall, Keith McClelland and Jane Rendall (2000: 106).
63. Sandra Stanley Holton (1996: 10–11).
64. The Acts were eventually repealed in 1886.
65. Sandra Stanley Holton (1998).
66. Catherine Hall, Keith McClelland and Jane Rendall (2000: 131).
67. Laura E. Nym Mayhall (2000: 343–4).
68. Sandra Stanley Holton (1996: 27).
69. Jane Rendall (1987); Susan Kingsley Kent (1987); Sandra Stanley Holton (1986).
70. Brian Harrison (1978).
71. Harling (2004: 221).
72. K. Theodore Hoppen (1996: 571).
73. John Brewer (1976); Frank O'Gorman (1989); Nicholas Rogers (1989); Kathleen Wilson (1995).
74. Jon Lawrence (2001: 211).
75. D. A. Hamer (1977).
76. Laura E. Nym Mayhall (2000).
77. Jon Lawrence (2001: 223).
78. Jon Lawrence (2006: 203–12).

References

Adams, Tony (1990) 'Labour and the First World War: Economy, Politics and the Erosion of Local Peculiarity?', *Journal of Regional and Local Studies*, 10: 23–47.

Adelman, Paul (1984) *Victorian Radicalism: The Middle-Class Experience, 1830–1914* (Harlow: Longman).

Adelman, Paul (1986) *The Rise of the Labour Party, 1880–1945*, 2nd edn (London: Longman).

Allen, Joan (2007) *Joseph Cowen and Popular Radicalism on Tyneside, 1829–1900* (Monmouth: Merlin Press).

Arnstein, W. L. (1965) *The Bradlaugh Case: A Study in Late Victorian Opinion and Politics* (Oxford: Clarendon Press).

August, Andrew (2001) 'A Culture of Consolation? Rethinking Politics in Working-Class London, 1870–1914', *Historical Research*, 74: 193–219.

Bailey, Peter (1979) 'Will the Real Bill Banks Stand Up? Towards a Role Analysis of Mid-Victorian Working-Class Respectability', *Journal of Social History*, 12: 336–53.

Barbary, V. C. (2008) 'Reinterpreting "Factory Politics" in Bury, Lancashire, 1868–1880', *Historical Journal*, 51: 115–44.

Beales, Derek (1999) 'The Idea of Reform in British Politics, 1829–1850', in *Reform in Great Britain and Germany 1750–1850* (Oxford: Oxford University Press for The British Academy).

Bebbington, David W. (1984) 'Nonconformity and Electoral Sociology, 1867–1918', *Historical Journal*, 27: 633–56.

Belchem, John (1982) '1848: Feargus O'Connor and the Collapse of the Mass Platform', in James Epstein and Dorothy Thompson (eds), *The Chartist Experience: Studies in Working-Class Radicalism and Culture, 1830–1860* (London: Macmillan).

Belchem, John (1990) *Class, Party and the Political System in Britain, 1867–1914* (Oxford: Blackwell).

Belchem, John (1996) *Popular Radicalism in Nineteenth-Century Britain* (Basingstoke: Macmillan).

Belchem, John (2005) 'Radical Language, Meaning and Identity in the Age of the Chartists', *Journal of Victorian Culture*, 10: 1–14.

Belchem, John and Epstein, James (1997) 'The Nineteenth-Century Gentleman Leader Revisited', *Social History*, 22: 173–92, reprinted in James Epstein (2003).

Bentley, Michael (1987) *The Climax of Liberal Politics: British Liberalism in Theory and Practice, 1868–1918* (London: Edward Arnold).

Bentley, Michael (1999) 'Victorian Politics and the Linguistic Turn', *Historical Journal*, 42: 883–902.

Bernstein, George L. (1983) 'Liberalism and the Progressive Alliance in the Constituencies, 1900–1914', *Historical Journal*, 26: 617–40.

Bernstein, George L. (1986) *Liberalism and Liberal Politics in Edwardian England* (London: Allen & Unwin).

Bevir, Mark (1999) 'The Labour Church Movement, 1891–1902', *Journal of British Studies*, 38: 217–45.

Biagini, Eugenio F. (1992) *Liberty, Retrenchment and Reform: Popular Liberalism in the Age of Gladstone, 1860–1880* (Cambridge: Cambridge University Press).

Biagini, Eugenio F. and Reid, Alistair J. (eds) (1991) *Currents of Radicalism: Popular Radicalism, Organised Labour and Party Politics in Britain, 1850–1914* (Cambridge: Cambridge University Press).

Black, Lawrence (2003) '"What Kind of People Are You?" Labour, the People and the "New Political History"', in John Callaghan, Steven Fielding and Steve Ludlam (eds), *Interpreting the Labour Party: Approaches to Labour Politics and History* (Manchester: Manchester University Press).

Bonner, Hypatia Bradlaugh (1908) [1894] *Charles Bradlaugh: His Life and Work*, 2 vols (London: T. Fisher Unwin).

Boyd, Kelly and McWilliam, Rohan (2007) 'Introduction: Rethinking the Victorians', in Kelly Boyd and Rohan McWilliam, *The Victorian Studies Reader* (Oxford: Routledge).

Brewer, John (1976) *Party Ideology and Popular Politics at the Accession of George III* (Cambridge: Cambridge University Press).

Briggs, Asa (1956) 'Middle-Class Consciousness in English Politics, 1780–1846', *Past and Present*, 9: 65–74.

Briggs, Asa (1959a) 'The Local Background of Chartism', in Asa Briggs (ed.), *Chartist Studies* (London: Macmillan).

Briggs, Asa (1959b) *The Age of Improvement, 1783–1867* (London: Longman).

Briggs, Asa (ed.) (1959c) *Chartist Studies* (London: Macmillan).

Brodie, Marc (2003) 'Free Trade and Cheap Theatre: Sources of Politics for the Nineteenth-Century London Poor', *Social History*, 28: 346–60.

Brodie, Marc (2004) *The Politics of the Poor: The East End of London, 1885–1914* (Oxford: Clarendon Press).

Browne, Harry (1979) *The Rise of British Trade Unions, 1825–1914* (London: Longman).

Burn, W. L. (1964) *The Age of Equipoise: A Study of the Mid-Victorian Generation* (London: Allen & Unwin).

Burness, Catriona (2002) 'The Making of Scottish Unionism, 1886–1914', in Stuart Ball and Ian Holliday (eds), *Mass Conservatism: The Conservatives and the Public since the 1880s* (London: Frank Cass).

Cain, Peter J. (ed.) (1995) *Political and Economic Works of Richard Cobden*, 6 vols (London: Routledge).

Cain, Peter J. (2006) 'Character and Imperialism: The British Financial Administration of Egypt, 1878–1914', *Journal of Imperial and Commonwealth History*, 34: 177–200.

Cain, P. J. and Hopkins, A. G. (1987) 'Gentlemanly Capitalism and British Expansion Overseas II: New Imperialism, 1850–1945', *Economic History Review*, 40: 1–26.

Chase, Malcolm (1991) 'Out of Radicalism: The Mid-Victorian Freehold Land Movement', *English Historical Review*, 106: 319–45.

Chase, Malcolm (2000a) *Early Trade Unionism: Fraternity, Skill and the Politics of Labour* (Aldershot: Ashgate).

Chase, Malcolm (2000b) 'Republicanism: Movement or Moment?', in David Nash and Antony Taylor (eds), *Republicanism in Victorian Society* (Stroud: Sutton Publishing).

Chase, Malcolm (2007) *Chartism: A New History* (Manchester: Manchester University Press).

Childs, Michael (1995) 'Labour Grows Up: The Electoral System, Political Generations, and British Politics 1890–1929', *Twentieth Century British History*, 6: 123–44.

Claeys, Gregory (ed.) (2001) *The Chartist Movement in Britain, 1838–1850*, 6 vols (London: Pickering & Chatto).

Clark, Anna (1992) 'The Rhetoric of Chartist Domesticity: Gender, Language and Class in the 1830s and 1840s', *Journal of British Studies*, 31: 62–88.

Clark, Anna (1995) *The Struggle for the Breeches: Gender and the Making of the British Working Class* (Berkeley: University of California Press).

Clark, Anna (1996) 'Gender, Class and the Nation: Franchise Reform in England, 1832–1928', in James Vernon (ed.), *Re-Reading the Constitution: New Narratives in the Political History of England's Long Nineteenth Century* (Cambridge: Cambridge University Press).

Clark, Anna (2003) 'Changing Concepts of Citizenship: Gender, Empire and Class', *Journal of British Studies*, 42: 263–70.

Clark, David (1981) *Colne Valley: Radicalism to Socialism* (London: Longman).

Clarke, Peter (1971) *Lancashire and the New Liberalism* (Cambridge: Cambridge University Press).

Clarke, Peter (1972) 'Electoral Sociology of Modern Britain', *History*, 57: 31–55.

Coetzee, Frans (1990) *For Party or Country: Nationalism and the Dilemmas of Popular Conservatism in Edwardian England* (New York: Oxford University Press).

Cole, G. D. H. (1948) *A Short History of the British Working Class Movement, 1789–1947* (London: George Allen & Unwin).

Coleman, Bruce (1988) *Conservatism and the Conservative Party in Nineteenth Century Britain* (London: Edward Arnold).

Coohill, Joseph (2005) '"The Liberal Brigade": Ideas of Co-operation between Liberal MPs in 1835', *Parliamentary History*, 24: 231–6.

Cook, Chris (1976) 'Labour and the Downfall of Liberalism', in Chris Cook and Alan Sked (eds), *Crisis and Controversy: Essays in Honour of A. J. P. Taylor* (London: Macmillan).

Cook, Chris and Stevenson, John (1988) *The Longman Handbook of Modern British History, 1714–1987*, 2nd edn (Harlow: Longman).

Cooke, A. B. and Vincent, J. (1974) *The Governing Passion: Cabinet Government and Party Politics in Britain, 1885–86* (Brighton: Harvester).

Cooper, Timothy (2005) 'London-over-the-border: Politics in Suburban Walthamstow, 1870–1914', in Matthew Cragoe and Antony Taylor (eds), *London Politics, 1760–1914* (Basingstoke: Palgrave).

Cornford, James (1963) 'The Transformation of Conservatism in the Late Nineteenth Century', *Victorian Studies*, 7: 35–77.

Cowling, Maurice (1971) *The Impact of Labour: The Beginning of Modern British Politics* (Cambridge: Cambridge University Press).

Cowman, Krista (2002) 'Incipient Toryism'? The Women's Social and Political Union and the Independent Labour Party, 1903–14', *History Workshop Journal*, 53: 129–40.

Cox, Gary (1986) 'The Development of a Party-Orientated Electorate in England, 1832–1918', *British Journal of Political Science*, 16: 187–216.

Craig, F. W. S. (1981) *British Electoral Facts, 1832–1980* (Chichester: Parliamentary Research Services).

Cragoe, Matthew (2000) '"Jenny Rules the Roost": Women and Electoral Politics, 1832–68', in Kathryn Gleadle and Sarah Richardson (eds), *Women in British Politics, 1760–1860: The Power of the Petticoat* (Basingstoke: Macmillan).

Cragoe, Matthew (2004) *Culture, Politics and National Identity in Wales, 1832–1886* (Oxford: Clarendon Press).

Crick, Martin (1994) *The History of the Social Democratic Federation* (Keele: Keele University Press).

Crossick, Geoffrey (1978) *An Artisan Elite in Victorian Society: Kentish London, 1840–1880* (London: Croom Helm).

Crossick, Geoffrey (1987) 'The Classes and the Masses in Victorian England', *History Today*, 37(3): 29–35.

Crowson, Nicholas (2001) *The Longman Companion to the Conservative Party since 1830* (Harlow: Pearson Education).

Cunningham, Hugh (1981) 'The Language of Patriotism, 1750–1914', *History Workshop Journal*, 12: 8–33.

Davidoff, Leonore and Hall, Catherine (1987) *Family Fortunes: Men and Women of the English Middle Class, 1780–1850* (London: Routledge).

Davis, David Brion (1996) [1988] *The Problem of Slavery in Western Culture* (Oxford: Oxford University Press).

Davis, John and Tanner, Duncan (1996) 'The Borough Franchise after 1867', *Historical Research*, 69: 306–27.

Dawson, Michael (1995) 'Liberalism in Devon and Cornwall, 1910–1931: "The Old-Time Religion"', *Historical Journal*, 38: 425–37.

Dolléans, Edouard (1949) *Le Chartisme, 1831–1848* (Paris: M. Rivière).

Doyle, Barry (1995) 'Urban Liberalism and the "Lost Generation": Politics and Middle-Class Culture in Norwich, 1900–1935', *Historical Journal*, 38: 617–34.

Drescher, Seymour (1981) 'Cart Whip and Billy Roller: Antislavery and Reform Symbolism in Industrializing Britain', *Journal of Social History*, 15: 3–24.

Driver, Cecil (1946) *Tory Radical: The Life of Richard Oastler* (New York: Oxford University Press).

Driver, Felix (1991) 'Tory-Radicalism? Ideology, Strategy and Popular Politics during the Eighteen-Thirties', *Northern History*, 27: 120–38.

Dunbabin, J. P. D. (1980) 'British Elections in the 19th and 20th Centuries: A Regional Approach', *English Historical Review*, 95: 241–67.

Dunbabin, J. P. D. (1994) 'Some Implications of the 1885 Shift Towards Single-Member Constituencies: A Note', *English Historical Review*, 109: 241–67.

Durbach, Nadja (2005) *Bodily Matters: The Anti-Vaccination Movement in England, 1853–1907* (Durham, NC: Duke University Press).

Eastwood, David (1992) 'Peel and the Conservative Party Reconsidered', *History Today*, 42(3): 31.

Epstein, James (1982) 'Some Organisational and Cultural Aspects of the Chartist Movement in Nottingham', in James Epstein and Dorothy

Thompson (eds), *The Chartist Experience: Studies in Working-Class Radicalism and Culture, 1830–1860* (London: Macmillan).

Epstein, James (1989) 'Understanding the Cap of Liberty: Symbolic Practice and Social Conflict in Early Nineteenth-Century England', *Past and Present*, 122: 75–118.

Epstein, James (1990) 'The Constitutional Idiom: Radical Reasoning, Rhetoric and Action in Early Nineteenth-Century England', *Journal of Social History*, 3: 553–74.

Epstein, James (1994) *Radical Expression: Political Language, Ritual and Symbol in England, 1790–1850* (Oxford: Oxford University Press).

Epstein, James (1996) '"Our Real Constitution": Trial Defence and Radical Memory in the Age of Revolution', in James Vernon (ed.), *Re-Reading the Constitution: New Narratives in the Political History of England's Long Nineteenth Century* (Cambridge: Cambridge University Press).

Epstein, James (2003) *In Practice: Studies in the Language and Culture of Popular Politics in Modern Britain* (Stanford: Stanford University Press).

Evans, Eric J. (1985) *Political Parties in Britain 1783–1867* (London: Methuen).

Evans, Eric J. (2000) *Parliamentary Reform, c.1770–1918* (London: Longman).

Fforde, Matthew (1990) *Conservatism and Collectivism, 1880–1914* (Edinburgh: Edinburgh University Press).

Fielding, Steven (1993) *Class and Ethnicity: Irish Catholics in England, 1880–1939* (Buckingham: Open University Press).

Finn, Margot C. (1993) *After Chartism: Class and Nation in English Radical Politics, 1848–1874* (Cambridge: Cambridge University Press).

Fladeland, Betty (1982) '"Our Cause being One and the Same": Abolitionists and Chartism', in James Walvin (ed.), *Slavery and British Society 1776–1846* (London: Macmillan).

Ford, C. S. (2002) *Pastors and Polemicists: The Character of Popular Anglicanism in South-East Lancashire* (Manchester: Chetham Society).

Foster, John (1974) *Class Struggle and the Industrial Revolution* (London: Weidenfeld & Nicolson).

Foster, R. F. (1983) 'Tory Democracy and Political Elitism: Provincial Conservatism and Parliamentary Tories in the early 1880s', in A. Cosgrove and J. McGuire (eds), *Parliament and Community* (Belfast: Appletree Press).

Francis, Martin and Zweiniger-Bargielowska, Ina (eds) (1996) *The Conservatives and British Society, 1880–1990* (Cardiff: University of Wales Press).

Fraser, Derek (1976) *Urban Politics in Victorian England: The Structure of Politics in Victorian Cities* (Leicester: Leicester University Press).

Fraser, Derek (1980) 'Politics and Society in the Nineteenth Century', in Derek Fraser (ed.), *A History of Modern Leeds* (Manchester: Manchester University Press).

Freeden, Michael (1978) *The New Liberalism: An Ideology of Social Reform* (Oxford: Clarendon Press).

Gadian, David (1996) 'Radicalism and Liberalism in Oldham: A Study of Conflict, Continuity and Change in Popular Politics, 1830–52', *Social History*, 21: 265–80.

Gambles, Anna (1999) *Protection and Politics: Conservative Economic Discourse, 1815–1852* (Woodbridge: Boydell Press).

Garrard, John (1977) 'Parties, Members and Voters after 1867', *Historical Journal*, 20: 145–63.

Garrard, John (2002) *Democratisation in Britain: Elites, Civil Society and Reform Since 1800* (Basingstoke: Palgrave).

Gash, Norman (1953) *Politics in the Age of Peel: A Study in the Technique of Parliamentary Representation, 1830–50* (London: Longman, Green).

Gash, Norman (1972) *Sir Robert Peel: The Life of Sir Robert Peel After 1830* (London: Longman).

Gleadle, Kathryn (2001) *British Women in the Nineteenth Century* (Basingstoke: Palgrave).

Gleadle, Kathryn and Richardson, Sarah (eds) (2000) *Women in British Politics, 1760–1860: The Power of the Petticoat* (Basingstoke: Palgrave).

Good, Kit (2007) '"Quit Ye Like Men": Platform Manliness and Electioneering, 1895–1939', in Matthew McCormack (ed.), *Public Men: Masculinity and Politics in Modern Britain* (Basingstoke: Palgrave Macmillan).

Gray, R. Q. (1976) *The Labour Aristocracy in Victorian Edinburgh* (Oxford: Clarendon Press).

Gray, Robert (1981) *The Aristocracy of Labour in Nineteenth-Century Britain, c.1850–1900* (Basingstoke: Macmillan).

Gray, Robert (1996) *The Factory Question and Industrial England, 1830–1860* (Cambridge: Cambridge University Press).

Green, E. H. H. (1995) *The Crisis of Conservatism: The Politics, Economics and Ideology of the British Conservative Party, 1880–1914* (London: Routledge).

Green, E. H. H. (2002) *Ideologies of Conservatism: Conservative Ideas in the Twentieth Century* (Oxford: Oxford University Press).

Gregory, James (2007) *Of Victorians and Vegetarians: The Vegetarian Movement in Victorian Britain* (London: I. B. Tauris).

Griffin, Ben (2003) 'Class, Gender and Liberalism in Parliament, 1868–1882: The Case of the Married Women's Property Acts', *Historical Journal*, 46: 59–87.

Hall, Catherine (2000) 'The Rule of Difference: Gender, Class and Empire in the Making of the 1832 Reform Act', in Ida Blom, Karen Hagemann and Catherine Hall (eds), *Gendered Nations: Nationalism and Gender Order in the Long Nineteenth Century* (Oxford: Berg).

Hall, Catherine, McClelland, Keith and Rendall, Jane (2000) *Defining the Victorian Nation: Class, Race, Gender and the Reform Act of 1867* (Cambridge: Cambridge University Press).

Hall, Robert G. (1999a) 'Chartism Remembered: William Aitken, Liberalism, and the Politics of Memory', *Journal of British Studies*, 38: 445–70.

Hall, Robert G. (1999b) 'Creating a People's History: Political Identity and History in Chartism, 1832–1848', in Owen Ashton, Robert Fyson and Stephen Roberts (eds), *The Chartist Legacy* (Woodbridge: Merlin Press).

Hall, Robert G. (2007) *Voices of the People: Democracy and Chartist Political Identity, 1830–1870* (Monmouth: Merlin Press).

Hamer, D. A. (1972) *Liberal Politics in the Age of Gladstone and Rosebery* (Oxford: Clarendon Press).

Hamer, D. A. (1977) *The Politics of Electoral Pressure: A Study in the History of Victorian Reform Agitations* (Hassocks: Harvester Press).

Hampton, Mark (2001) ' "Understanding Media": Theories of the Press in Britain, 1850–1914', *Media, Culture and Society*, 23: 213–31.

Hanham, H. J. (1959) *Elections and Party Management: Politics in the Time of Disraeli and Gladstone* (London: Longman).

Hannam, June (1987) ' "In the Comradeship of the Sexes Lies the Hope of Progress and Social Regeneration": Women in the West Riding ILP, c.1890–1914', in Jane Rendall (ed.), *Equal or Different: Women's Politics, 1800–1914* (Oxford: Basil Blackwell).

Harling, Philip (1995) 'Rethinking "Old Corruption"', *Past and Present*, 147: 127–58.

Harling, Philip (1996) *The Waning of "Old Corruption": The Politics of Economical Reform in Britain, 1779–1846* (Oxford: Oxford University Press).

Harling, Philip (2001) *The Modern British State: An Historical Introduction* (Cambridge: Cambridge University Press).

Harling, Philip (2003) 'Equipoise Regained? Recent Trends in British Political History, 1790–1867', *Journal of Modern History*, 75: 890–918.

Harling, Philip (2004) 'The Centrality of Locality: The Local State, Local Democracy, and Local Consciousness in Late-Victorian and Edwardian Britain', *Journal of Victorian Culture*, 9: 216–34.

Harrison, Brian (1978) *Separate Spheres: The Opposition of Women's Suffrage in Britain* (London: Croom Helm).

Harrison, Brian and Hollis, Patricia (1967) 'Chartism, Liberalism and Robert Lowery', *English Historical Review*, 82: 503–35.

Hart, Michael (1982) 'The Liberals, the War and the Franchise', *English Historical Review*, 97: 820–32.

Hawkins, Angus (1989) '"Parliamentary Government" and Victorian Political Parties, c.1830–c.1880', *English Historical Review*, 104: 638–69.

Hawkins, Angus (1998) *British Party Politics, 1852–1886* (Basingstoke: Macmillan).

Hewitt, Martin (1996) *The Emergence of Stability in the Industrial City: Manchester, 1832–67* (Aldershot: Scolar Press).

Hill, R. L. (1929) *Toryism and the People, 1832–1846* (London: Porcupine Press).

Hilton, Boyd (2006) *A Mad, Bad and Dangerous People? England, 1783–1846* (Oxford: Clarendon Press).

Himmelfarb, Gertrude (1966) 'The Politics of Democracy: The English Reform Act of 1867', *Journal of British Studies*, 6: 97–138.

Hobsbawm, Eric J. (1968a) *Industry and Empire: From 1750 to the Present Day* (London: Weidenfeld & Nicolson).

Hobsbawm, Eric J. (1968b) [1964] 'The Labour Aristocracy in Nineteenth-Century Britain', in Eric J. Hobsbawm, *Labouring Men: Studies in the History of Labour* (London: Weidenfeld & Nicolson).

Hobsbawm, Eric J. (1984) 'The Making of the Working Class 1870–1914', in Eric Hobsbawm, *Worlds of Labour: Further Studies in the History of Labour* (Weidenfeld & Nicolson).

Hollis, Patricia (1987) *Ladies Elect: Women in English Local Government, 1865–1914* (Oxford: Oxford University Press).

Hoppen, K. Theodore (1985) 'The Franchise and Electoral Politics in England and Ireland, 1832–1885', *History*, 70: 202–17.

Hoppen, K. Theodore (1994) 'Grammars of Electoral Violence in England and Ireland', *English Historical Review*, 109: 597–620.

Hoppen, K. Theodore (1996) 'Roads to Democracy: Electioneering and Corruption in Nineteenth-Century England and Ireland', *History*, 81: 553–71.

Hoppen, K. Theodore (1998) *The Mid-Victorian Generation, 1846–1886* (Oxford: Clarendon Press).

Hovell, Mark (1918) *The Chartist Movement* (Manchester: Manchester University Press).

Howell, David (1983) *British Workers and the Independent Labour Party, 1881–1906* (Manchester: Manchester University Press).

Innes, Joanna (2003) '"Reform" in English Public Life: The Fortunes of a Word', in Arthur Burns and Joanna Innes (eds), *Rethinking the*

Age of Reform: Britain 1780–1850 (Cambridge: Cambridge University Press).

Jaggard, Edwin (1999) *Cornwall Politics in the Age of Reform, 1790–1885* (Woodbridge: Boydell Press).

Jaggard, Edwin (2004) 'Small Town Politics in Mid-Victorian Britain', *History*, 89: 3–29.

James, David (1995) *Class and Politics in a Northern Industrial Town: Keighley, 1880–1914* (Keele: Keele University Press).

Jefferys, Kevin (2007) *Politics and the People: A History of British Democracy Since 1918* (London: Atlantic Books).

Jenkins, T. A. (2004) 'Political Life in Late Victorian Britain: The Conservatives in Thornbury', *Parliamentary History*, 23: 198–224.

Jones, David (1975) *Chartism and the Chartists* (London: Allen Lane).

Joyce, Patrick (1982) [1980] *Work, Society and Politics: The Culture of the Factory in Later Victorian England* (London: Methuen).

Joyce, Patrick (1991) *Visions of the People: Industrial England and the Question of Class, 1848–1914* (Cambridge: Cambridge University Press).

Joyce, Patrick (1993) 'The Imaginary Discontents of Social History: A Note of Response', *Social History*, 18: 81–5.

Joyce, Patrick (1994) *Democratic Subjects: The Self and the Social in Nineteenth-Century England* (Cambridge: Cambridge University Press).

Joyce, Patrick (1996) 'The Constitution and the Narrative Structure of Victorian Politics', in James Vernon (ed.), *Re-Reading the Constitution: New Narratives in the Political History of England's Long Nineteenth Century* (Cambridge: Cambridge University Press).

King, J. E. (1982) 'The Limits of Paternalism: The Cotton Tyrants of North Lancashire, 1836–1854', *Social History*, 7: 59–73.

Kingsley Kent, Susan (1987) *Sex and Suffrage in Britain, 1860–1914* (New Jersey: Princeton University Press).

Kinzer, Bruce L. (1978) 'The Un-Englishness of the Secret Ballot', *Albion*, 10: 237–56.

Kirk, Neville (1985) *The Growth of Working-Class Reformism in Mid-Victorian England* (London: Croom Helm).

Kirk, Neville (1987) 'In Defence of Class: A Critique of Recent Revisionist Writing upon the Nineteenth-Century English Working Class', *International Review of Social History*, 32: 2–47.

Kirk, Neville (1994a) 'History, Language, Ideas and Postmodernism: A Materialist View', *Social History*, 19: 221–40.

Kirk, Neville (1994b) 'Post-Modernism and the Sublime Myth of the Backward March of Democracy in Nineteenth-Century England', *Labour History Review*, 59: 71–8.

Kirk, Neville (1998) *Change, Continuity and Class: Labour in British Society, 1850–1920* (Manchester: Manchester University Press).

Kirk, Neville (2000) 'Decline and Fall, Resilience and Regeneration: A Review Essay on Social Class', *International Labor and Working-Class History*, 57: 88–102.

Knott, John (1986) *Popular Opposition to the 1834 Poor Law* (London: Croom Helm).

Koditschek, Theodore (1990) *Class Formation and Urban Industrial Society: Bradford, 1750–1850* (Cambridge: Cambridge University Press).

Lawrence, Jon (1991) 'Popular Politics and the Limitations of Party: Wolverhampton, 1867–1900', in Eugenio F. Biagini and Alistair J. Reid (eds), *Currents of Radicalism: Popular Radicalism, Organised Labour and Party Politics in Britain, 1850–1914* (Cambridge: Cambridge University Press).

Lawrence, Jon (1992) 'Popular Radicalism and the Socialist Revival in Britain', *Journal of British Studies*, 31: 163–86.

Lawrence, Jon (1993) 'Class and Gender in the Making of Urban Toryism, 1880–1914', *English Historical Review*, 108: 628–52.

Lawrence, Jon (1997) 'The Dynamics of Urban Politics, 1867–1914', in Jon Lawrence and Miles Taylor (eds), *Party, State and Society: Electoral Behaviour in Britain Since 1820* (Aldershot: Scolar Press).

Lawrence, Jon (1998) *Speaking for the People: Party, Language and Popular Politics in England, 1867–1914* (Cambridge: Cambridge University Press).

Lawrence, Jon (1999) 'The Complexities of English Progressivism: Wolverhampton Politics in the Early Twentieth Century', *Midland History*, 24: 147–66.

Lawrence, Jon (2001) 'Contesting the Male Polity: The Suffragettes and the Politics of Disruption in Edwardian Britain', in Amanda Vickery (ed.), *Women, Privilege and Power: British Politics, 1750 to the Present* (Stanford: Stanford University Press).

Lawrence, Jon (2003) 'Political History', in Stefan Berger, Heiko Feldner and Kevin Passmore (eds), *Writing History: Theory and Practice* (London: Hodder Arnold).

Lawrence, Jon (2006) 'The Transformation of British Public Politics after the First World War', *Past and Present*, 190: 185–216.

Lawrence, Jon and Elliot, Jane (1997) 'Parliamentary Election Results Reconsidered: An Analysis of Borough Elections, 1885–1910', *Parliamentary History*, 16: 18–28.

Lawrence, Jon and Taylor, Miles (1993) 'The Politics of Protest: Gareth Stedman Jones and the Politics of Language – A Reply', *Social History*, 18: 1–15.

Laybourn, Keith (1994) 'The Failure of Socialist Unity in Britain, c.1893–1914', *Transactions of the Royal Historical Society*, Sixth Series, 4: 153–75.

Laybourn, Keith (1995) 'The Rise of Labour and the Decline of Liberalism: The State of the Debate', *History*, 80: 207–26.

Laybourn, Keith (1997) *The Rise of Socialism in Britain, c.1881–1951* (Stroud: Sutton Publishing).

Laybourn, Keith and Reynolds, Jack (1984) *Liberalism and the Rise of Labour 1890–1918* (London: Croom Helm).

Levy, Carl (1987) *Socialism and the Intelligentsia, 1880–1914* (New York: Routledge).

Light, Julie (2005) ' " . . . Mere Seekers of Fame?": Personalities, Power and Politics in the Small Town: Pontypool and Bridgend, c.1860–95', *Urban History*, 32: 88–99.

Lynch, Patricia (2003) *The Liberal Party in Rural England, 1885–1910: Radicalism and Community* (Oxford: Clarendon Press).

MacCoby, S. (ed.) (1952) *The English Radical Tradition 1763–1914* (London: Nicholas Kaye).

Macleod, Hugh (1984) *Religion and the Working Class in Nineteenth-Century Britain* (London: Macmillan).

Mandler, Peter (1990) *Aristocratic Government in the Age of Reform: Whigs and Liberals, 1830–1852* (Oxford: Clarendon Press).

Mandler, Peter (2001) 'Review of *Defining the Victorian Nation: Class, Race, Gender and the Reform Act of 1867*' [Catherine Hall, Keith McClelland and Jane Rendall (2000)], *Parliamentary History*, 20: 272–5.

Mares, Detlev (2005) 'Transcending the Metropolis: London and Provincial Popular Radicalism', in Matthew Cragoe and Antony Taylor (eds), *London Politics, 1760–1914* (Basingstoke: Palgrave Macmillan).

Mather, F. C. (1972) *Chartism* (London: Historical Association).

Matthew, H. C. G.; McKibbin, R. I. and Kay, J. (1976) 'The Franchise Factor in the Rise of the Labour Party', *English Historical Review*, 91: 723–52.

Mayfield, David and Thorne, Susan (1992) 'Social History and its Discontents: Gareth Stedman Jones and the Politics of Language', *Social History*, 17: 165–88.

Mayhall, Laura E. Nym (2000) 'Defining Militancy: Radical Protest, the Constitutional Idiom, and Women's Suffrage in Britain, 1908–1909', *Journal of British Studies*, 39: 340–71.

McBriar, A. M. (1962) *Fabian Socialism and English Politics* (Cambridge: Cambridge University Press).

McCalman, Iain (1993) *Radical Underworld: Prophets, Revolutionaries, and Pornographers in London, 1795–1840* (Oxford: Clarendon Press).

McCormack, Matthew (2004) 'The Independent Man: Gender, Obligation, and Virtue in the 1832 Reform Act', in Michael J. Turner (ed.), *Reform and Reformers in Nineteenth Century Britain* (Sunderland: Sunderland University Press).

McCormack, Matthew (2005) *The Independent Man: Citizenship and Gender Politics in Georgian England* (Manchester: Manchester University Press).

McCormack, Matthew (2007) 'Men, "The Public" and Political History', in Matthew McCormack (ed.), *Public Men: Masculinity and Politics in Modern Britain* (Basingstoke: Palgrave Macmillan).

McCormack, Matthew and Roberts, Matthew (2007) 'Conclusion: Chronologies in the History of British Political Masculinities, c.1700–2000', in Matthew McCormack (ed.), *Public Men: Masculinity and Politics in Modern Britain* (Basingstoke: Palgrave Macmillan).

McKenzie, R. and Silver, A. (1968) *Angels in Marble: Working-Class Conservatism in Urban England* (London: Heinemann).

McKibbin, Ross (1974) *The Evolution of the Labour Party, 1910–1924* (Oxford: Clarendon Press).

McKibbin, Ross (1984) 'Why Was There No Marxism in Great Britain?', *English Historical Review*, 99: 297–331.

McLeod, Hugh (1984) *Religion and the Working Class in Nineteenth-Century Britain* (London: Macmillan).

McLeod, Hugh (1996) *Religion and Society in England, 1850–1914* (Basingstoke: Macmillan).

McWilliam, Rohan (1991) 'Radicalism and Popular Culture: The Tichborne Case and the Politics of "Fair Play"', in Eugenio F. Biagini and Alistair J. Reid (eds), *Currents of Radicalism: Popular Radicalism, Organised Labour and Party Politics in Britain, 1850–1914* (Cambridge: Cambridge University Press).

McWilliam, Rohan (1998) *Popular Politics in Nineteenth-Century England* (London: Routledge).

McWilliam, Rohan (2007) *The Tichborne Claimant: A Victorian Sensation* (London: Hambledon).

Messner, Andrew (1999) 'Land, Leadership, Culture, and Emigration: Some Problems in Chartist Historiography', *Historical Journal*, 42: 1093–109.

Midgley, Clare (1992) *Women Against Slavery: The British Campaigns 1780–1870* (London: Routledge).

Moore, D. C. (1966) 'Concession or Cure: The Sociological Premises of the First Reform Act', *Historical Journal*, 4: 39–59.

Moore, James R. (2001) 'Progressive Pioneers: Manchester Liberalism, the Independent Labour Party, and Local Politics in the 1890s', *Historical Journal*, 44: 989–1013.

Moore, James R. (2003) 'Liberalism and the Politics of Suburbia: Electoral Dynamics in Late Nineteenth-Century South Manchester', *Urban History*, 30: 225–50.

Moore, James R. (2006) *The Transformation of Urban Liberalism: Party Politics and Urban Governance in Late Nineteenth Century England* (Aldershot: Ashgate).

Morgan, Kenneth (1973) 'The New Liberalism and the Challenge of Labour: The Welsh Experience, 1885–1929', *Welsh History Review*, 6: 288–312.

Morgan, Simon (2007) *A Victorian Woman's Place: Public Culture in the Nineteenth Century* (London: Tauris Academic Studies).

Morley, John (1906) *The Life of Richard Cobden* (London: T. Fisher Unwin).

Newbold, Ian (1983) 'Sir Robert Peel and the Conservative Party: A Study in Failure?', *English Historical Review*, 98: 529–57.

Nicholls, David (1996) 'The New Liberalism – After Chartism?', *Social History*, 21: 330–42.

Nicholls, David (1997) 'Friends of the People: Parliamentary Supporters of Popular Radicalism, 1832–1849', *Labour History Review*, 62: 127–46.

Nordlinger, E. A. (1967) *The Working Class Tories: Authority, Deference and Stable Democracy* (London: MacGibbon & Kee).

Nossiter, T. J. (1975) *Influence, Opinion and Political Idioms in Reformed England: Case Studies from the North-East, 1832–74* (Hassocks: Harvester Press).

O'Gorman, Frank (1989) *Voters, Patrons and Parties: The Unreformed Electoral System of Hanoverian England* (Oxford: Clarendon Press).

O'Gorman, Frank (1992) 'Campaign Rituals and Ceremonies: The Social Meaning of Elections in England, 1780–1860', *Past and Present*, 135: 79–115.

O'Gorman, Frank (1993) 'The Electorate Before and After 1832', *Parliamentary History*, 12: 171–83.

O'Leary, Sandra (2004) 'Re-thinking Popular Conservatism in Liverpool: Democracy and Reform in the Later Nineteenth Century', in Michael J. Turner (ed.), *Reform and Reformers in Nineteenth-Century Britain* (Sunderland: Sunderland University Press).

Ostrogorski, Moisei (1970) [1902] *Democracy and the Organization of Political Parties*, 2 vols (New York: Haskell).

Pack, Mark (1995) 'Aspects of the Electoral System, 1800–50: With Special Reference to Yorkshire', Unpublished PhD thesis, University of York.

Packer, Ian (2001) *Lloyd George, Liberalism and the Land: the Land Issue and Party Politics in England, 1906–1914* (Woodbridge: Boydell Press).

Paine, Thomas (1987a) [1792] *The Rights of Man, Part Two*, reprinted in Michael Foot and Isaac Kramnick (eds), *The Thomas Paine Reader* (London: Penguin).

Paine, Thomas (1987b) [1795] 'Dissertation on First Principles of Government', reprinted in Michael Foot and Isaac Kramnick (eds), *The Thomas Paine Reader* (London: Penguin).

Parry, J. P. (2006) 'Liberalism and Liberty', in Peter Mandler (ed.), *Liberty and Authority in Victorian Britain* (Oxford: Oxford University Press).

Parry, Jonathan (1993) *The Rise and Fall of Liberal Government in Victorian Britain* (New Haven: Yale University Press).

Pelling, Henry (1967) *Social Geography of British Elections, 1885–1910* (London: Macmillan).

Phillips, Gordon (1992) *The Rise of the Labour Party, 1893–1931* (London: Routledge).

Phillips, John A. and Wetherell, Charles (1991) 'The Great Reform Bill of 1832 and the Rise of Partisanship', *Journal of Modern History*, 63: 621–46.

Phillips, John A. and Wetherell, Charles (1995) 'The Great Reform Act and the Political Modernisation of England', *American Historical Review*, 100: 411–36.

Pickering, Paul A. (1986) 'Class Without Words: Symbolic Communication in the Chartist Movement', *Past and Present*, 112: 144–62.

Pickering, Paul A. (1991) 'Chartism and the "Trade of Agitation" in Early Victorian Britain', *History*, 76: 221–37.

Pickering, Paul A. (2001) ' "And Your Petitioners &c": Chartist Petitioning in Popular Politics, 1838–1848', *English Historical Review*, 116: 368–88.

Pickering, Paul A. (2003) ' "The Hearts of the Millions": Chartism and Popular Monarchism in the 1840s', *History*, 88: 227–48.

Pickering, Paul A. and Tyrrell, Alex (2000) *The People's Bread: A History of the Anti-Corn Law League* (Leicester: Leicester University Press).

Pocock, J. G. A. (1975) *The Machiavellian Moment: Florentine Political Thought and the Atlantic Republican Tradition* (New Jersey: Princeton).

Price, Richard (1972) *An Imperial War and the British Working Class* (London: Routledge & Kegan Paul).

Price, Richard (1996) 'Historiography, Narrative and the Nineteenth Century', *Journal of British Studies*, 35: 220–56.

Price, Richard (1999) *British Society, 1680–1880: Dynamism, Containment and Change* (Cambridge: Cambridge University Press).

Pugh, Martin (1985) *The Tories and the People 1880–1935* (Oxford: Basil Blackwell).

Pugh, Martin (1988) 'Popular Conservatism in Britain: Continuity and Change, 1880–1987', *Journal of British Studies*, 27: 254–82.

Pugh, Martin (2002a) 'The Rise of Labour and the Political Culture of Conservatism, 1890–1945', *History*, 87: 514–37.

Pugh, Martin (2002b) 'Working-Class Experience and State Social Welfare, 1908–1914: Old Age Pensions Reconsidered', *Historical Journal*, 45: 775–96.

Purdue, A. W. (1981) 'The Liberal and Labour Parties in North-Eastern Politics 1900–14: The Struggle For Supremacy', *International Review of Social History*, 36: 1–24.

Ramsden, John (1999) *An Appetite for Power: A History of the Conservative Party Since 1830* (London: HarperCollins).

Randall, Timothy (1999) 'Chartist Poetry and Song', in Owen Ashton, Robert Fyson and Stephen Roberts (eds), *The Chartist Legacy* (Rendlesham: Merlin Press).

Readman, Paul (1999) 'The 1895 General Election and Political Change in Late Victorian Britain', *Historical Journal*, 42: 467–93.

Readman, Paul (2001a) 'The Liberal Party and Patriotism in Early Twentieth Century Britain', *Twentieth Century British History*, 12: 269–302.

Readman, Paul (2001b) 'The Conservative Party, Patriotism and British Politics: The Case of the General Election of 1900', *Journal of British Studies*, 40: 107–45.

Reid, Alastair J. (1991) 'Old Unionism Reconsidered: The Radicalism of Robert Knight, 1870–1900', in Eugenio F. Biagini and Alistair J. Reid (eds), *Currents of Radicalism: Popular Radicalism, Organised Labour and Party Politics in Britain, 1850–1914* (Cambridge: Cambridge University Press).

Rendall, Jane (ed.) (1987) *Equal or Different: Women's Politics 1800–1914* (Oxford: Basil Blackwell).

Rendall, Jane (1999) 'Women and the Public Sphere', *Gender and History*, 11: 475–88.

Reynolds, Jack and Laybourn, Keith (1978) 'The Emergence of the Independent Labour Party in Bradford', *International Review of Social History*, 30: 313–46.

Roberts, Andrew (1999) *Salisbury: Victorian Titan* (London: Weidenfeld & Nicolson).

Roberts, Matthew (2003) 'W. L. Jackson, Leeds Conservatism and the World of Villa Toryism, c.1867–c.1900', Unpublished PhD thesis, University of York.

Roberts, Matthew (2006a) 'Constructing a Tory World-View: Popular Politics and the Conservative Press in Late Victorian Leeds', *Historical Research*, 79: 115–43.

Roberts, Matthew (2006b) 'Currents of Electoral Independence: James Lowther and Popular Politics in York, c.1865–1880', *Yorkshire Archaeological Journal*, 78: 217–40.

Roberts, Matthew (2006c) ' "Villa Toryism" and Popular Conservatism in Leeds, 1885–1902', *Historical Journal*, 49: 217–46.

Rogers, Helen (2000) *Women and the People: Authority, Authorship and the Radical Tradition in Nineteenth-Century England* (Aldershot: Ashgate).

Rogers, Nicholas (1989) *Whigs and Cities: Popular Politics in the Age of Walpole and Pitt* (Oxford: Clarendon Press).

Rowbotham, Sheila and Weeks, Jeffrey (1977) *Socialism and the New Life: The Personal and Sexual Politics of Edward Carpenter and Havelock Ellis* (London: Pluto Press).

Rowe, D. J. (1967) 'The London Working Men's Association and the People's Charter', *Past and Present*, 36: 73–86.

Royle, Edward (1971) *Radical Politics, 1790–1900: Religion and Unbelief* (London: Longman).

Royle, Edward (1976) *The Infidel Tradition: From Paine to Bradlaugh* (London: Macmillan).

Royle, Edward (1980) *Radicals, Secularists and Republicans: Popular Freethought in Britain, 1866–1915* (Manchester: Manchester University Press).

Royle, Edward (1996) *Chartism*, 3rd edn (Harlow: Pearson Education).

Royle, Edward (2000) 'Chartists and Owenites – Many Parts But One Body', *Labour History Review*, 65: 2–21.

Rubinstein, David (1978) 'The Independent Labour Party and the Yorkshire Miners: The Barnsley By-Election of 1897', *International Review of Social History*, 23: 102–34.

Salmon, Philip (2002) *Electoral Reform at Work: Local Politics and National Parties, 1832–1841* (Woodbridge: Boydell Press).

Salmon, Philip (2005) ' "Reform Should Begin at Home": English Municipal and Parliamentary Reform, 1818–32', in Clyve Jones, Philip Salmon and Richard W. Davis (eds), *Partisan Politics, Principle and Reform in Parliament and the Constituencies, 1689–1880: Essays in Memory of John A. Phillips* (Edinburgh: Edinburgh University Press).

Savage, Michael (1987) *The Dynamics of Working-Class Politics: The Labour Movement in Preston, 1880–1940* (Cambridge: Cambridge University Press).

Savage, Michael and Miles, Andrew (1994) *The Remaking of the British Working Class, 1840–1940* (London: Routledge).

Saville, John (1987) *1848: The British State and the Chartist Movement* (Cambridge: Cambridge University Press).

Schwarzkopf, Jutta (1991) *Women in the Chartist Movement* (Basingstoke: Macmillan).

Searle, G. R. (1983) 'The Edwardian Liberal Party and Business', *English Historical Review*, 98: 28–60.

Searle, G. R. (2004) *A New England? Peace and War, 1886–1918* (Oxford: Clarendon Press).

Seymour, Charles (1970) [1915] *Electoral Reform in England and Wales: The Development and Operation of the Parliamentary Franchise 1832–1885* (Newton Abbot: David & Charles Reprints).

Shannon, Richard (1996) *The Age of Salisbury: Unionism and Empire* (London: Longman).

Shepherd, John (1991) 'Labour and Parliament: the Lib.-Labs. as the First Working-Class MPs, 1885–1906', in Eugenio F. Biagini and Alistair J. Reid (eds), *Currents of Radicalism: Popular Radicalism, Organised Labour and Party Politics in Britain, 1850–1914* (Cambridge: Cambridge University Press).

Shipley, Stan (1971) *Club Life and Socialism in Mid-Victorian London* (Oxford: Ruskin College).

Simmons, James R., Jr (ed.) (2007) *Factory Lives: Working-Class Autobiographies* (Peterborough, Ontario: Broadview Press).

Skelly, Colin (2005) 'The Origins, Nature and Development of Moral Force Chartism, 1836–1850', Unpublished PhD thesis, University of York.

Smith, Jeremy (1997) *The Taming of Democracy: The Conservative Party, 1880–1924* (Cardiff: University of Wales Press).

Smith, Joan (1984) 'The Labour Tradition in Glasgow and Liverpool', *History Workshop Journal*, 17: 32–56.

Snowden, Viscount (1934) *An Autobiography*, 2 vols (London: Ivor Nicholson & Watson).

Stanley Holton, Sandra (1986) *Feminism and Democracy: Women's Suffrage and Reform Politics in Britain, 1900–1918* (Cambridge: Cambridge University Press).

Stanley Holton, Sandra (1996) *Suffrage Days: Stories from the Women's Suffrage Movement* (London: Routledge).

Stanley Holton, Sandra (1998) 'British Freewomen: National Identity, Constitutionalism and Languages of Race in Early Suffragist Histories', in Eileen Janes Yeo (ed.), *Radical Femininity: Women's Self-Representation in the Public Sphere* (Manchester: Manchester University Press).

Stedman Jones, Gareth (1974) 'Working-Class Culture and Working-Class Politics in London, 1870–1900: Notes on the Remaking of a Working Class', *Journal of Social History*, 7: 460–508, reprinted in Gareth Stedman Jones (1983).

Stedman Jones, Gareth (1976) [1971] *Outcast London: A Study in the Relationship between the Classes in Victorian Society* (Harmondsworth: Penguin Books).

Stedman Jones, Gareth (1982) 'The Language of Chartism', in James Epstein and Dorothy Thompson (eds), *The Chartist Experience: Studies in Working-Class Radicalism and Culture, 1830–1860* (London: Macmillan).

Stedman Jones, Gareth (1983) *Languages of Class: Studies in English Working Class History, 1832–1982* (Cambridge: Cambridge University Press).

Stevens, Christopher (1997) 'A Study of Urban Conservatism with reference to Sheffield', Unpublished PhD thesis, University of Teesside.

Stewart, Robert (1978) *The Foundation of the Conservative Party, 1830–1867* (London: Longman).

Swift, R. E. (2007) 'Policing Chartism, 1839–1848: The Role of the "Specials" Reconsidered', *English Historical Review*, 122: 669–99.

Szreter, Simon (1997) 'Economic Growth, Disruption, Deprivation, Disease and Death: On the Importance of the Politics of Public Health for Development', *Population Development Review*, 23: 693–729.

Tanner, Duncan (1990) *Political Change and the Labour Party, 1900–1918* (Cambridge: Cambridge University Press).

Tanner, Duncan (1997) 'Class Voting and Radical Politics: the Liberal and Labour Parties, 1910–31', in Jon Lawrence and Miles Taylor (eds), *Party State and Society: Electoral Behaviour in Britain since 1820* (Aldershot: Scolar Press).

Taylor, Antony (1995) ' "Commons-Stealers", "Land-Grabbers" and "Jerry-Builders": Space, Popular Radicalism and the Politics of Public Access in London, 1848–1880', *International Review of Social History*, 40: 383–408.

Taylor, Antony (1997) ' "The Best Way to Get What He Wanted": Ernest Jones and the Boundaries of Liberalism in the Manchester Election of 1868', *Parliamentary History*, 16: 185–204.

Taylor, Antony (1999a) *'Down With the Crown': British Anti-Monarchism and Debates about Royalty since 1790* (London: Reaktion Books).

Taylor, Antony (1999b) 'Commemoration, Memorialisation and Political Memory in Post-Chartist Radicalism: The 1885 Halifax Chartist Reunion in Context', in Owen Ashton, Robert Fyson and Stephen Roberts (eds), *The Chartist Legacy* (Rendlesham: Merlin Press).

Taylor, Antony (2002) 'Shakespeare and Radicalism: The Uses and Abuses of Shakespeare in Nineteenth-Century Popular Politics', *Historical Journal*, 45: 357–79.

Taylor, Antony (2004a) *Lords of Misrule: Hostility to Aristocracy in Late Nineteenth- and Early Twentieth-Century Britain* (Basingstoke: Palgrave).

Taylor, Antony (2004b) 'After Chartism: Metropolitan Perspectives on the Chartist Movement in Decline, 1848–1860', in Michael J. Turner (ed.), *Reform and Reformers in Nineteenth-Century Britain* (Sunderland: Sunderland University Press).

Taylor, Antony (2005a) ' "A Melancholy Odyssey among London Public Houses": Radical Club Life and the Unrespectable in Mid-Nineteenth-Century London', *Historical Research*, 78: 74–95.

Taylor, Antony (2005b) 'Post-Chartism: Metropolitan Perspectives on the Chartist Movement in Decline, 1848–80', in Matthew Cragoe and Antony Taylor (eds), *London Politics 1760–1914* (Basingstoke: Palgrave Macmillan).

Taylor, Barbara (1983) *Eve and the New Jerusalem: Socialism and Feminism in the Nineteenth Century* (London: Virago).

Taylor, Miles (1991) 'The Old Radicalism and the New: David Urquhart and the Politics of Opposition, 1832–1867', in Eugenio F. Biagini and Alistair J. Reid (eds), *Currents of Radicalism: Popular Radicalism, Organised Labour and Party Politics in Britain, 1850–1914* (Cambridge: Cambridge University Press).

Taylor, Miles (1995) *The Decline of British Radicalism, 1847–1860* (Oxford: Clarendon Press).

Taylor, Miles (1996) 'Rethinking the Chartists: Searching for Synthesis in the Historiography of Chartism', *Historical Journal*, 39: 479–95.

Taylor, Miles (1997) 'Interests, Parties and the State: The Urban Electorate in England, c. 1820–72', in Jon Lawrence and Miles Taylor (eds), *Party, State and Society: Election Behaviour in Britain Since 1820* (Aldershot: Scolar Press).

Taylor, Miles (1999) 'The Six Points: Chartism and the Reform of Parliament', in Owen Ashton, Robert Fyson and Stephen Roberts (eds), *The Chartist Legacy* (Woodbridge: Merlin Press).

Taylor, Miles (2003) *Ernest Jones, Chartism and the Romance of Politics, 1819–1869* (Oxford: Oxford University Press).

Taylor, P. F. (1995) *Popular Politics in Early Industrial Britain: Bolton, 1825–1850* (Ryburn Publishing: Keele).

Thane, Pat (1991) 'Labour and Local Politics: Radicalism, Democracy and Social Reform, 1880–1914', in Eugenio F. Biagini and Alistair J. Reid (eds), *Currents of Radicalism: Popular Radicalism, Organised Labour and Party Politics in Britain, 1850–1914* (Cambridge: Cambridge University Press).

Thane, Pat (1984) 'The Working Class and State "Welfare" in Britain, 1880–1914', *Historical Journal*, 27: 877–900.

Tholfsen, Trygve R. (1976) *Working-Class Radicalism in Mid-Victorian England* (London: Croom Helm).

Thompson, Andrew (2005) *The Empire Strikes Back? The Impact of Imperialism on Britain From the Mid-Nineteenth Century* (Harlow: Pearson).

Thompson, Dorothy (1984) *The Chartists: Popular Politics in the Industrial Revolution* (New York: Pantheon Books).

Thompson, Dorothy (1996) 'Who were "the People" in 1842?', in Malcolm Chase and Ian Dyck (eds), *Living and Learning: Essays in Honour of J. F. C. Harrison* (Aldershot: Scolar Press).

Thompson, E. P. (1960) 'Homage to Tom Maguire', in Asa Briggs and John Saville (eds), *Essays in Labour History in Memory of G. D. H. Cole* (London: Macmillan).

Thompson, E. P. (1966) [1963] *The Making of the English Working Class* (New York: Vintage Books).

Thompson, J. A. (1990) 'The Historians and the Decline of the Liberal Party', *Albion*, 22: 65–83.

Thompson, James (2007) ' "Pictorial Lies"? – Posters and Politics in Britain, c.1880–1914', *Past and Present*, 197: 177–210.

Thompson, Noel (1996) *Political Economy and the Labour Party: The Economics of Democratic Socialism, 1884–1995* (London:Routledge).

Thompson, Paul (1967) *Socialists, Liberals and Labour: The Struggle for London, 1885–1914* (London: Routledge & Kegan Paul).

Toole, Janet (1998) 'Workers and Slaves: Class Relations in South Lancashire in the Time of the Cotton Famine', *Labour History Review*, 63: 160–81.

Torr, Dona (ed.) (1936) *Karl Marx and Frederich Engels: Correspondence, 1846–1895: A Selection with Commentary and Notes* (London: Lawrence & Wishart).

Trentmann, Frank (2008) *Free Trade Nation: Commerce, Consumption, and Civil Society in Modern Britain* (Oxford: Oxford University Press).

Turner, Michael J. (2001) 'Thomas Perronet Thompson, "Sensible Chartism" and the Chimera of Radical Unity', *Albion*, 33: 51–74.

Vernon, James (1993) *Politics and the People: A Study in English Political Culture, c.1815–1867* (Cambridge: Cambridge University Press).

Vernon, James (1994) 'Who's Afraid of the "Linguistic Turn"? The Politics of Social History and its Discontents', *Social History*, 10: 81–97.

Vernon, James (ed.) (1996) *Re-Reading the Constitution: New Narratives in the History of England's Long Nineteenth Century* (Cambridge: Cambridge University Press).

Vincent, David (1989) *Literacy and Popular Culture: England, 1750–1914* (Cambridge: Cambridge University Press).

Vincent, John (1967) *Pollbooks: How Victorians Voted* (Cambridge: Cambridge University Press).

Vincent, John (1972) [1966] *The Formation of the Liberal Party, 1857–1868* (London: Penguin).

Wahrman, Dror (1995) *Imagining the Middle Class: The Political Representation of Class in Britain, c.1780–1840* (Cambridge: Cambridge University Press).

Wald, K. D. (1983) *Crosses on the Ballot: Patterns of British Voter Alignment Since 1885* (Princeton: Princeton University Press).

Walker, Linda (1987) 'Party Political Women: A Comparative Study of Liberal Women and the Primrose League, 1890–1914', in Jane Rendall (ed.), *Equal or Different: Women's Politics, 1800–1914* (Oxford: Basil Blackwell).

Waller, P. J. (1981) *Democracy and Sectarianism: A Political and Social History of Liverpool, 1868–1939* (Liverpool: Liverpool University Press).

Walsh, David (1991) 'Working-Class Political Integration and the Conservative Party. A Study of Class Relations and Party Development in the North-West, 1800–1870', Unpublished PhD thesis, University of Salford.

Ward, John (2002) *W. B. Ferrand: 'The Working Man's Friend', 1809–1889* (East Linton: Tuckwell Press).

Wasserman, Justin and Jaggard, Edwin (2007) 'Electoral Violence in Mid-Nineteenth-Century England and Wales', *Historical Research*, 80: 124–55.

Weaver, Stewart Angas (1987) *John Fielden and the Politics of Popular Radicalism, 1832–1847* (Oxford: Clarendon Press).

Weisser, Henry (1981) 'Chartism in 1848: Reflections on a Non-Revolution', *Albion*, 13: 12–26.

Williams, Raymond (1988) *Keywords: A Vocabulary of Culture and Society* (London: Fontana).

Williamson, Philip (2002) 'The Conservative Party, 1900–1939: From Crisis to Ascendancy', in Chris Wrigley (ed.), *A Companion to Early Twentieth-Century Britain* (Oxford: Blackwell).

Wilson, Kathleen (1995) *The Sense of the People: Politics, Culture and Imperialism in England, 1715–1785* (Cambridge: Cambridge University Press).

Windscheffel, Alex (2000) 'Villa Toryism? The Making of London Conservatism, 1868–1896', Unpublished PhD thesis, University of London.

Windscheffel, Alex (2005) '"In Darkest Lambeth": Henry Morton Stanley and the Imperial Politics of London Unionism', in Matthew Cragoe and Antony Taylor (eds), *London Politics, 1760–1914* (Basingstoke: Palgrave).

Windscheffel, Alex (2007) *Popular Conservatism in Imperial London, 1868–1906* (Woodbridge: Boydell Press).

Winstanley, Michael (1993) 'Oldham Radicalism and the Origins of Popular Liberalism, 1830–52', *Historical Journal*, 36: 619–43.

Wright, D. G. (1966) 'Politics and Opinion in Nineteenth-Century Bradford', Unpublished PhD thesis, University of Leeds.

Yeo, Eileen Janes (1981) 'Christianity in Chartist Struggle, 1838–1842', *Past and Present*, 91: 109–39.

Yeo, Eileen Janes (1998) 'Introduction: Some Paradoxes of Empowerment', in Eileen Janes Yeo (ed.), *Radical Femininity: Women's Self-Representation in the Public Sphere* (Manchester: Manchester University Press).

Yeo, Stephen (1977) 'A New Life: The Religion of Socialism in Britain, 1883–1896', *History Workshop Journal*, 4: 5–56.

Index